THE POPULATION OF LATIN AMERICA

The Population of Latin America

A HISTORY

Nicolás Sánchez-Albornoz

TRANSLATED BY W. A. R. RICHARDSON

UNIVERSITY OF CALIFORNIA PRESS

BERKELEY · LOS ANGELES · LONDON

University of California Press
Berkeley and Los Angeles, California
University of California Press, Ltd.
London, England
Copyright © 1974 by
The Regents of the University of California
ISBN: 0–520–01766–8
Library of Congress Catalog Card Number: 77–123621
Printed in the United States of America
Designed by Dave Comstock

To Graciela

CONTENTS

LIST OF ILLUSTRATIONS

Maps

Figures

LIST OF TABLES

Preface

*T*HE scope of the present work extends from the time when primitive hunters and gatherers discovered the New World, to the future year 2000. At the rate of less than one page per century for the four hundred known so far, condensation is essential. The text must necessarily survey events that one would like to study in more detail. Otherwise, the book would fail in its main purpose, that of presenting an accessible, comprehensive view of one of the most fascinating aspects of human history in Latin America. An understanding of the overall development of the region is made much easier once one has grasped the basic facts of its demographic evolution.

This work does not seek to give equal coverage to all periods. It passes rapidly over the early and last spans for which conjecture plays so great a part, and examines in some detail those periods for which more reliable historical information is available. Archaeology is a fascinating exercise, but reason has to set bounds to extravagant flights of fancy when seeking to interpret the evidence of inert matter. By inspired conjecture or logical inference, prehistorians have managed to reconstruct the general trends of evolution, even though factual lacunae and differing interpretations still exist. As for the future, the present generation mistrusts utopias and dares to go no further than to hazard a guess as to what lies ahead for the person of average age. These predictions, though based on accurate mathematical calculations, can do no more than outline future probabilities, with no guarantee of fulfillment.

Historical times link the remote past with the immediate future.

The reliability of documentary evidence varies with the periods studied; the evidence is sometimes firsthand, sometimes from secondary sources; conclusions will consequently be more reliable in some cases than in others. The study of Latin America's population development during historical times can be divided into three subperiods: the Conquest, colonial and neocolonial times, and the present-day population explosion. Some attempt has been made here to balance the space allotted to cover all three. By chapters, the main emphasis is, however, on events closest to us—three chapters out of the five discussing the historical period.

This book synthesizes a vast amount of research, but is not the outcome of special investigation. It is deeply indebted to previous works of others, whether of a general or a specific nature. The bibliography appended to this volume is both long and incomplete; it indicates the breadth of studies in the field, even though the subject still has no wide academic recognition. The present volume stems from a shorter, less complete version, published by Editorial Paidós in Buenos Aires in which José Luis Moreno wrote the section dealing with more recent history. All that remains of that volume is its outline and a set of arguments. The text has been completely rewritten, and the factual content considerably expanded.

In recent years publications dealing with the population of Latin America have multiplied. The whole canvas, past, present, and future, has been reworked. On this occasion I have been fortunate enough to have at my disposal the resources not only of the New York Public Library but also of the libraries of the universities of Yale and Columbia. No library in the whole of Latin America can rival the combined resources of the three for a comparative study like this covering twenty-one nations. The author has traveled widely in Latin America in recent years in an endeavor to supplement deficient information whenever possible. A list of all those to whom the author is indebted for assistance would be exceedingly long. A general acknowledgment is extended here with warmest thanks.

In order to indicate the authority of statements and also to guide readers in further study, an abbreviated system of reference has been used which, it is hoped, will not prove too distracting. Instead of footnotes, the author and date of publication have been included in the text for any article or book referred to. Authors are listed alphabetically in the bibliography at the end of the book. The books have been listed in order of date of publication, and when more than one work is cited in any given year, a distinctive letter has been appended. Works written in collaboration have been listed after the books by individual authors, and the collaborators themselves have been listed alphabetically. Page numbers and other references have likewise been omitted to lighten the text. The author hopes he will be forgiven for this procedure to which, understandably, some readers may object.

The term Latin America to be read in the title and frequently throughout the text is used in the widely accepted American sense; it applies to the whole of non-Anglo-Saxon America south of the Rio Grande. This originally exclusive expression has now been adopted and accepted by those to whom it refers in a contrasting and self-assertive sense. The term Latin is also frequently given such a wide interpretation that it may shortly even be extended to include the countries of the American Third World of African or Asiatic descent whose native tongue is English, such as Jamaica, Trinidad-Tobago and Guiana. The etymological sense of the word might even become so distorted as to be used in reference to a country such as Surinam, which is Dutch in its ties. These newly independent countries are drawing closer to their neighbors; they are beginning to share both their problems and their anxieties. The time will come when it will no longer be possible to deal with them in isolation, least of all for the demographic questions discussed in this book. A new expression will then be needed.

The meaning given here to "Latin America" is restricted to its original sense, referring to Spanish America and Brazil—Ibero-America—and Haiti. Puerto Rico also comes within its scope, even after 1898. Although statistics, which are subject to administrative canons, sometimes omit Puerto Rico and thus make comparisons difficult, demographically there is no difference whatsoever between the problems that beset Puerto Rico in this century and those confronting the rest of Latin America. The island's distinct political situation is irrelevant in this instance.

I

The Demographic History of Latin America

*P*OPULATION history is a new discipline in both Latin America and the rest of the world. Although interest in the subject is of long standing, it tended to concentrate on certain problems which, because of alterations in methods and the precision of scientific content, have now been abandoned. No more than ten years ago the main points under discussion were usually the size of the population at major historical junctures and, secondly, the racial composition and mixture occasioned by centuries of living in close proximity.

One can easily appreciate why these two features should have been the ones to attract the attention both of historians and of the general public. A sequence of population counts provided one way of comparing population growth, or occasionally the opposite. The rise and fall of populations has always been of interest to historians. The analytical tools they use may change, but the purpose is a legitimate one.

Secondly, the study of the mixture and merging of Latin American populations developed when there was a renewed interest in ideas about the inherent qualities of ethnic and racial groups. During the nineteenth and twentieth centuries racist ideas were very much in vogue, and, of course, Latin America did not escape the current fashions. Paradoxically, instead of bringing about racial segregation or a hierarchical stratification of different racial groups, the opposite occurred. Simultaneously in both Spanish America and Brazil there arose the belief that there was some sort of merit implicit in miscegenation. Far from leading to the deterioration of the human species, *mestizaje* was regarded as leading to qualitative improvement. The Mexican philosopher Vasconcelos used a hyperbolic phrase, "the cosmic race," to describe the end product of the process.

With some inevitable exceptions, this idea that Latin America was bound to become a racial melting pot was widely shared. The notion of *mestizaje* was advanced as a strong integrating force within Latin America, helping to stress its differences from the rest of the world. By rejecting the predominance of any one particular racial group and asserting the mestizo nature of Latin-American peoples and their culture, the interplay of ethnic groups became a focal point in the historical process and a matter of interest to all.

To assign permanent characteristics to each race and rank them accordingly is evidence of blunt prejudice. Also the whole view of social history has been altered by developments in sociological knowledge. It is economic activity, among other things, rather than pigmentation or blood, that determines the conditions for one's position in society. Color cannot be disregarded, because of its broad social significance, but it should only be considered as one more differentiating factor and perhaps not the most important.

On the other hand, when demographers did historical research, they did not always take the racial variant into account, for the simple reason that national censuses do not record such information, on the ground that citizens are equal. Thus studies of the recent past differ from those of more distant times such as the colonial period, because of the variety of data and methods to be used. This unevenness in demographic material and research points out the disparate nature of the two disciplines that join in population history: scientific demography, with little historical perspective, and history, endowed with a deeper temporal dimension but inexpert in demographic methodology.

These two disciplines tend, however, to converge on each other. Demography, somewhat restricted by the narrow chronological span to which its investigations are limited, found itself looking to the dimension of the past for explanations of long term trends. As soon as it strays from mere technical exercises and starts elaborating theories of demographic change, it resorts to history. Recent investigations such as those of Collver (1965) and Arriaga (1968a and 1970a) concerning Latin America as a whole, or the more restricted ones of Recchini de Lattes and Lattes (1969) and Somoza (1971a), show clearly that this is no mere fad. These are not the only studies, nor will they be the last. The manual of Henry (1967), its English equivalent by Wrigley (1966), and the source evaluation study made by Hollingsworth (1969) are all the work of demographers who have given to demographic history the best descriptions of the tools of their trade.

As a result of the advances in methods for population study the historian, for his part, is confronted with a whole new set of problems and has acquired more accurate measuring techniques than a mere comparison of inaccurate estimates. When general census figures and reports are not available, other material can make up for the deficiency. New techniques can be applied to broaden the range of source material; discarded sources can be found to be productive; and both can provide new ways of expressing the dynamic of population. The line joining two points on a graph was formerly a monotonous inclined plane. Now, we have become aware of sudden fluctuations, rapid oscillations, accidents with startling results, compensations, ups and downs, with sections of the population or age groups wiped out; a seething mass of life, in fact, both tragic and happy, but a very different picture from that presented by a steady statistical increase on a graph.

Short-term changes, seasonal movements, and even the sampling of relevant universes, which have their morphology and biological behavior accurately measured, have been brought into the historian's stock-in-trade. This "microdemography," made possible by the resources now available and induced by a reaction against studies broader in scope but more sterile, shows a desire to know everything in as full and detailed a way as possible. This new attitude does not a priori exclude mere comparison between census figures, but no one nowadays will claim an understanding of the processes without disclosing the complex factors of change indiscernible in the global data. To sum up, it can be said that historical analysis has been refined by demography.

A complete adjustment has not yet been achieved between demographers and historians. Some talk of demographic history, others of historical demography, a semantic distinction of little import to those who wish to come to an understanding. It is more difficult to overcome differences in academic training and professional habits. But in any case the views of both historians and demographers have been represented in this book as the need has arisen.

A start will be made with a rapid survey of the Latin American world. It is also intended to compare or contrast the trends in this region with those in the other major areas of the world, especially those best documented: North America—which separated from the region under study in the sixteenth century—Europe, and Russia.

In the second part of the chapter, the sources available in each period will be enumerated and classified according to abundance and wealth of information. It is important that the reader realize that only well-documented facts are cited, and that the research opportunities open to the historian are much greater than those he has already explored. Despite deficiencies, these primary sources are capable of quantitative elaboration and provide more reliable information than any narrative testimony.

THE POPULATION OF
LATIN AMERICA AND WORLD HISTORY

From the ethnic point of view, the history of the population of Latin America could be divided into two main periods. The first began when primitive man entered the New World and ended when Columbus set foot in the West Indies in the late fifteenth century A.D. At that time America was an ethnic extension of Asia. Columbus therefore was not so far astray when he presumed that he had landed somewhere in the Far East. What he lacked was a geographical and historical view of the question. The geographical aspect was soon resolved by the speculations of Amerigo Vespucci and those who came after him: a continent blocked the route west. The historical aspect has only been resolved in our day by archaeologists. The links of the original native population of America with Asia were already very distant in time.

After 1492, the American continent began to look toward the Atlantic, which previously had been ignored. There arrived from this direction, in successive waves, the European and African substrata. The present-day population of Latin America is the result of the juxtaposition and intermingling of these three elements, with a recent minor influx from the Near and the Far East.

Three events of a technological and sociological nature had a significant effect on demographic development. The Agricultural Revolution made possible a greater control over the forces of nature by man. Farming led to a more intensive occupation of the land than had been possible in the preceding period when nomadic hunting and gathering tribes wandered over the plains and mountains. Peasants established themselves on the land, first building villages and later cities.

The conquest by Europeans brought about an abrupt end to this independent expansion and established a new point of departure intimately linked with overseas history. The technology and the requirements of the Old World thereafter set the priorities for the development of the region. Also the infectious diseases brought by the newcomers wrought havoc with the native population. Numbers were so drastically reduced that a fresh labor supply had to be imported from Africa.

Once stability was achieved, the population embarked on a new demographic cycle. Then, a century later, the Industrial Revolution shook Europe, and in due course its effects were felt throughout the rest of the world. The new methods of production had no immediate direct impact on Latin America, but soon led to an increase in the demand for certain primary products from the area and even to such subsidiary benefits as improvements in communications. Nevertheless, these effects were restricted to relatively few areas, and the demographic changes that followed in the wake of the Industrial Revolution were only of very local significance in Latin America. In spite of this, the region was not quite the same as it had been before. Other people had migrated to America, new ideas were in the air, hopes and expectations were growing, and mechanized production methods were making inroads on traditional societies.

Applied science then suddenly revolutionized the situation, and the slow, steady increase in population became a flood. The discovery of antibiotics and pesticides caused a sudden fall in both the regular death rate and that caused by disasters and epidemics. The consequences of this graft from another civilization, as Sauvy calls it, are comparable to those of the agricultural and industrial revolutions in scope and significance. The contemporary "population explosion" is one of the most important and significant periods in the history of the population of Latin America.

The sudden fall in the death rate that occurred from the 1940s onward brought about the survival of enormous numbers of children who would formerly have died at birth. Moreover, it acted as a spur to fertility. This sudden, uncontrolled growth inevitably gave rise to endless problems. Unemployment and undernourishment aggravated former living conditions. The growth rate shows no sign of abating for many years to come, according to latest forecasts.

The European pattern, which has been used for so long as a model for the study of world population, is thus not applicable to Latin America. The former pattern can be summarized as follows: first was a centuries long series of demographic fluctuations—rather, of leaps and ceilings—within the limits imposed by agrarian technology; then, from the eighteenth century onward, the death rate declined, owing to better control of epidemics and disasters, and a fall in the natural death rate; the birth rate dropped in the third phase, leading to a slowing down in the rate of population growth.

In Latin America, however, the fall in the death rate came with an increase in the birth rate some three quarters of a century later than in most of the Old World. Also, the early part of the model is different. According to recent research, the native population of America fluctuated within certain limits, much in the same way as happened in Europe; but the Old World never suffered—at least in modern historical times—a catastrophe such as that which was brought about by the Conquest. Nor was the population explosion in Europe or North America as violent as it is in Latin America today. Arriaga (1970a and b) has accurately pointed out how widely the fertility and birth rates in Latin America differ from "Western" norms. The quantitative difference is so great that it should be regarded as a distinct natural phenomenon rather than as a variant from the *norm*. The Latin-American model can hardly be described in linear form. Its profile is more like a tub with two high walls.

Between the Conquest and the population explosion there is a stretch of nearly four centuries in which it is possible to distinguish subperiods. In view of this, and taking the pre-Columbian era into account, the general history of population in Latin America appears divided finally into subperiods: those of the hunting peoples, the native agrarian communities, the Conquest, the colonial and neocolonial era, and the present population explosion.

As the size of the population prior to the discovery of America is still in doubt, and the figures for other periods are not very reliable, only the general outlines of the period after 1750 will be examined now. Figure 1 compares the growth of the population of Latin America with that of North America, Europe, and Russia since 1750, and projects forward in time to the year 2000 in accordance with the latest forecasts. Needless to say, all the figures are somewhat tentative. The scale used is semilogarithmic.

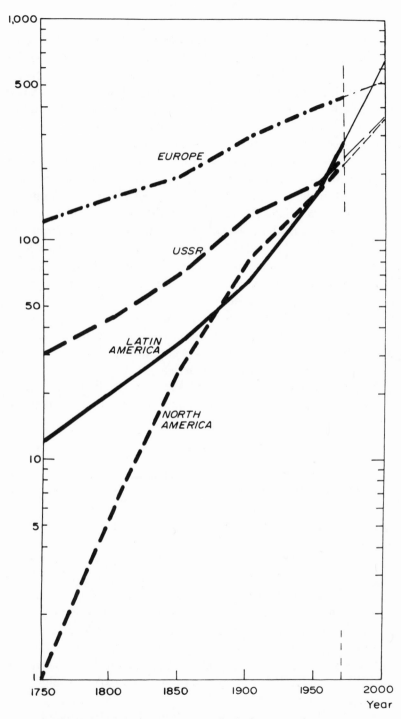

FIGURE 1. Population growth in Latin America compared with that in other regions, 1750–2000. (Sources: for 1750–1900, Durand, 1967a; for 1950 and 2000, U.N., 1967.)

Since the matter will be discussed later, only one or two major points should be stressed here. In 1750, Latin America's population was only 10 percent of that of Europe, or 40 percent of that living then within the present-day boundaries of the Soviet Union. Since then it has always remained lower than that of the other two areas until the last decade. At that time it overtook the Soviet figure; in about the year 1990, it will also exceed that of Europe.

The lines tracing the demographic evolution of Latin America and North America show a more complex movement. At first they were related in the proportion of 12 to 1, but the figures gradually approached each other. Because of natural increase and immigration, the numbers in the north went up without pause. Eventually, about 1880, the U.S.A. and Canada together caught up with their neighbors in Central and South America, and held their lead for about three quarters of a century when the growth rate in the north slackened. In 1951, the populations of the two areas were again equal. Latin America reached the population of the U.S.A. alone as early as 1946. Since then the discrepancy between the two has widened. By the end of the century the population of North America will be just over half that of Latin America.

In the year 2000, the region will have a population larger than any of the other areas under consideration, though not as great as the Far East, southern Asia, or Africa.

SOURCES

There are two types of written sources that describe any population: those which refer to the characteristics or morphology of the group at any given point in time, and those which concern the vital statistics—births, marriages, and deaths. The first examines a static situation, and the second traces population movements. Both sources are complementary, since they explain the demographic structure of the area described, whether town, district, nation, or continent. Sequences of general censuses and accurate vital statistics permit a comparison of results, which may serve to determine their consistency and consequently their degree of accuracy and validity.

Besides these two basic types there is yet another, which records population shifts, and especially international migration. Whenever these sources are lacking, the population growth due to migration can be estimated from census statistics of the host countries.

As all of these sources are seldom found for each period of time, the researcher is compelled to supplement his information by resorting to a variety of subsidiary data. For instance, the prehistorian will have to study the extent of cultivation and the type of production to determine the density of a rural population; the size and number of population centers to estimate the degree of urban development; and even, perhaps, the corpses in a cemetery to estimate average life expectancy. These are but a few examples of how ingenuity can make up for deficient information in the study of what has come to be called paleodemography. For historical times it is not always possible to obtain adequate documentary evidence. There are no counts, for example, of the aboriginal population on the eve of discovery and during the Conquest, yet it is very important that the size of population should be established. The historian can refer to the reports of soldiers, clerics, and royal functionaries, as well as to extant native traditions. Two scholars, in particular (Cook and Borah, 1966 and 1971, and Borah, 1970) have taken pains to demonstrate the relative validity of many of these accounts after submitting them to an appropriately critical appraisal.

In the following pages only those sources will be considered which were compiled for statistical, even if not for specifically demographic, purposes. During the colonial period, the authorities took censuses for fiscal, military, and administrative purposes, and the church also enumerated the recipients of some sacraments and other clerical services. Only in certain cases, such as the *statua animarum*, or state of the souls of a parish or diocese, was it the express intention to discover the characteristics of the religious community. Therefore information is generally indirect, although demographically significant.

As time passed, registration was improved, the scope of the categories included was broadened, and the documents became more and more specific. For these reasons, periods will henceforward be differentiated in accordance with the type and accuracy of the census information. It would be, however, misleading to presume that the most up-to-date information is necessarily the most reliable. Records for the seventeenth century are generally fewer and more inaccurate than those for the sixteenth; the first censuses in the newly independent republics, were, on the whole, less trustworthy than the last ones taken during the late colonial regime. Naturally, the quality of recording depends on administrative efficiency, and it is well known that bureaucratic efficiency deteriorated in the latter half of the seventeenth century and in the first half of the nineteenth century.

Despite substantial deficiencies, both types of sources—those recording population data at a specific time, and those regularly registering vital statistics—gradually became more reliable. Thus it is possible to recognize a pre-statistical period (1555–1774), during which the majority of the documents have an incidental, indirect demographic value; another, proto-statistical period (1775–1880), in which one can see the beginning of a deliberate intention to count inhabitants for population purposes; and finally, after 1800 an entirely statistically based period, when the gathering of such information was the exclusive responsibility of governments. During the first period the counts were usually more sporadic and imperfect than in the second, and, of course, during the third they were carried out more systematically. The dates indicated are approximate.

In 1555 the First Provincial Council held in Mexico ordered parish priests to keep baptismal and matrimonial registers of both Indians and Spaniards, years before the Council of Trent issued a general order. The measure was not put into effect immediately throughout Spanish America owing to the difficulties involved. A widespread adoption of the register came only later; however, the gesture was in itself very significant. In addition, it was then that a new system of taxing the Indian population was introduced in the viceroyalty of New Spain, different from the one previously used, which had been based on Aztec practice. The new system was to influence the methods adopted later in the other dominions of the Spanish crown and, with some variations, was to remain in force in some places as late as the middle of the nineteenth century, well into the period when the colonial regime had been replaced by independent republics.

In 1775 the first census in Cuba was held; on November 20 of the following year, a royal decree was issued at the palace of San Lorenzo de El Escorial, on the initiative of José de Gálvez, instructing viceroys and governors to carry out a census. This was undertaken throughout nearly the whole of Spanish America during the following two years. The intention was to carry out periodic surveys in the future. At about the same time, the Portuguese crown asked parish priests for information on the number of inhabitants of Brazil, and this was provided (IBGE, 1951). Apparently, the population was counted at that time also in Haiti (Victor, 1944). Thus by mere chance a general recording was taken simultaneously of the area later to be known as Latin America. The very scale of the undertaking makes it reasonable to regard this date as the beginning of the proto-statistical period.

About the year 1880, of the then eighteen independent states of Latin America, eleven had carried out some form of national census, and one, Chile, was taking a census once every decade. At approximately the same time, legislation had been introduced or drawn up in eleven republics creating civil registries of births, marriages, and deaths. As in the sixteenth century, the recording of vital statistics was not introduced automatically. Years were to pass before the practice became generalized and even more before coverage was complete.

Administrative changes, which influence deeply the gathering of statistical data, suggest that subdivisions should be distinguished within the three periods mentioned above. During the pre-statistical era, the first period lasted from the mid-sixteenth century to 1646, when Díez de la Calle made the last attempt to estimate the overall population of the Indies. After that, documentary evidence becomes fragmentary; figures are few and far between, and tend to refer just to single territories. Colonial administration was chaotic and poorly financed. The recording of general demographic data was resumed later by an order of the crown to Viceroy Fuenclara of New Spain in 1741. Similar instructions were sent to the viceroys of New Granada and Peru. In all cases the crown's instructions were carried out. It is therefore possible to make a documented estimate of the population of Spanish America for the middle of the eighteenth century.

The proto-statistical period can be divided, for obvious administrative reasons, into a colonial and a national phase. In the statistical period one needs to recognize a first stage during which each government gathered demographic information in accordance with its own means and purposes, and a later one when international initiative brought about homogeneity of criteria and systematized the gathering of information. After lengthy planning under the auspices of the Inter-American Statistical Institute, the majority of the nations in the region carried out censuses simultaneously in 1950 (IASI, 1953). For some countries—Ecuador and Haiti—it was their first census since independence. Since then the Inter-American Statistical Institute, together with the Population Division and CELADE of the United Nations, have coordinated efforts and when necessary have provided advice and even material assistance for the gathering of information and the analysis of census results.

The basis of these time divisions having been explained, a brief examination of the materials available in each period and subperiod seems in order. During the early pre-statistical subperiod and in much of the following subperiod, the commonest and most methodically kept demographic records were of a fiscal nature: Indian tribute rolls. In principle every male Indian between the ages of eighteen and fifty had to pay a fixed tribute as vassal of the king, and this exempted him from taxes levied on other subjects. There were variations in age limits, type of exemptions, and the rate to be paid, depending on the area and period concerned, but in general those required to pay were the adult male members of the population. If the recorded figures concern only this group, in order to estimate the total population it is necessary to add all the females and children, as well as those Indians exempted from paying tribute who were over fifty years of age. It is, however, by no means unusual for the census to include women, the young, and the *reservados* (those exempted).

Ideally, the making of the roster (*matrícula*) or roll (*padrón*) entailed a tour of inspection (*visita*), place by place and house by house. Later inspections (*revisitas*) revised the original figures in accordance with new demographic conditions. The sharp fall in the Indian population during the sixteenth and seventeenth centuries made such revisions (*retasas*) necessary. The latter were usually prepared only after a long and costly judicial process paid for by the people concerned. They were, of course, always completed well in arrear of events. During this delay the Indians' financial burden rose sharply. One special section of the Real Hacienda (Royal Treasury) was in charge of the tax rolls—the Contaduría General de Reales Tributos, Real Servicio y Azogues in New Spain and the Contaduría General de Retasas in Peru.

The king kept an eye upon the number of his subjects overseas and the amount of tribute they brought in. Accordingly many reports were collected on individual Indian towns and on the tribute they paid; but in order to have systematic information the crown also instructed Juan de Ovando to tally the whole population of its American realms. Once the data were gathered by him from among the financial records held by the Consejo de Indias (Council of the Indies), the cosmographer and chief chronicler of the Indies, Juan López de Velasco, prepared a summary for the public, which preserved this information for posterity, since the original Ovando papers have been lost. The *Geografía y descripción universal de las Indias* by López de Velasco, which he finished in 1574, lists nine thousand Indian towns and two hundred Spanish ones. Ovando remained for a long time afterwards in charge of the collection of demographic data for the council which required the colonial authorities to continue to make counts of Spaniards and Indians. The *Relaciones geográficas* assembled between 1575 and 1585 owe their origin in part to these intentions. They might be compared to the surveys made in Spain itself on the orders of Philip II (Konetzke, 1948).

Between 1604 and 1614 the crown made another attempt, less successful than the first, to gather fiscal and geographical data on its American dominions. The inquiries made in Peru by the viceroy, the marquis of Montesclaros, were part of this effort. In contrast to official documents is the work of Antonio Vázquez de Espinosa, an itinerant friar who traveled throughout the New World from 1612 to 1622 taking notes. His book, *Compendio y descripción de las Indias Occidentales*, published six years after his return, was the last general description of the Spanish empire in the seventeenth century. A later book by Díez de la Calle, *Memorial y noticias sacras y reales del imperio de las Indias Occidentales* (1646), was intended as a general survey but was not comprehensive because of a lack of material on Peru. His work brought to an end a succession of attempts to estimate the number of inhabitants of the New World. No similar efforts would be made for another century. Basically, these researches relied on the records kept of tribute-paying Indians, who were by far the most numerous element in the population of America. Scattered, incomplete figures relating to the Spanish inhabitants were also collected.

As for vital statistics, the Third Mexican Church Council in 1585 confirmed the resolution of the First and ordered that two other kinds of parish records should be kept—of deaths and confirmations —thus anticipating Pope Paul V's decision of 1614 (Lodolini, 1958). The Pope required yet a fifth register to be kept, *de statu animarum*, of the members of all families living in the parish, but this record was sporadically maintained. The church complied thoroughly with the other rules to the point that, in Mexico and Peru, the officials carrying out revisions of Indian rolls used to compare the new ones with the lists of deaths and baptisms provided by the parish priests, in order to ascertain how accurate the records were. Each ethnic group was registered in the parish separately: the Indians, the Negroes and mulattoes together, and lastly the whites.

The Casa de Contratación (House of Trade) in Seville wrote down the names of those who crossed the Atlantic legally with the fleets, but obviously these were but a fraction of the total number. Research in the unpublished files of the *Archivo de Indias* has produced new estimates of Transatlantic migration which may be unreliable but are nevertheless interesting. Involuntary migration has also been studied. Data on persons are lacking, but such migration can be estimated from the shipping records of the infamous traffic in slaves across the Atlantic.

During the period of imperial decadence, the tribute roll revisions were more sporadic, and the administration, unable to carry out the task, relied on the church to provide it with information. Parish registers covered new areas and remained at least as accurate as they had been before, as the recent study by Carmagnani (1970) has shown. Pastoral visits became more frequent. Important additional information is provided by records such as those of tithes and the half-*real* tribute levied to maintain the cathedral of Mexico City. Among official initiatives were the *Razón de las ciudades, villas y lugares, vecindarios y tributarios* carried out in the audiencia of Guatemala in 1683 and the contemporary count carried out in Peru by the viceroy, the duke of La Palata, because of the sudden drop in the population of the viceroyalty. His successor, the count of Monclova, completed it in 1690, lowering tributes in accordance with the lower number of taxpayers. The plague of 1719 at last made necessary a new *revisita* during the administration of the marquis of Castelfuerte.

The censuses by Fuenclara, Solís, and Superunda, which have already been referred to, were carried out during the third subdivision of the pre-statistical period. The results of these for Mexico were published by José Antonio Villaseñor in his *Teatro americano* (1748), and for Peru, by Cosme y Bartolomé Bueno in their *Descripción del Virreinato* published later (1774). The administration in this subperiod made great efforts to improve the collection of taxes and consequently had to improve the records of taxpayers. Proof of these efforts are the *retasas* made in Peru during the administration of Viceroy Amat and the reform of data-collecting processes contained in the *Instrucciones* of Leuro (1769) and Escobedo (1784). In a *real órden* of 1749, the crown also reminded the bishops of church responsibilities so far as the correct keeping of parish registers was concerned.

These timid steps culminated in the vast general census undertaken by Gálvez (1776), which has already been mentioned. In table 1.1 it can be seen that this was no isolated phenomenon but the beginning of an as yet irregular series of individual censuses in different administrative areas, such as those of Las Casas, Revillagigedo, Gil de Taboada, and Abascal, to mention some of the more important ones. The new interest in population matters was quite in accord with preoccupations typical of the century of the Enlightenment. The authorities began to be able to rely on a body of efficient civil servants to carry out the task, especially after the Reforma de Intendentes. Baron Humboldt, like his predecessors López de Velasco, Villaseñor, and Bueno, made the results of the *relevamientos* widely known. Enlightened monarchy, availing itself of its royal privileges, led the government to overstep the bounds of its jurisdiction when, by a *real órden* of 1801, it in effect turned the clergy into civil servants by requiring them to remit monthly reports concerning the vital statistics of their parishes.

The Portuguese crown, for the same motives, but with a colonial administration less subject to central control, required priests to supply demographic information. As the Brazilian census of 1775 was ecclesiastical rather than secular in origin, it has been omitted from table 1.1.

The importance of the native Indian element fell with the increase of Negroes, mestizos, and whites. The Real Hacienda did not lose interest in the Indians on this account but, on the contrary, sought to record them even more rigorously. Regular five-year counts were carried out. Despite their imperfections and their one-sided nature, they are nevertheless regular records of a segment of the total population.

With the coming of independence, the colonial civil service disintegrated to a level which took many years to overcome. Intense political and military activity together with a new fiscal policy of relying on customs duties rather than on head taxes, lessened the fiscal need for censuses. Nevertheless, in some former colonies, such as Chile, the United Provinces of the River Plate, and Gran Colombia, censuses were hurriedly prepared. Other states also held them, principally for electoral purposes (table 1.1). Because of their bearing on the distribution of disputed parliamentary seats, it is doubtful that accurate population counts were made. There were heated debates over the reliability of many censuses.

Census statistics again became important when the economic progress of the third quarter of the nineteenth century reemphasized the significance of human resources. By then, several important countries, such as Brazil, Argentina, and Venezuela, carried out their first national censuses.

One thus enters the statistical period. Table 1.2 shows that, at

TABLE 1.1 General Population Censuses. The First Century, 1775–1874

	Captaincy General of Cuba	Viceroyalty of New Spain	Captaincy General Of Guatemala	Viceroyalty of New Granada
1775	De la Torre 1775			
		Bucareli 1777		
			Mayorga 1778	Flórez 1778
1785				Caballero y Góngora 1782
	Las Casas 1791	Revillagigedo 1791		
1795				
1805			Anguiano 1803 (Honduras)	Mendinueta 1803
			Gutiérrez y Ulloa (El Salvador) 1807	Villavicencio 1810
1815	Cienfuegos 1817			
		1821		
1825	Vives 1827		Constituent Assembly 1824 (Costa Rica)	Gran Colombia Census 1825
1835				II National Census (Colombia) 1835
	O'Donnell 1841			III National Census 1843
1845				
1855	Spanish National Census 1860			IV National Census 1859
			I National Census (Costa Rica) 1864	V National Census 1864
1865				
				VI National Census 1869
1874				

Captaincy General of Venezuela	Viceroyalty of Peru	Captaincy General of Chile	Viceroyalty of the River Plate	Brazil
	Guirior 1777	Jáuregui 1777		
			Vértiz 1778	
	Croix 1785			
Castro y Araúz 1787				
	Gil de Taboada 1790			
				Rosende 1798
				Ministry of War 1808
		1810		
	Abascal 1813	Congress 1813	Constituent Assembly 1813	
			1822	
		I National Census 1832		
	I National Census 1836			
Census 1838				
Censuses 1844–47		II National Census 1844		
	II National Census 1850		I National Census (Uruguay) 1852	
Census 1854		III National Census 1854		
Census 1857			General Census (Bolivia) 1854	
	III National Census 1862		Census of the Argentine Confederation 1857	
		IV National Census 1865		
			II National Census (Uruguay) 1860	
I National Census 1873			I National Census (Argentina) 1869	Imperial Census 1872

TABLE 1.2 Dates of Laws Establishing National Civil Registers of Births, Marriages, and Deaths

Peru	1852	Chile	1885
Mexico	1859	Cuba	1885
Venezuela	1863	Costa Rica	1888
Guatemala	1877	Brazil	1889
El Salvador	1879	Ecuador	1901
Nicaragua	1879	Paraguay	1914[b]
Uruguay	1879	Panama	1914
Honduras	1882	Haiti	1922
Dominican		Colombia	1938
Republic	1884	Bolivia	1940[b]
Argentina	1884–1904[a]		

[a]Federal law for the capital and national territories. Each province established its own law between 1885 and 1904.

[b]Paraguay and Bolivia had established marriage registers as early as 1898 and 1911 respectively.

SOURCE: U.N., 1955*b*.

the beginning of the twentieth century, more than two-thirds of the countries of Latin America had started keeping state-organized vital statistics. The dates in Table 1.2 do not give the precise years when registration began in each nation but show the approximate time that the state arrogated to itself the tasks hitherto carried out by the church. Conflict between liberals and conservatives often delayed the establishment of civil registers. Liberals favored public registration, but they could not always enforce the laws they enacted. In Mexico, for example, despite the date given, the Civil Register did not start functioning until 1867, after the defeat of Maximilian's empire. Even if the law was not immediately implemented, the decision still reveals an important change of attitude.

As should be expected, during the early stages the recording was inefficient. There are several studies under way now which are endeavoring to determine the extent to which registers fell short. Thus it is hoped to correct the series in order to have reliable information. For examples of this task, see the works of Recchini de Lattes (1967) and Cordero (1968).

Table 1.3 gives the dates of national censuses taken from 1875 on. During the last quarter of the nineteenth century there were thirty censuses in the whole of Latin America. Leaving aside the eight countries where no census was held, the average is close to two per country, including the dubious ones for El Salvador and some other nations.

The censuses are recorded in the appropriate year by a figure indicating their official numbering in the state concerned. The Span-

TABLE 1.3 General Population Censuses. The Second Century, 1875–1974

	1875–1884	1885–1894	1895–1904	1905–1914	1915–1924	1925–1934	1935–1944	1945–1954	1955–1964	1965–1974
Argentina			2	3				4	5	6
Bolivia			2					3		P
Brazil		2	3		4		5	6	7	8
Chile	5	6	7	8	9	10	11	12	13	14
Colombia				7 8	9	10	11	12	13	P
Costa Rica	2	3				4		5	6	P
Cuba		S	W	1	2	3	4	5		6
Dominican Republic					1		2	3	4	5
Ecuador				U				1	2	P
Guatemala	2	3			4		5	6	7	P
Haiti					U			1		U
Honduras	1	2	3 4	5 6	7	8 9	10 11	12 13	14	15
Mexico			1 2	3	4	5	6	7	8	9
Nicaragua				U	1		2	3	4	5
Panama				1	2	3	4	5	6	7
Paraguay		1	2				3	4		5
Peru	4						5		6	7
Puerto Rico	S	S	S W	13	14	15	R 16	17	18	19
Salvador (El)	1* 2*	3* 4*	5* 6*			1		2	3	4
Uruguay				3					4	P
Venezuela	2	3			4	5	6 7	8	9	10

S Spain
W U.S. War Department
R Puerto Rico Reconstruction Administration

* El Salvador, first series
P Proposed census
U Unofficial Census

ish colonial administration and, in 1899, the United States War Department were responsible for the earliest censuses in Cuba and Puerto Rico. The later numbering for Puerto Rico follows the United States census sequence.

During the first quarter of the twentieth century there were thirty-two censuses taken, including those open to objection. Although only two countries, Costa Rica and Peru, did not hold any census during that period, the overall average was lower. The practice had become more widespread but had not increased in frequency. Some nations—Mexico, Honduras, and the countries within the U.S. sphere of influence (Cuba, Puerto Rico, and Panama)—began to hold regular censuses. Chile and Colombia had been doing this at regular intervals.

The first census forms simply asked for personal details such as sex, age, marital status, and perhaps nationality, place of birth, color, and some information concerning trade or profession and economic status. Gradually the questions became more numerous, requiring information concerning legitimacy, family, education, and sometimes race. The latest ones ask for information about fertility and type of personal relationship—marriage or free union.

During the second quarter of this century, which was, in general, a period of economic depression, four republics (Uruguay, Bolivia, Ecuador, and Haiti) took no census. The total taken shrunk slightly to thirty, but it should be noted that this reduction was compensated for by the new practice of holding censuses in the years ending in zero. This spread in 1950 when, as has already been mentioned, all the governments except two took censuses on or about that date. The so-called Census of the Americas made possible a reasonably reliable count of the population of the whole continent. It was a real landmark in the history of censuses in the area. From then on no country has failed to take a census. The principle of having them every ten years has been accepted, but the proposal to take them simultaneously in every country has proved too ambitious. In the hundred years covered by table 1.3 there is reflected a development in the field of demography parallel with the ups and downs in the institutional and socioeconomic life of the region. The average number of censuses per country is seven, that is, one every fourteen years, although the reliability of many is open to question. No one would accept them at their face value without submitting them to detailed internal examination, such as any historian carries out with the documents on which he is working. For some of the first investigations of this nature, see Somoza and Lattes (1967), Lattes (1968), and Lattes and Poczter (1968).

The present frequency of censuses is reasonable, if not ideal, and places Latin America first among the less advanced regions of the world. No account has been taken of the numerous provincial censuses, which also contain valuable demographic information.

Finally, with reference to contemporary international migration, the figures are to be found in the periodical publications of the government departments responsible—the ministry of the interior in some countries, the ministry of agriculture or of foreign affairs in others. Government-controlled statistical institutes can also provide this information.

To conclude these introductory notes on the materials available, one may read what Hollingsworth (1969) has to say about those involved in this field:

> The ideal historical demographer will need to have a keen historical sense and a command of all the knowledge and resources of modern demography, requiring a thorough acquaintance with the methods and findings of every national system of census and vital registration in the world. He will be deeply versed in economics, sociology, religious observance, archaeology, anthropology, climatology, epidemiology, and gynaecology; and he will understand the mathematical techniques of the statistician so well that he can advance improvements on them of his own. He will be a good palaeographer, an expert on taxation law and practice, on town planning and agricultural methods, at all times and places; he will know how to collect quantitative information, to code and punch it on cards or tapes, and to produce an analysis of it by computer. He will be a voracious reader, with a command of at least a dozen languages, reading a hundred issues of learned periodicals and as many books, emanating from every part of the world, from cover to cover every year.

Hollingsworth concludes: "The ideal historical demographer, of course, does not exist."

II
The Population of
Pre-Columbian America

A T the time of the Conquest, the native population
was distributed unevenly throughout the continent. Some areas were
densely populated, while others were practically uninhabited. Settlement was concentrated in the mountains and on the Pacific coastline,
while the great plains bordering on the Atlantic coast were thinly
peopled. The contrast was dictated by the conditions on the land,
since natural obstacles are hard to overcome in primitive societies.

But the differential distribution of the population was due to
historical as well as environmental circumstances. Many ethnic,
socioeconomic, and cultural factors had a bearing on the situation.
For example, although the vegetation and relief of many parts of the
Caribbean area are close to that of the peninsula of Yucatán, it was
only in the latter that a civilization such as that of the Mayas flourished. Similarly, in the southern Andean area, the slopes of the cordillera are not topographically or climatically very different from the
central Andean area, but the civilization in the south was never so
highly developed as in the area occupied by the Incas. The Inca
civilization of the central Andes took a very long time to spread
south. Consequently, it would be wrong to assume that, at the arrival
of the Spaniards, the native population and nature were in a stable
adjustment. The Indians had been living on the continent for thou-

sands of years and, during this time, had suitably modified the productive capacity of the soil by increasingly complex technical means.

THE DISPERSION OF
THE HUNTING AND GATHERING PEOPLES

For some time it was thought that American man was indigenous. This misconception was due to an inaccurate examination of human remains in remote geological strata and the very fragmentary nature of our knowledge of the evolution of the higher mammals at that time. Nowadays it is believed that man's presence on the American continent is relatively recent, especially in comparison with Asia and Africa. In both of these two continents remains have been found of anthropoid primates ancestral to our species whereas none have been found in America. This does not imply that American man is as recent as was imagined during the period of reaction against the theory of his indigenous origin. As finds become more numerous and dating methods improve, his arrival in the New World recedes in time. Although new discoveries may well push this date back even further, it is now thought that he has been in America between forty and a hundred thousand years.

Thus it was an empty continent that, tens of thousands of years ago, witnessed the arrival of the first human beings on American soil. They came from Asia and crossed the Bering Strait, which separates Alaska from Siberia. During the Ice Age that stretch of sea was not the same obstacle that it is today. The bands that arrived were extremely primitive; they lived by gathering wild fruit, fishing, and hunting small game. Their way of life drove them to fresh sources of subsistence once the resources of one area were exhausted. Nomadic existence prevented the formation of large or stable communities. As soon as a band grew too large, one part had to move on to new lands. This migration safety valve must have worked well, for despite the brake put on their reproduction by the type of life they led, the pressure was sufficiently high for some tribes to reach the far south of South America in some thousands of years. A recent sensational archaeological discovery has established the passage of these primitive hunters and gatherers through Peru about twenty-two thousand years ago (MacNeish, 1971). Climatic changes must also have caused human migration to kindlier and more favorable lands.

The second series of invasions brought big-game hunters through the interior of Alaska. Like their predecessors, they spread out through the whole continent. Archaeological remains provide evidence of their arrival at the extreme south, in Patagonia, about the year 9000 B.C. Their passage through Mexico, Venezuela, Ecuador, Peru, and Chile many thousands of years previously has also been proved. These hunters possessed improved stone projectiles and lived by killing big game. Until the arrival of the Europeans they roamed the great plains of the north and south of the continent, where they exercised their extraordinary hunting skills. They, likewise, never formed very large groups, and it is doubtful whether their capacity for increase was much greater than that of the early hunters.

In caves in Tamaulipas and in the Valley of Tehuacán in Mexico, archaeologists have identified the wild plants that formed part of the diet of the gathering tribes. Among the more important are pumpkins, beans, and maize. Driven by sheer necessity, influenced by certain observations, and guided by subsequent experiments—or even taught by other peoples, as some authorities maintain—those primitive men managed to domesticate these plants. The same may well be true of the potato in Peru. It is possible that cultivation of the pumpkin began between 7000 and 5000 B.C., of beans between 5000 and 3000 B.C., and of maize between 3000 and 2300 B.C. This domestication, the significance of which escaped the people who achieved it, was to bring about an utterly profound change in the history of the continent.

THE AGRICULTURAL REVOLUTION

In its social and economic results, the domestication of plants prompted a revolution as significant in its day as the Industrial Revolution for the Contemporary Age. Agriculture created an economy which, by giving men a more reliable supply of food, permitted them to multiply to a hitherto unknown degree. Industrialization, in its turn, made possible a sustained growth of population by overcoming the economic dependence on land. Both of these technological changes were followed by a violent population explosion. Agriculture reached its natural limit in a new balance between man and the land. In our day, industrial society seems to be heading toward a new demographic equilibrium, even though it is as yet a long way off.

In both cases a stage of preparation preceded the explosion. American prehistorians date this period of adaptation between 2000 and 800 B.C. In the modern era, such processes become much more rapid, requiring only a few decades or a century at the outside.

During the formative period, horticulture settled men on the land, gave them permanent lodging, and concentrated them together. As a result of this, more complex and more widely differing social and political patterns emerged, together with a multiplicity of new ideas. Agriculture therefore set in motion processes whose consequences could not have been foreseen.

It would seem irrelevant to our purpose of tracing the growth of the native population of America, to note that the domestication of plants first occurred in the Near East, some seven to eight thousand years B.C. It is possible that this constitutes a factor in support of the diffusionist theory, according to which the innovation was brought from the Old World to the New. The same applies for the opposite opinion, the evolutionist hypothesis, which holds that domestication was discovered independently in the American continent. Even more, among those subscribing to the latter theory are those who also accept the possibility that there were four independent centers of domestication within the American continents: two in so-called nuclear America—Central America and Peru—another in the Amazon basin, and the last in the Mississippi Valley. However, if agriculture spread from the Near East to America via the Pacific route, as the first thesis maintains, a new migratory wave brought it. The great variety of racial groups among the indigenous inhabitants certainly leads one not to exclude the possibility. The widely differing achievements of agriculturists in the four areas mentioned cannot easily be explained by ecological factors alone, since areas with similar potentials did not achieve a similar degree of development. If this was the case, then—as on later occasions—a paramount change was introduced from abroad. Immigration must again have played a salient role.

Whichever theory one subscribes to, the contrast between the agriculture of the Amazon and Mississippi basins and that of the nuclear American region is remarkable. In both of the river basins, agriculture fed only a scanty population in villages, frequently shifted elsewhere when the cultivation system required it. In the mountains, agriculture went through increasingly intensive phases which culminated with irrigation. The advanced cultures developed in these latter areas. Irrigation, especially that carried out on terraced cultivated mountain slopes such as in the Peruvian coastal valleys, not only demanded an intensive use of labor, but provided regular subsistence for it at the same time. The same applies to the *chinampas* of the Valley of Mexico. This type of agriculture favored stable settlement. The population became gradually more concentrated, first in villages, and then later in cities, some of which became the capitals of kingdoms or even empires.

Whatever is said about the demography of this period can only be conjectural, apart from the fact that the increasing size and number of archaeological finds seem to provide evidence for rise in population. Actually, the hypotheses depend upon how one answers the question about the way in which those societies applied the greater productivity drawn from the new methods of cultivation and the new food sources. Generally speaking it could have led to improvement in material well-being, or may merely have ended in the maintenance of the previous subsistence level; all the excess could have been used up in providing for increased population. It might also have been used to maintain numerous parasitic classes, such as craftsmen, the nobility, and the priesthood, or have been invested in the construction of such unproductive works as monuments. The answer should probably be a compromise among the possibilities.

Living standards presumably improved in comparison with earlier periods, that is, there was more regular and more abundant food, more comfortable accommodation, and more leisure time. Such improvement undoubtedly led to a slightly longer life expectancy and to a slight slowing down in the rate of generation replacement. Prehistoric demographic studies—which are still in their infancy as far as the New World is concerned, but full of promise if we are to believe the suggestive studies of Vallois (1960)—have the last word in the matter. The increasing number of populated regions, and the migration of people to areas where cultures developed later, bear witness to a high fertility rate. In archaeological remains and even in the writings of the chroniclers, there is evidence of such population displacements. On the other hand, the development of parasitic classes and urban growth point to the fact that not all the new resources can have been used up on population expansion alone. Moreover, there is astonishing evidence in stone of the architectural effort expended for religious purposes.

Thus both the refinements of material life and the satisfaction of less immediate social or cultural demands absorbed part of the agricultural surplus, and consequently checked population growth, preventing it from reaching its maximum potential. Despite this brake, was population ever in equilibrium with environmental forces, social structure, and technical resources? In other words, did the population ever reach a ceiling or peak, which could only be passed by means of technological changes? Did the Spaniards, on the contrary, find the Indian population halfway in its evolution, when there was still room for population expansion under the prevailing social and technical order?

The results published by the Peabody Foundation archaeological expedition to the Valley of Tehuacán, northwest of Oaxaca and southeast of Puebla in Mexico, suggest a lineal progression of the population of the area excavated. Many will consider that the conclusions reached there can be applied to the general process. The aim of the expedition was to identify the stages of human settlement that could be detected in a restricted area, in order to attempt to establish the density of people in each stage. When the exhaustive investigation of the valley was concluded, 453 archaeological sites had been found, many of which had been occupied over several different eras. Depending on the area occupied by the remains of each phase, and employing a changing factor according to the social and cultural level of each epoch, MacNeish (1970) ventured an estimate of probable population densities.

Expressing the figures as the number of inhabitants per 100 square kilometers, the earliest must have been about 0.5 before the year 7000 B.C., which suggests a very sparse population, appropriate to the hunting stage. Before the year 5000 B.C. the figure is 2.2, and between 3400 and 2300 B.C., 13.7, reaching 42.6 in the agricultural period called Late Ajalpan. This period was marked by the cultivation of slopes. Forty-three percent of the diet was from cultivated plants.

At a more advanced stage (Santa María) which covered the span 900–100 B.C., irrigation fostered production, and the population almost quadrupled. The growth rate speeded up even more in the following period. Between 100 B.C. and A.D. 700, the Palo Blanco period, the density of population reached 11.1 per square kilometer. Finally, during the eight centuries before the Conquest (the Venta Salada phase), density rose to no less than 36.29 per square kilometer. At that time cultivated plants accounted for three-quarters of the diet.

Within this development, the jump represented by the step from the hunting to the agricultural stage becomes extremely clear. Finally the latter density cannot be explained, in fact, without reference to a process of urban concentration that will be dealt with later.

According to the edaphological studies carried out by S. F. Cook (1949), first in the Teotlapan and later in the Mixteca Alta, Puebla, Valley of Mexico, Michoacán, Veracruz, and the Bajío—

that is, in a fairly broad and varied series of samples, even though restricted to Mexico—there appear to have been three phases of erosion, the result of man's intensive exploitation of the soil. The erosion was more profound than that caused later by the cattle introduced by the conquistadores. Agricultural production must have fallen off on each occasion, and the population must have suffered the consequences of deteriorating soil. Both Cook and his colleague, W. Borah, are inclined to believe that the native population of central Mexico must have experienced successive expansions and contractions rather than a gradual rate of increase. The studies of J. R. Parsons (1968) on the settlement patterns in the valley of Texcoco confirm the existence of demographic oscillations in the era immediately preceding the arrival of Cortés. If this is so, then it is quite possible that the Indian population had reached a new maximum expansion on the eve of the Spanish Conquest, and that such saturation would inevitably have brought about its decline even had the invasion not occurred (Cook, 1947). It is thus not surprising that the Conquest did have such a tremendous impact on the native population.

There are several factors that lend support to this idea of relative saturation within the bounds of the state of the agricultural technology of the time. Cook (1946a) observed that the Aztecs' *guerras floridas* (wars of the flowers) and their massive sacrifices of captives in honor of the gods could not be comprehended if there had been a shortage of human resources, since it would then have been in their interests to conserve lives. This waste would therefore seem to have been an unconscious mechanism for the control of population expansion. The practice of sacrificing young children, which was so characteristic, for example, of the *santamariana* culture of northern Argentina, was likewise a kind of birth control of an equally violent kind. Thousands of extremely beautiful funeral urns can be seen in museums, or still lie in the earth, containing evidence of such macabre rites.

THE RISE OF TOWNS AND CITIES

In pre-Columbian times a long chain of cities developed on the strip which goes from Tzintzuntzan, in Michoacán (Mexico), to Tiahuanaco, on the Peruvian altiplano, or, if we include places of a smaller rank, from Chihuahua to Atacama. Only on the Isthmus of Panama did a gap separate the two areas of highly developed cultures in Central and South America. Both had large rural populations whose high productive capacity made possible the creation of great political or ceremonial centers.

Between pre-Conquest and colonial towns there is sometimes a physical continuity which often runs on up to the present. Modern nations, such as Mexico and Ecuador, still have the capital city on the site of the earlier pre-Hispanic native capital. In such cases, the primitive city plan has disappeared. On sites that are now uninhabited, however, such outlines are readily identifiable under layers of earth or scrub, while excavation reveals the splendors of earlier civilizations. Very few of these prehistoric urban centers have been even half-investigated. While the sites await systematic exploration, only an occasional outstanding monument has been thought worthy of reconstruction.

The great buried cities mark the end of a process that began with modest Neolithic villages and reached highest expression in the late metropolises of Tenochtitlán or Cuzco. In the present state of our knowledge, it would seem that both areas developed without any extra-continental influence, and independently of each other. There is no evidence that the Central American civilizations exercised any influence over the South American ones, or vice versa, though both passed through parallel and contemporary stages.

There are serious conceptual difficulties involved in any attempt to trace the beginnings of indigenous American urbanization. On the basis of what size and what population density can one state when a cluster of dwellings becomes a hamlet? At what stage does it rank successively as village, town, city, or even metropolis? The quantitative criteria in use today are not suitable or appropriate, even for the colonial town or city. Archaeological finds or fragmentary demographic information are insufficient to determine their true dimensions. On the other hand, commercial, administrative, religious, and other functions carried out by a given center are more significant, though difficult, regrettably, to measure numerically. Consequently, in both this chapter and the next, it is impossible to use an exact terminology.

The first places to attract considerable numbers of rural inhabitants were religious ceremonial complexes such as Chavín de Huantar in the mountains of northern Peru, the centers of the Olmec culture (La Venta, in Tabasco) or Maya centers like Dzibilchaltún, in Yucatán, both in the Gulf of Mexico area.

In Peru ceremonial complexes appeared when irrigation, even

in its most primitive form, was bringing new land into cultivation. The population grew as a result of this innovation, forming clustered hamlets of adjacent dwellings, which were built according to no pre-established plan. Then fortified hilltop centers were also established. These forts provided protection for villages in the vicinity.

In the classical period, that is, during the first eight centuries A.D., the areas devoted to agriculture expanded once again. In the Virú Valley of northern Peru, for example, the area increased by 40 percent as a result of the construction of a vast network of irrigation canals. The population, of course, expanded with the availability of increased resources. This fact is confirmed by the greater concentration in already established areas and the building of villages in places hitherto uninhabited. In Mexico, MacNeish (1970) has found, in the case of Tehuacán already quoted, significant changes in the size of the population, in the extension of the agriculturally productive area, and in settlement patterns: villages and towns built like camps on hilltops, with the individual buildings more regularly distributed.

The gap between the ordinary peasants and the military and priestly castes became wider at this time, developing into a stratified society. The military expansion of some centers led to the formation of miniature states. However, the priests managed to control the military. Ceremonial centers grew in size and number, and it was precisely around certain of these that the first cities flourished, on the Andean altiplano, in the Petén area of Yucatán and Guatemala, and on the plateau of central Mexico (Anáhuac). In due course, governmental functions were added to the religious ones of these cities; such was the case at Tiahuanaco, near Lake Titicaca in present-day Boliva, at Tikal, in the Petén jungles of Guatemala, and at Teotihuacán near Mexico City.

The Akapana or the Kalasasaya at Tiahuanaco, the stepped pyramids around the central square at Tikal, the Sun and Moon pyramids which line the Calle de los Muertos at Teotihuacán—all are magnificent religious monuments, which the ravages of time have not succeeded in demolishing. The earliest excavations paid the greatest attention to the most impressive religious monuments, while more recent ones have revealed—especially at Tikal and Teotihuacán—palaces and houses indicative of complete settlements. Of the three sites mentioned, two were unique within their respective zones of influence. Tiahuanaco in Peru and Teotihuacán in Mexico were in positions of unrivaled predominance. In the Maya area, however,

Tikal eventually had to compete for supremacy with such other sites as Palenque in Chiapas, Copán in Honduras, and Chichén Itzá on the Yucatán peninsula. It is disputed whether these and other sites ever actually became real cities, in view of the scant evidence of extensive occupation and the apparently unimportant nature of their administrative functions.

Urban development is more obvious in the Postclassical Period. In the early stages urban centers were like compact villages with spacious houses, evidently arranged according to a plan allowing for ease of movement within the inhabited area. There was sometimes even a surrounding wall to cut off the residential area from the country outside. Community buildings arose, and religious ones no longer predominated among these. Some of the towns had so many functions, and such a size, and concentration, that they should be classified as cities.

Gradual political centralization, such as occurred during this period, led to the formation of confederations and kingdoms. When the city became the seat of local or "national" political power, it expanded, and population growth became a matter of concentration in the city itself rather than of more intensive settlement on the land.

The culminating point in this process was reached with true cities, such as Tenochtitlán, the capital of the Aztec empire, and the Inca empire's capital, Cuzco. The splendor of these two somewhat outshines that of other equally worthy cities like Tula, Cholula, Xochicalco, and Monte Albán in Mexico, or Chan Chan, Cajamarquilla, Pachacamac, and Machu Picchu in Peru. Tula and Xochicalco were Toltec capitals, and Monte Albán, the Mixtec capital. In Peru, Chan Chan was the capital of the Chimú kingdom on the northern coast, near present-day Trujillo, while Cajamarquilla and Pachacamac were the greatest centers on the central coast, near Lima. All of these cities antedate the formation of the Aztec and Inca empires. Machu Picchu, on the other hand, was one of the last refuges of the Incas in the Andes. The above is but a very abbreviated list of the cities that are only just beginning to be excavated.

Cuzco, "the other Rome of those Antarctic lands," as Vázquez de Espinosa called it, was a vast city in which the palaces of royalty and nobility stood side by side with religious monuments. They were erected on vast stone platforms, which still serve as the foundations for the houses and religious buildings constructed in the colonial period. Two main axes divided the city into four parts, thus giving it an ordered appearance. In the center lived the upper classes, near the public and religious buildings, while those lower down the social scale occupied districts that looked less and less typically urban as one moved toward the outskirts. A city of such opulence could only exist when backed by the human and material resources of a vast empire.

The chroniclers attribute to Tenochtitlán a population of several hundreds of thousands on the arrival of Cortés. If this is correct, then it had a larger population than most European urban centers of the time. It was, of course, the largest city on the American continent, and its existence presupposes an extremely strong political power, capable of exploiting much greater resources than could be found in the valley of Mexico and the surrounding areas. The precise size of Tenochtitlán is still disputed, but in any case it was unusually large for that age. Like the Inca empire's capital, Cuzco, it was a more secular city than those of the preclassical period. Religious monuments occupied the center, and houses spread toward the periphery subject to no preordained plan. The Aztec rulers did, however, insist on providing Tenochtitlán with an adequate communications network, thus making it appear more orderly. Four causeways led from the central square to the four points of the compass to facilitate access to the city. Moctezuma, moreover, built an aqueduct from Chapultepec to ensure a regular supply of drinking water.

SIZE OF THE ABORIGINAL POPULATION
ON THE EVE OF THE CONQUEST

The conquistadores, the missionaries, and the chroniclers took naturally an interest, even for practical reasons, in the size of the aboriginal populations they visited or conquered. Their rough estimates, some quite wild, were soon disregarded and the consequent vacuum of knowledge was not filled for a long time, not, in fact, until modern investigators attempted to make estimates that were apparently more scientifically based.

The desire to obtain reliable figures does not stem from idle speculation among scholars, since the knowledge we may get of the size of the indigenous population of America is of enormous significance to the whole history of man's occupation of the continent. There are two widely differing interpretations how the population rose from minute beginnings to its present-day level. One suggests a gradual increase, while the other asserts that, when two peoples and two ways of life clashed, there was a drastic reduction in the population so profound in its consequences that it only really recovered its earlier numbers around the middle of the past century. Dobyns (1966) has rightly said that "the idea that social scientists hold of the size of the aboriginal population of the Americas directly affects their interpretation of New World civilization and cultures." Since population density can be an indicator of cultural development, the nature and extent of indigenous civilization, the nature of the contact between both worlds, the nature of the colonial regime, the character of its society—all are dependent upon our adoption of one criterion or the other.

It has been pointed out with some scorn that contemporary scientists—realizing how little they still know about the Indians in spite of the arduous hours of research devoted to them—are reluctant to admit that the conquistadores, lacking their scientific knowledge and not having the same sympathy for the natives, actually knew more about the Indians than they do. Joking apart, geographers and anthropologists, while systematically rejecting early testimony, had to think up indirect methods in order to arrive at overall estimates of the size of the indigenous population on the eve of the Conquest. We shall continue to include in this the primitive hunters and gatherers of what is now Canada and the U.S.A.; their small numbers would have an insignificant effect on the overall picture, and it helps to avoid the anachronism of trying to distinguish between a Latin and an Anglo-Saxon America before Columbus.

Among the various methods used to arrive at an approximate figure, two are particularly noteworthy. The first consists of multiplying by 3 the number of indigenous inhabitants who still survived some decades ago in the present century. This calculation is based on the hypothesis that, from the sixteenth century onward, they had been reduced by that amount. The second evaluated the ecological potential of each region and attributed a typical population density figure to each one. This latter procedure embodies the implicit idea— which we discounted in the first paragraph of this chapter—that the part played by historical and cultural factors in the distribution of the indigenous population of America is considered of secondary importance. However, each using a different method, Rivet and Sapper both arrived at the remarkably similar figures of forty and fifty million respectively.

A so-called skeptical school of thought, which was originated by the anthropologist Kroeber and which culminated with the philologist Rosenblat (1954 and 1967), set about reducing these figures. Kroeber maintained that there were only 8.5 million Indians in the whole of America at the time of the Conquest. This figure presupposes an average density of only 0.2 inhabitants per square kilometer. Kroeber came to this conclusion after a careful examination of the indigenous population of specific areas in the U.S.A., California in particular, and the backward projection of the growth rate of the indigenous population of Mexico, recorded between the estimate of Humboldt at the end of the eighteenth century and the 1930 national census. The last operation is based on the supposition that there had been a regular rate of growth since the Conquest. Among other things, it did not take into account either the formidable losses caused by Spanish rule or the debilitating effects of the continual epidemics, which were far more serious then than in the nineteenth and twentieth centuries. Kroeber thus assigned to the highly developed cultures of the continent a total of 3 million each. Rosenblat (1954), however, estimated the Indian population of America at that time, within the administrative limits of the present-day states, as 13 million. He arrived at this figure by adding together the estimates of various ethnographers in specific area studies and then adjusting the total in accordance with his own personal "verisimilitude" criterion. He allowed Mexico 4.5 million, Peru only 2 million, to which should be added the 1,300,000 Indians of Bolivia and Ecuador.

Quite as arbitrary as the above estimates, but vastly higher, is that of another American anthropologist. His method is simple and clear, and, moreover, he does not disguise its theoretical nature nor hide his basic assumptions. Nor does he attempt to arrive at an exact figure. Dobyns, the anthropologist concerned, assumes that the Indian population was reduced, after contact with the Europeans, by approximately 95 percent for reasons that will be examined in the next chapter. Using some relatively recent examples and some very early ones, he comes to a variety of different results. The whole sum of his accumulated materials leads him to conclude that it is justifiable to multiply by 20 or 25 the lowest Indian population figure recorded, that is, before their numbers started to increase again. According to him, this lowest point was not reached everywhere simultaneously, but varied from region to region. It occurred late, for example, in those few groups that first came into contact with Europeans in the eighteenth century or even later. In the remainder it was reached in the seventeenth century.

On the basis of such arguments, Dobyns calculates a pre-Columbian population of between 90 and 112 million, of whom 60 million would be equally divided between central Mexico and Peru.

His reasoning is actually less haphazard than it appears in a summary as brief as this. Dobyns critically reexamines all the hypotheses and methods previously formulated and raises to the status of a generalization the results reached by the detailed historical studies of Cook, Borah, and Simpson. These three were themselves too cautious to apply their conclusions to the continent as a whole.

The historical line of inquiry carried out by the California school, made up of the above-mentioned authors, seems a more promising one than that followed by others. Their studies so far refer to one portion of the old viceroyalty of New Spain, but the techniques they have developed can equally well be applied anywhere else where similar sources are available.

The estimates of Cook, Borah, and Simpson concerning the population of central Mexico, the region bounded by the Isthmus of Tehuantepec and the frontier of the Chichimecas and of the kingdom of New Galicia, are based on well-defined methods of backward projection. Having been able to establish the population of the area in about 1565 from counts of the Indians made for fiscal purposes, and taking into account that several local samples suggest that there was at least a 40 percent demographic decline between 1519 and 1565, Cook and Simpson in 1948 ventured to suggest a population figure. They multiplied the 1565 base and attributed to the area, on the eve of the Conquest, a population of 11 million.

Nearly a decade later, Cook and Borah again took up the question. They then made a more thorough study of the rate at which the population had dropped, and found that between 1550 and 1570 the average annual rate was 3.8 percent, a higher figure than had previously been acknowledged. Moreover it was such despite the fact that during the period examined there had been no epidemics that were anywhere near as disastrous as those which had occurred both before and after. Thus the rate of depopulation in the earlier years after the Conquest may well have been higher. In any case, Cook and Borah (1957), using the annual depopulation figure of 3.8 percent as a constant, estimated the Indian population of central Mexico on the arrival of Cortés as 25.3 million. Later, Borah and Cook suggested that the figure should be raised to 30 million; however, they reduced their estimate again to a figure of 25.2 million—almost identical with their original 1957 projection—after a study of the tribute received by the Indian Triple Alliance on the basis of information recorded by the viceregal authorities from the verbal statements of old people.

Thus, with examination of new documents and refinement of technical methods, historians' estimates of the size of the indigenous population of central Mexico has tended to increase. Although the estimates vary as more and more careful studies are made, the three professors from the University of California have shown remarkable ingenuity and persistence in their endeavors to make their investigations more reliable; while their estimates have fluctuated, they are all significantly higher than those of their predecessors. In the opinion of Cook and Borah (1966), these figures revalidate the evidence provided by many chroniclers whose statements were proclaimed exaggerated, and they accord fully with the impression given by archaeological evidence that the area had reached demographic saturation.

Subsequent studies on agricultural productivity (for example, those of Wagner, 1964, and West, 1970), nutrition, and pathology of pre-Columbian social conditions, as well as the discovery of new demographic sources, will shed new light on a subject that is still much in dispute and that fascinates scholars, for strictly scientific reasons, and a wider public, for profoundly intellectual ones.

III

The Conquest

*N*OT even in prehistoric times was America completely isolated from other continents. Successive contacts with Asia contributed to the variety of its cultures and languages, and to the physical features of its inhabitants, such as their stature, cranial structure, and pigmentation. On one occasion there was even a link with Europe: the Scandinavians set foot on the northeast coast and maintained colonies there from the ninth to the fifteenth centuries, without realizing they had reached another continent. They thought that the lands they had discovered belonged to the chain of islands which, like Greenland, they had already found. When the Nordic settlements disappeared, their achievement was forgotten; their incursion went almost unrecognized in Europe and had no lasting effect on the events in the New World.

The second invasion from Europe was a different matter: its effects were irreversible. At the end of the fifteenth century, the Spaniards landed in the West Indies, and within half a century of rapid and continuous advance, they dominated a large part of the New World. Their success was not due to their numbers, which were actually small, nor to a technology so overwhelmingly more advanced as to cancel out the Indians' natural advantages of numerical superiority and local knowledge. This is proved by the success of some resistance put up by the indigenous population. Although the conquistadores did possess superior technology, their triumph is to be explained rather by political circumstances.

Both the Aztecs and the Incas were encountered at a time of great political instability in both empires. Fierce internal dissensions were undermining the hitherto solid fabric of their institutions, and this had undoubted moral repercussions on the native Indians. The people subjugated by the Aztecs were longing to shake off the yoke of their oppressors. The Tlascalans, for example, far from opposing Cortés, became his valuable allies. Peru, at that time, was in the midst of a large-scale civil war between two rival pretenders to the throne, Huáscar and Atahualpa. In yet another case, that of the Chibchas, Jiménez de Quesada managed to lay hands on their rich empire by exploiting the dissensions between two local leaders.

The armies of the conquistadores, moreover, were not fighting on their own initiative. A strong, unified state backed them, and it provided them with objectives, support, and lines of communication. Thanks to this, a few thousand men spread out over a vast continent were able to overcome the disintegrating effects of distance. Moreover, the Spaniards were possessed of a tradition of conquest. For eight centuries they had learned not to be put off by the superior numerical strength of the enemy, and to dominate other peoples. Of all European states, it was Castile that was best qualified to confront the Indian masses. The nations that followed her to join in the division of America were restricted to the relatively unpopulated Atlantic coastline.

External causes, then, disrupted the course of the indigenous world. The population began to drop alarmingly once the balance of their economy, society, and culture was disturbed. This fact is no longer denied, but an attempt is now being made to establish the extent of the drop, the factors responsible for it, and the relative importance of each one of them.

The term Conquest is here used to refer to the period from the discovery of the New World to the time when the native population of America reached its nadir. It thus exceeds the temporal limits usually assigned to the term when considered from a political or military point of view. In our opinion, it seems more appropriate in a demographic study to restrict the adjective colonial to the period following the nadir, when the society that emerged from the upheaval of the Conquest had reached a new equilibrium and was starting on a second cycle of expansion. From this point of view, the sixteenth century and part of the seventeenth are, in brief, the antithesis of the indigenous phase. The later colonial period was to witness yet another demographic change of direction, which would reverse the trends of the previous disastrous phase.

The lowest point in the decline of the indigenous population was reached a century and a half after the first contacts between the conquered and the conquerors, that is, in the middle of the seventeenth century in New Spain and later in parts of Peru.

THE COLLAPSE OF THE INDIGENOUS POPULATION

Having established the meaning and limits of the period, let us consider the extent of the decline of the indigenous population during that time. This, of course, inevitably depends on what we consider the initial and final population figures to have been.

Rosenblat (1954), typical of those who hold that the indigenous population on the eve of the Conquest was quite small, thinks that between 1492 and 1650 the inhabitants of America were reduced from 13.3 million to 10 million, a loss of a quarter of the original total. For any people that retains its internal cohesion and suffers no external disruptive interference, such a reduction in a century and a half is, of course, a very considerable one. Spain itself lost less than this proportion, and in a shorter space of time, during the famous decadence of the seventeenth century, and this is generally admitted to have been very serious. Nevertheless, in the nature of the crisis there was nothing like the disaster which affected America. The population of the Iberian peninsula became discouraged on account of economic depression; but the social, political, and cultural framework survived and did not suffer the disruption which the New World experienced. It is therefore not surprising that the population decline in America should have been greater.

For those who accept an initially high population figure the decline seems catastrophic. Dobyns, whom we have already mentioned, considers it likely that the decline resulting from contact with Europeans was so great as to leave only 4 or 5 percent of the original native population. He suggests a reduction from 90–112 million to about 4.5 million by the middle of the seventeenth century, an even lower figure than that quoted by Rosenblat. According to the latter, the indigenous population reached its lowest point later, in 1825, with 8.5 million.

Thus we are faced with two opposing theses, which it would be pointless to discuss in general terms. Only a regional examination, based on reliable local sources, would allow one to make reasonable generalizations. We may begin by seeing what happened in the area that has been most reliably studied to date, central Mexico, referring again to the studies of the California school.

In moving from prehistoric to historic times, we leave the field of crude inferences based on secondary sources, such as archaeological and other less usual evidence. For lack of more reliable data, we have had to refer to them in order to be able to give an overall picture of demographic evolution. But for the period we are going to consider, there is one source which—though not ideal—is at least more closely related to demography: the counts made for fiscal, administrative, or religious purposes. The most frequent and exact are those carried out by the Real Hacienda.

Because they were prepared for strictly practical reasons, the counts omit important segments of the population. In the majority of cases only male adults were recorded, since this was the tribute-paying section of the population and consequently the administration gave it the greatest attention. The later processing of this fiscal data to obtain population data demands an accurate knowledge of the Indians' family structure and of the Spanish tribute system. Without this knowledge one runs the risk of making serious mistakes, such as that of Kubler in an early statement about the population trends in central Mexico in the sixteenth century. In a work published in 1942, this distinguished historian maintained that the Indian population had increased in the middle of the century. Later investigations have proved, however, that the rise was only an apparent one. It was due to a tax reform that brought into the tax-paying class certain groups that had previously been exempt, in particular the Chichimecas, slaves, and *mayeques*.

To obtain the total population figure for a locality or region from this fiscal information, the recorded numbers should be multiplied by a factor representing each individual's dependents. Then the omitted categories should be estimated and added. Finally, after using all the available sources, the gaps should be filled in by extrapolations. In order to complete the first operation, the California school empirically adopted, after several attempts, the conversion factor of 2.8 when dealing with tribute-payers recorded after the fiscal reform, and of 3.3 for the earlier period, when only married males were subject to the tax. These are the lowest factors that have ever been employed. Basing their estimates on documentary evidence from New Granada, the Colombian historians Friede (1965 and 1967) and Jaramillo Uribe (1963 and 1964) recommend higher ratios and deny that any one factor can be applied in the variety of situations that occur. Whenever the documents do not give the number of *tributarios* but indicate the payments made in kind, then, if the price of the goods and the head tax are known, the number of tributarios could be determined and total population figure calculated.

After various steps indicated in the previous chapter, Cook and Borah proposed the following figures for the Indians of central Mexico:

1519	25.3 million
1523	16.8 "
1548	6.3 "
1568	2.6 "
1580	1.9 "
1595	1.3 "
1605	1.0 "

According to these figures, one-third of the Indians died off in the early years of the Conquest, and in each subsequent quarter-century more than half of the remainder disappeared. At the beginning of the seventeenth century only 4 percent of the original population was left. The drop shows no pause, nor any sign of leveling off. Even architecture can provide evidence for the demographer. As Phelan (1956) has shown in his analysis of the Franciscan churches, at the beginning of the Conquest period, this order built open chapels at the west end of their churches from which services could be conducted in the open air for the crowds of newly converted Indians. By the end of the sixteenth century, mass was celebrated inside the churches at the high altar or even in the side chapels.

Was the evolution of central Mexico exceptional or was the situation similar over the whole continent? The sources are equally fragmentary concerning the rest of America, but, contrary to the instance of Mexico, they lie neglected. For the time being, therefore, one is treading on uncertain ground. Future studies will weigh, compare and relate the samples already available in order to establish with greater certainty what reliance can be placed upon them and, consequently, to what extent it is legitimate to generalize from such partial results. One may say, for the moment, that it appears from all the cases so far investigated that, despite local variations and differences of degree, the precipitate fall in Mexico is noted elsewhere.

The Antilles, the oldest of the examples in question, fully corroborates the idea of a fall of catastrophic proportions. Cook and

Borah (1971) have recently caused yet another stir by putting forward a proposition as daring as the one they formulated some years ago concerning central Mexico. The Berkeley scholars, referring to Hispaniola, the island now divided between Haiti and the Dominican Republic, suggest a pre-Columbian population similar to that of today. This figure is far higher than the three or four million suggested by Bartolomé de las Casas, an estimate that has been criticized and challenged for centuries. The Cook and Borah figure is based not on newly discovered data, but on a critical reexamination of facts that are already known and on a backward projection of the demographic trend. The decline was undoubtedly of disastrous proportions. Even accepting conservative estimates, the pre-Columbian population of Hispaniola must have fallen from about one hundred thousand to only a few hundred in 1570. To make up for the lack of natives, Negro slaves and Indians from the Bahamas were introduced at an early date. That measure alone proves that depopulation there was worse than on the mainland.

Jaramillo Uribe (1964) has carried out an exhaustive and careful review, region by region, of the literature left by the conquistadores, chroniclers, and missionaries in Colombia. From his detailed study, and despite his reservations, one receives a clear impression of disaster. More limited in its compass, Friede followed up his original thesis dealing with the Quimbaya tribe (1963) by examining the whole of the province of Tunja, also situated in the eastern Andean cordillera (1965). In both cases Friede resorted to the *visita* records and the tribute rolls prepared by royal officers. According to these documents, the 232,407 Indians in Tunja in 1537 were reduced by over a quarter to 168,444 by 1564. Later there was a further decline, and by 1636 only a fifth of the original number were left, 44,691. Whole towns had been abandoned. Although somewhat reluctantly, the Indians at that time were concentrating into recently built villages, not always carefully planned. A later revision of the Tunja case by Colmenares (1970) has provided adjusted figures and added previously unknown material, but has not altered the picture outlined by Friede's study. The even more recent study of the same data by Cook and Borah (1971) just adds more details to the analysis.

Recent monographs on other parts of the eastern region have reexamined the tribute visitas. In Vélez (Fajardo, 1969) and Pamplona (Colmenares, 1969), the indigenous population also shrank to about one-fifth of its original size by 1640. However, the greatest contribution of the new studies by Fajardo and Colmenares is not that they confirm the accuracy of the trend shown, but that they present the question from a new angle. Fajardo found data for constructing age pyramids of several mining towns. The serious epidemics that afflicted the Nuevo Reino de Granada, especially the one that occurred in 1587, left a very noticeable gap in the age group concerned, both in Vélez and in Pamplona. It is also easy to visualize the gradual decline of the population by noting how the base of the successive pyramids shrinks. There appears to have been a halt in the middle of the seventeenth century, when the age structure began to take on a more youthful appearance again. This recovery was also partly due to the departure of the large number of adult migrants who had flocked to the mines.

In neighboring Venezuela, the evidence gathered by Arcila Farías (1957) agrees that the number of tributarios declined shortly after the founding of Caracas. Contemporaries disagreed about the extent of the decline: some maintained that the numbers fell by one-half, others that they fell to a quarter of the original figure; in any case it was a substantial drop.

In a paper presented to the American Historical Association in Boston, N. D. Cook (1970) has recently foreshadowed important information concerning the demography of Peru, which he studied in an as yet unpublished thesis. His study starts with the *visita general* carried out by Viceroy Toledo in the 572 repartimientos of Indians that existed in the country in 1572, and continues with the periodic *revisitas* carried out from then on. After several years' research in Spanish and Peruvian archives, he was fortunate enough to find copies of the actual rosters or their summaries. His study goes up to 1620, thus covering half a century. N. D. Cook naturally has filled in the gaps in his documentary evidence, and he has arranged the erratic figures into ten-year intervals. The results of his investigations and calculations are shown in table 3.1, which he has kindly allowed us to reproduce. According to this, between 1570 and 1620 the indigenous population of Peru was reduced by approximately half, from 1,264,530 inhabitants of all ages and both sexes to 589,033. Although the rate of decline seems somewhat slower than in the cases of Tunja and central Mexico over equivalent periods, it is nevertheless rapid.

N. D. Cook's investigations do not yet cover the period between Pizarro's arrival and the beginning of Viceroy Toledo's term of office, a decisive one so far as the fate of the Indian population is concerned. For lack of data, all one can do is to compare the figures given

TABLE 3.1 Indigenous Population of Peru, 1570–1620

	1570		1580		1590	
Region	Tributarios	Total	Tributarios	Total	Tributarios	Total
North Coast	20,401	77,529	15,353	60,651	11,759	48,270
Central Coast	25,189	128,820	20,567	101,399	17,082	82,044
South Coast	8,711	36,587	6,403	26,406	4,936	19,883
Northern Sierra	42,677	209,057	34,544	180,753	30,224	163,366
Central Sierra	42,024	241,143	36,955	207,381	33,025	181,111
Southern Sierra	176,003	571,394	103,739	506,910	93,465	452,961
Totals	315,005	1,264,530	217,561	1,083,500	190,491	947,301

	1600		1610		1620	
Region	Tributarios	Total	Tributarios	Total	Tributarios	Total
North Coast	9,160	39,062	7,252	32,131	5,835	22,815
Central Coast	14,331	67,710	12,140	56,942	10,374	42,323
South Coast	3,935	15,394	3,193	12,164	2,668	8,168
Northern Sierra	26,002	146,274	22,372	131,034	19,356	106,125
Central Sierra	29,731	159,082	26,874	139,998	24,431	109,792
Southern Sierra	84,599	406,266	76,905	365,644	70,242	299,810
Totals	167,758	833,788	198,736	737,913	132,900	589,033

SOURCE: N. D. Cook, 1970.

for the early visitas with the number of tributarios of the Incas which local chieftains noted on quipus. Indian authorities rapidly passed through their experienced, agile fingers the conventional knots tied in the *quipu* cords by their ancestors, and in the presence of the Spanish census officials deciphered the figures that a notary public wrote down. Thus in 1567, the Indian chief Martín Cari read before the visitador Garcí Díez de San Miguel the quipus that listed town by town the number of Aymarás and Urus tributary in the province of Chucuito (Espinoza Soriano, 1964). According to Indian sources, before the campaigns of Huayna Capac and the civil war between Huáscar and Atahualpa, Chucuito had 20,280 tributarios aged between thirty and sixty. As is the case in flourishing rural communities, this group would have made up about 12 percent of the population, so that the inhabitants of this Indian district must have numbered about 170,000. Less than half a century later, in 1567, according to the visitador, the same valleys and mountains had only 63,012 people, a third of their previous number.

One can clearly see the extensive nature of this catastrophe when examining the demographic profile of Chucuito in search of corroborative evidence. Boys and girls aged between eleven and

each township before the regrouping took place. These figures have been obtained by dividing the numbers recorded in 1575 by the number of settlements in order to produce an average per township. It is not suggested that the inhabitants were equitably distributed among all the centers in the district—some would have been larger, some smaller; but their overall scarcity, together with the drastic reduction in the number of population centers, suggests that depopulation was continuing. Archaeology will perhaps be able to confirm or reject our guess that villages and townships were larger prior to the Conquest. By comparing the surface of each repartimiento with the number of original and new Indian settlements we may realize how much waste land was left between new townships under the regrouping arrangements. In view of this, it could be argued that the pre-Hispanic Indian population was several times greater than that recorded during the visita.

It may also be mentioned in passing that the first, very fragmentary figures concerning the reduction in the native population of the central valley of Chile in the late sixteenth and early seventeenth centuries have been made available in the study by Góngora (1970) on the formation of encomiendas in that region.

Since it has been suggested that altitude and climate may, to varying degrees, have affected the rate of decline of the native population, let us examine what happened on the coast of Peru compared with what we have already seen concerning the mountain and plateau areas. According to the suggestion put forward by Rowe (1946) on rather scanty evidence, the population of the coastal zone declined in the first decades of the Conquest period until it was reduced to 5 percent or even less of its original size. Keith (1970) still holds to this opinion when examining the valley of Chancay. An economy dependent on irrigation would probably be more vulnerable to any disturbance that upset the complicated mechanism controlling it, and this would apply equally to the pre- and post-Conquest periods. In addition when we look closely at the six zones into which N. D. Cook divided Lower Peru, the coastal ones registered a sharp decline between 1570 and 1620, while the mountain zones, on the other hand, were declining only slowly. The coast, already less populated, fell to one-third or one-quarter of its original size, while the mountain zones only went down to one-half. The difference between these highland and coastal rates was particularly noticeable in the south. There, the mountain areas declined at the rate of -1.1 percent annually, while that of the coastal zones was almost -4 percent.

The comparison between coast and mountain is a subject to which Cook and Borah have frequently paid attention. They have just dealt with the topic in their recent examination of the case of Colombia (1971), which we have already referred to; but the classic, careful, and detailed treatment of the subject is that dealing with Mexico (1960). Cook and Borah assembled the data available on the region in such a way as to construct two demographic curves. One was based on data concerning the highlands of the central plateau and central Veracruz, as well as the areas of Oaxaca-Mixteca, Michoacán, and Jalisco-Zacatecas; the other was based on data concerning the *tierras calientes* of the Gulf of Mexico and Pacific coastlines, that is, the Pánuco-Valles and Alvarado-Coatzacoalcos coast in the east, and the Oaxaca-Costa, Zacatula-Guerrero, and Colima-Nayarit coast in the west. The contraction of the first group was as follows: 1534–38, −6.53 percent per year; 1539–43, −5.01; 1544–48, −4.27; 1549–53, −3.97; 1554–58, −4.33; 1559–63, −0.95; 1564–68, −4.85; and 1569–73, −2.79. Without exception, the annual rates show a negative sign and are higher at the beginning of the period. During the same quinquennia, the corresponding tierras calientes percentage figures were as follows: −9.11; −6.92; −7.15; −10.25; −6.88; −4.34; −6.18; and −9.84. Thus the coastal areas suffered a more pronounced decline than the interior. For the whole period, the yearly average is −6.87 percent on the coast, and nearly half that figure, −3.74, on the plateau. (See also fig. 2.)

It is hard to grasp what these cold figures mean in human terms. Even minds accustomed to the hard facts of Old World demography find it difficult to conceive such huge losses. In the studies on European society in the seventeenth and eighteenth centuries, historians use the expression demographic crisis to describe a situation when a third of the inhabitants of a locality or region died off within the short term of two or three years. Such a setback was serious, but of only passing significance, since natural recovery from such a catastrophe was very rapid. A high marriage rate made up for the low rate during the crisis and led to a boom in the birth rate. The latter was also partially caused by the desire of many couples to enlarge their families after an involuntary postponement. When these extra births were added to the normal rate, the losses were soon made good, and after a while the only evidence of the crisis was the slightly unusual composition of certain age groups. Thus the depletion in one generation was counteracted by the natural birthrate reaction in another.

Plateau   Coast
Population (millions)   Population (millions)

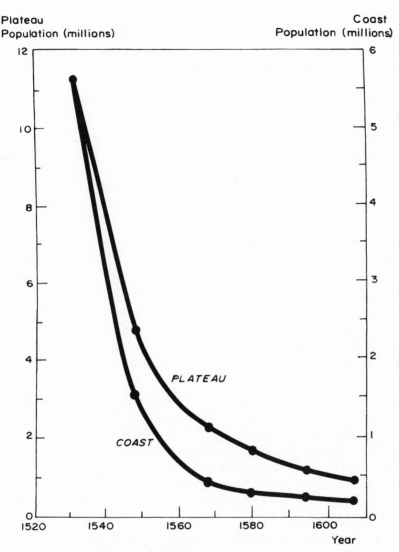

FIGURE 2. Population of plateau and coastal areas of central Mexico, 1532–1608. (Source: Cook and Borah, 1971.)

The size of each generation might fluctuate, but the population as a whole remained steady or actually increased.

But the downfall of the Indian population of America was not like this. Crises caused by famine and epidemics had also existed there before the arrival of the Spaniards (Álvarez Amézquita, 1960). Aztec codices record, for example, the famine of 1453, when men sold themselves as slaves in order to remain alive. Similar records exist of the 1504 famine caused by drought (Rosenblat, 1954, and Cook, 1946a). Nevertheless, however severe and long-lasting was the havoc wrought by both events, they never threatened the vitality of pre-Columbian society in Mexico.

Nor did wars have serious or lasting results. There have been two wars of unprecedented scope and intensity since registers of vital statistics, containing regular and reliable information, were started in the majority of countries in the world. The use of war materiel and the mobilization of resources were on a massive scale, as were the human and material losses. Nevertheless, the destruction suffered on the battlefield and behind the lines, and other indirect losses such as those caused by the postponement of marriages, fall in the birth rate, and economic disorganization (for example, greater prenatal mortality rate), were quite easily compensated for in the postwar period. After a couple of decades all traces of the conflict had vanished. Recent experiences seem to prove that, in the long run, war fortunately does not have such disastrous consequences as one might expect, at least provided that the damage does not exceed recognized limits. This opinion is by no means intended to excuse war—it is readily admitted that a whole generation is seriously affected—but it does suggest that recovery is possible.

In view of the number of combatants and the type of weapons available, the wars of the Conquest could not possibly have caused greater damage proportionately than the last two World Wars. On the other hand, in the pre-Cortesian period, the so-called guerras floridas of the Aztec empire ended (according to Cook, 1946a) with the sacrifice of more than fifteen thousand captives per year, the majority on the altars of Tenochtitlán. Not even butchery on this scale endangered Indian society. On the contrary, it is quite possible that, despite its unpleasantness, it actually helped to relieve incipient population pressure.

The reader will forgive this attempt to deal with the problem of population decline and its causes by means of comparison and contrast rather than by use of historical evidence. The well-known phrase "You can't see the forest for the trees" suggests why it was considered that an accumulation of evidence might easily lessen the reader's understanding of what happened. The explanations contained in documentary evidence deal with the impressions or beliefs of contemporaries, but these people were not always in the best position to disentangle the reasons behind events. What have present-day theorists to say about this decline in the population of America?

The Homicide Theory

Let us examine first the homicide theory (Kubler, 1942). It would be more accurate to term it the genocide theory, since the action described affected not only individuals but whole ethnic groups. Although the title of this theory is a misnomer, it has been widely accepted because it embraces a wide variety of offensive actions against the Indian masses.

The theory was inspired by the famous pamphlet *Breve relación de la destrucción de las Indias Occidentales* by the militant Fray Bartolomé de Las Casas. It was soon translated into several languages, and became the prime base of the arguments giving rise to the Black Legend. Allegation is implicit in its very title. The praiseworthy zeal that engendered it has for centuries kept alive the moral stature of Las Casas but, on the other hand, has prevented the proper analysis of the information it contains, as it is impossible for historians to separate fact from prejudice.

Las Casas attributes the population losses to direct action on the part of the conquistadores. He denounces them for systematic killing, appalling cruelty, and excessive overwork. Kubler consequently calls the book a catalogue of horrors. The Dominican, who later became bishop of Chiapas, was a leading figure among the pro-Indian, anti-settler humanitarians, who also included other clerics like Fray Toribio de Motolinía, and royal officials like Alonso de Zorita. This group came to acquire such influence that it managed to obtain from the Spanish crown protective powers over the Indians, in both the legal and the economic fields.

The homicide theory shows manifest signs of a voluntarist concept of man and of the world and includes a variety of features, which must be elucidated in any detailed analysis.

First of all, it lists factors of a military nature. Deaths resulting from military encounters are mentioned, and yet, as we have seen, these cannot have been too significant from a demographic point of view. The same applies to deliberate acts committed by isolated forces in areas not then effectively controlled. Systematic terror as a psychological weapon made up for the numerical inferiority of the Spaniards. Las Casas relates the use of such tactics within cities that had offered no resistance, for the sole purpose of ensuring the submission of the inhabitants through fear. Regrettably, this measure has been employed only too frequently in colonial, international, and civil wars, even in the present century.

The list of horrors committed could not, of course, fail to include the forcible requisitioning of supplies for the occupying troops and the repressive measures employed to "persuade" those suppliers who were uncooperative. In a subsistence economy like that of the Indians, any significant loss in food reserves was as serious as the partial or total loss of a crop and certainly led to famine and death. Similar results must have ensued when male, native labor was forcibly recruited either for military construction work or to serve as auxiliaries in operations against neighboring peoples. Las Casas recounts how Indians were pressed into service in Nicaragua to transport timber from the forests to the coast for the construction of ships for the Spanish Pacific fleet. The enslaving of Panamanian Indians for transport to Peru falls into the same sort of category.

Equally credible are the scenes describing arbitrary acts committed during the search for plunder or ransom, or those which portray sexual abuses. Strictly speaking, such behavior falls within the military tradition of the period. It is not difficult to imagine, either, a whole string of vicious acts such as figure in every account of violence. In the same category of deeds imputed to the Spaniards must be included the massacre of whole villages of sedentary and peaceful Indians by unsubmissive, rebellious, or nomadic factions. Such acts certainly occurred. Thiel (1951) assembles information concerning their occurrence in Guatemala; Sauer (1935) mentions them in northwestern Mexico, and Friede (1963) gives details of some in his study of the Quimbayas.

In time, when the conquistadores had settled down in the new dominions, the denunciators of the colonial process changed their line of attack: allegations of a military nature were replaced by those of an economic nature. In common with the accusations above, there is a core of truth. Friede (1967) is quite correct when he states that labor in the mines was the prime cause of depopulation in the mining areas of Muzo, in present-day Colombia. But one should also bear in mind that the example quoted is late, occurring as it did in the seventeenth century. The extent of the loss of life among Indians employed in the mines was such as to lead to the issuance of a royal cedula in April 1549 prohibiting the use of native labor in the mines of New Spain. The measure was later extended to New Galicia and Peru, but never enforced. On the contrary, the *mita* and repartimientos—the results rather than the causes of depopulation—were institutionalized. Mellafe (1965) has quite rightly asserted: "Work in the mines, together with the military and political events of the Conquest, are phenomena constantly quoted as being the causes of depopulation, but they are only minor contributing factors to the demographic disaster of the first half of the sixteenth century. It should be realized that when work in the mines was organized on a massive and compulsory scale, the native population of America had already been reduced by more than 50 percent."

Perhaps some day soon it may be possible to abandon the ever scurrilous field of speculation for firmer ground, which will enable us to measure the incidence of each of the factors enumerated by the homicide theory. It will only be possible to evaluate each of the individual elements featured in this thesis when enough age pyramids are available showing indisputable evidence of the deaths attributable to the conquistadores or the excessive exploitation of labor by encomenderos. Both inevitably affected the adult male section of the population more seriously, since they were the ones fit for the bearing of arms or for hard labor. Women, children, and old people usually took less of the immediate impact of the hardships or war and exploitation. The sex and age structure of Huánuco (Ortiz de Zúñiga, 1967) shows this very clearly. The men who could be used by the army or for forced labor during the Conquest, and whose age by 1562 no longer made it necessary for them to hide, are conspicuously less numerous than the women of their generation. But if one were to generalize concerning the population decline as a whole on the basis of this case, one would have to be very careful. Such an irregular sex distribution does not mean that the community was irreparably affected. If the female portion of the population was thus preserved and if there were some relaxation of the monogamous nature of the society, then perhaps the long-term consequences on effective fertility would not have been serious, and the Indians of Huánuco could very soon have recovered from that unfortunate episode. The large numbers of children and young people recorded in the visita are perhaps evidence that some compensatory mechanism had already begun to operate for reasons as yet unknown to us.

Until such time as it becomes possible to assess the situation by means of reliable figures, one cannot but quote the sensible observations on the matter which the marquis of Castelfuerte wrote in a memoir to his successor in the government of the viceroyalty of Peru. Really worried because the Indians, even in his time, in 1736,

had not recovered from the demographic tragedy that had over-
taken them, he argued as follows concerning their obvious numerical
decline:

> The causes of the above-mentioned population decline in the Indies
> are various, and although all those who have dealt with and spoken
> of them assert that the main cause of the decline is also that of their
> continued existence, such as work in the mines, . . . nevertheless, the
> prime reason, which without any others would have led to the de-
> crease of the Indians' numbers, is the mere fact of their being sub-
> ject to the rule of an alien power, as has happened in all empires. . . .
> Many townships are deserted (in the province of Santa), but neither
> they nor the previous ones were destroyed by any positive action.
> The loss of political control, esteem, wealth, abundance, and strength
> to the conquering power naturally affects the will of the conquered
> to beget and bring up children they are unable to support. (*Memorias
> de los Virreyes*, vol. 3).

Loss of the Will to Survive

When examining the tax records in which both the tributary and
his family were noted, it is surprising to observe how small the family
unit was and how many men remained unmarried. Jaramillo Uribe
(1964) remarks that at the beginning of the seventeenth century it
was common in New Granada to find that half the Indian couples
had no children. On the average they had only two children, and the
family with four offspring was exceptional. Only polygamous chiefs
sometimes had more. One century earlier, in 1514, the repartimiento
of Indians on the royal haciendas in Santo Domingo recorded an
average of less than one child per family (Sauer, 1969). However,
Las Casas reported that Indian women had between three and five
children each at the time of the Spaniards' arrival. Thus a period of
satisfactory reproduction was followed by one of sterility. According
to González and Mellafe (1965), the pre-Conquest average family
of six in the Andean region of Huánuco became an average of two
and a half. This drop, according to them, suggests that after the Conquest nuclear families were biologically incomplete. It also reveals
a reduction in the number of children per family. It is evident that
the Indians decreased not only on account of deaths, but also partially because they did not ensure the normal replacement of the
generations.

Why should there have been such a drop in the fertility rate? In
general terms this may be due to psychological or socioeconomic

causes. These are not mutually exclusive, but rather complementary. A social or economic attitude is translated into a psychological one before motivating a conscious or unconscious resolve, just as a psychic predisposition has a bearing on the social and economic state. The accusations made by encomenderos decrying the aloofness and laziness of the Indians are well known. The Burgos laws of 1512, introduced precisely to protect the Indians, took the validity of this judgment of the Indians' character for granted. As with similar complaints made by modern colonial powers, this is clear evidence of the despondency of natives living in a society that was no longer theirs.

Little is yet known about demographic behavior that can be studied reasonably objectively, and of course still less is known about the psychological states that influence it! We can judge the state of mind of the natives only through the extreme reactions, which have left an indelible mark behind, but we shall never know their intimate thoughts, owing to the lack of literary testimony from the oppressed people themselves. Spanish sources, nevertheless, allow one to catch a glimpse of the deep impression made on the Indian conscience by the Conquest. The far-reaching and irreversible nature of its effects make the Indians' state of depression readily understandable. The rapid and unforeseen collapse of their conception of the world, of their beliefs and customs, could not but foster in the natives a feeling of complete and utter helplessness. They felt their gods had abandoned them. They were suddenly launched into a world over which they had no control, and they lost their will to live. Flight, which uprooted them from their homes and disrupted their family and community ties, was their instinctive reaction to the offensive and inescapable presence of the invader.

Ill-treatment, excessive work, and the desire to avoid payment of tribute often resulted in attempted suicide. Kubler (1942) quotes one particular, extreme case in which a medicine man persuaded a large number of people to commit suicide. The story leads us beyond the individual's feeling of frustration to that experienced by a whole community. The symptoms of this include continence, regular abortion, and even infanticide, carried out with the deliberate purpose of hastening the disappearance of the tribe.

In a letter sent from Santo Domingo expressing his astonishment and indignation, Fray Pedro de Córdoba, Dominican vice-provincial, described the following situation to the king (CDI, vol. 11):

The women, worn out with work, avoid conception and childbearing; lest, being pregnant or with young children, they have twice the work to do. The situation is so bad that many pregnant women seek and induce abortion, others have killed their children with their own hands so that they shall not have to endure the same hardships. . . . I have never read or heard of any nation, not even among the heathen, who have done such harm to their enemies as Christians have done to these unfortunate people who have helped and befriended them in their own land, for . . . they have caused these poor people to lose all desire to procreate. They neither breed nor multiply nor can breed or multiply, nor have they any posterity, which is a very parlous state.

No more complete proof of voluntary sterility seems needed besides the one given by an eyewitness of such probity as Fray Pedro; however, let us quote the following text, which contains a decisive argument. The paragraph was written centuries later by Father Gumilla, the author of *Orinoco ilustrado*, and is quoted by Jaramillo Uribe (1964).

. . . experienced observers have noted that in areas where the Indian population has been noticeably reduced, many Indian women are childless and completely sterile. . . ; in those same places and areas, Indian women married to Europeans and to mestizos, *cuarterones*, mulattoes, zambos, and Negroes are so fertile and produce so many children that they can rival Jewish women in this regard. . . . The difference is that the Indian woman with an Indian husband produces humble Indian children. . . . Indian children are subject to depression, are spiritless and fearful and obliged to pay tribute, which though not excessive is regarded as a burden and a stigma. . . ; the majority of Indians have one child only, to satisfy their creative instincts and then take herbs to prevent the arrival of others.

The same woman in geographically similar but socially different circumstances reacts differently. The better the social position, the higher the fertility rate.

Economic and Social Readjustment

During their first expeditions, the Spaniards had to be content to live off what the land produced. Once they became settlers, they quite naturally endeavored to revert to those foods to which they were accustomed. It was then a question no longer of mere survival, but of the realization of their dreams or, at the very least, of returning to their folkways. The diet of a Mediterranean country was based on products that were unknown in the New World, such as wheat, wine, olive oil, meat, and sugar. The climatic conditions of the Indies were ideally suited to the cultivation of sugar and the raising of cattle, but they were not so favorable as far as wheat was concerned. Wine and olive oil continued to be imported from the Iberian Peninsula.

Sugar plantations spread rapidly over the favorable tierras calientes, and simultaneously there grew up plantations of cacao and dye-producing plants, which provided profitable crops for export to Europe. The widespread cultivation of these products became an intrusive element among the native population and its economy. At first, an attempt was made to get the Indians to use part of their land to grow wheat and use the grain to pay their tribute; but in view of their reluctance to grow it and of its low yield, an alternative method was introduced, the distribution of land to the conquistadores for cultivation. It was thus that Indian property began to be expropriated. But none of these changes was as significant as those resulting from the rapid breeding of livestock in some areas.

Pigs, goats, and even "Castilian" sheep were soon introduced into the Indian economy, and in Peru they replaced the llamas and alpacas on which the Andean peoples based their wealth. But their introduction was not always beneficial. At times, as Thomas More said of English sheep, the peaceful sheep of Peru "devoured" men. Indians vanished from the land they occupied. But the really spectacular breeding rate was that of horses and cattle. In Cuba, cattle took over the land left vacant by the extinction of the Indians. On the central plateau and on the northern plains of Mexico the numbers of cattle and horses grew phenomenally, and the same occurred in the River Plate area. In the semidesert lands of the Chichimecas and on the pampas, this rapid reproduction was not a disadvantage; on the contrary, it allowed the Indians to advance from being mere hunters to being equestrian nomads.

In densely populated areas, however, cattle and horses became as much a pest as the plague. It was not unusual for wild cattle, or those from neighboring Spanish estancias, to invade the cultivated fields (the *milpas* in Mexico) and ruin the crops. According to Castilian tradition, the stubble fields had to be open to cattle, and when this right was strictly enforced it led to the destruction of sown land as well. In a reciprocal action, the growth of the estancias reduced the resources of the Indian villages, while the consequent depopulation led the colonists to steal more land from the Indian communities. Chevalier (1963) and Simpson (1952) have made masterly studies of this alteration in land use in Mexico, and Friede (1969) has analyzed the situation in New Granada. In Peru, according to Macera (1968), official policy tended to favor agriculture.

The shift to new productions became an indirect way of restructuring society, and of expropriation for the benefit of the privileged group, but naturally more direct means were also used, such as grants, purchases, and usurpation. A second stage of Spanish domination began after the booty from the Conquest had been squandered and the mirage of the mines had evaporated. It was also increasingly apparent that the crown intended to exercise close control over encomienda labor and revenue. Then the conquistadores, who were, after all, men from rural backgrounds, remembered the economic advantage and prestige inherent in landownership. In principle all vacant land belonged, as in Castile, to the crown. It was thus that the crown acquired domains that had belonged to the aboriginal state, the monarch, and to those chieftains who had perished in battle. It also confiscated the estates formerly reserved for the maintenance of priestly castes. In order to encourage the settlement of Spaniards, viceregal or municipal authorities made generous grants to new settlers. Despite the opposition of the crown, many of these concessions were strategically situated near an individual's own encomienda, so that the trustee and owner could easily obtain the work force necessary to develop his own properties.

This was how the appropriation of land started, but not all land changed hands in this manner. There were also purchases. Chevalier (1963) has pointed out that a phenomenon has passed unnoticed in Mexico: the ancient native nobility, profiting from the chaos of the early post-Conquest days, had taken possession of the lands belonging to the calpulli, or communities, as well as land belonging to Moctezuma and religious properties. But in the long run the advantages thus gained by the Indian nobility were short-lived. They were responsible for the collection of tributes at a time when Indian population was rapidly falling. What they could not collect from the Indians came out of their own pocket. Many were ruined as a consequence. It was then easy for Spanish settlers to buy up these properties very cheaply. On other occasions, the conquistadores took advantage of their position to compel Indians to sell, or simply stole land from them, with or without some pretense of due legal process. Despite the vigilant intervention of the viceregal authorities and of the religious orders, it proved impossible to curb such actions, which in the seventeenth century were legalized by the payment to the crown of a *composición de tierras*.

By use of these and other stratagems, the new occupants of the country dislodged the Indians from the most fertile land and drove them to the less profitable areas of their former territory. Thus there came to be two juxtaposed economies: the Indian one based on small landholdings suffering from diminishing returns, and the other based on latifundia, which tended to expand. This expansive tendency of the haciendas was based on the better quality of the land, the greater availability of capital, and the abundant cheap labor provided by encomiendas and repartimientos. The Indian economy was at an obvious disadvantage.

This altered economic environment inevitably induced biological changes, increasing the death rate and lowering the fertility rate. For the sake of analogy and because of the lines of thought it opens up, let us consider one late example, an exceptional one, but very much to the point. The factors involved are few and easily identifiable; the results were negative and unintentional and of no use to anyone. This is regrettable because it illustrates the failure of a generous intention.

In his study of Lower California, Aschmann (1959) describes the fate of the primitive hunting and gathering Indians. During the eighteenth century, the Jesuits and, after their expulsion, the Franciscans tried to collect them into missions. Their settlement meant a break with their past life, upset their dietary habits, and made them less resistant to disease. The problem was obviously an extremely serious one, but the missionaries were unable to come up with a solution. On the contrary, they wasted the economic and human resources of the mission. On land of limited capacity, on account of the aridity of the soil, the missionaries used the best-irrigated fields to produce cotton; this raw material was used to supply a primitive handicraft which absorbed most of the female labor. Clothes being available from local sources, they then insisted that the hitherto naked Indians should wear them, diverting the women from the gathering of wild fruits to an unproductive task. In addition, the Jesuits restricted the Indians' diet to a mere subsistence level, so that the surplus could be used to feed those who built the astonishing religious monuments which are still to be found in this inhospitable area. Such squandering of natural resources made it impossible for the region to support a population as great as that of prehistoric times. The Indians' resistance to disease was undermined to such an extent that the missions had to be abandoned for lack of people.

Before Aschmann, Cook (1937 and 1940) had shown that the

supposed growth of the missions in Upper California in fact disguised a very high death rate, which was only counterbalanced by the continual arrival of new converts. Sauer (1935) had written earlier concerning northwestern Mexico: "With the best of intentions, the missionaries, by 'reducing' the Indians to compact pueblos and gathering them together regularly for worship, instruction and joint labor, exposed them to contagion by European diseases." The same seems to have been the case in Brazil (Freyre, 1946).

Kubler (1942) and Borah (1951) have observed that the grandiose and lavish architectural program carried out enthusiastically by the monastic orders in Mexico between 1530 and 1570 was achieved at the expense of much human suffering. The ensuing crisis compelled a halt. Fray Toribio de Motolinía went so far as to call the reconstruction of the city of Tenochtitlán "the seventh plague," in view of its cost in human lives.

Epidemics

Lastly let us examine what most contemporary authors consider to have been the major cause of the population decline: epidemics. The Spaniards were aware of the spread of epidemics in the New World and that they occurred almost at regular intervals; nor did they fail to appreciate their gravity. The phenomenon was no surprise to them, since epidemics were so common in the Europe of the time. They took the same health precautions to combat and prevent them as were taken in the Old World, but when they came to assess the reasons for the extent of the tragedy in America, it was this very familiarity with the situation in Europe that prevented them from recognizing the features that were peculiar to America. As Kubler (1942) observed, it was quite natural that they should attribute the population decline to social rather than pathological causes. Opinions have changed with the passage of time, and now disease is recognized as being the prime cause of the decline.

The epidemics were introduced from beyond the continent and were spread by the usual means. But the economic and working conditions imposed by the Conquest had a very significant effect on their severity. Nutritional deficiencies and dietary changes had particularly disastrous results. Sauer (1969) has pointed out the relationship between the extinction of the Indian population on Hispaniola and the imposition of a monotonous diet, which consisted of an abundant supply of yucca (cassava) but was lacking in proteins. After centuries of isolation from other parts of the world, it is not surprising that the Indians should have developed immunity to their own endemic diseases. The sudden invasion, however, broke that isolation and rapidly introduced all sorts of viruses and bacteria unknown in America, but which, unfortunately, were well known to Europeans and Africans. Even before the maritime discoveries of the Portuguese, continuous contacts across the Sahara had spread the same infectious diseases throughout both black Africa and the Mediterranean basin, with the exception of a few tropical diseases which climatic differences prevented from spreading to Europe. The same must have occurred between Europe and the Far East, despite the greater distance involved. Borah (1962) therefore concludes that of all the areas of the world subject to colonization, only America and the Pacific islands lacked natural resistance to the diseases introduced by the invaders, and consequently the native population was particularly susceptible to them.

Smallpox was brought to the Caribbean from Europe shortly after the discovery of the New World. In May 1519 the royal officials on Hispaniola reported that it had wiped out most of the Indian inhabitants of the island. It then immediately went to Puerto Rico, according to Dobyns (1963), who gives an account we shall follow closely. Within a year, Cortés's soldiers had taken it on to the mainland. Nearly half the population of Tenochtitlán died as a result of the outbreak. It did, at the least, weaken the resistance of the Aztecs and killed Cuitláhuac, the emperor Moctezuma's successor. From Mexico it then spread to Guatemala, with similar results to the Cakchiqueles. From Central America it jumped to the Peruvian empire five years ahead of Spanish troops. It would appear that Huayna Capac, the Inca emperor, died of the disease in 1524, thus leaving vacant the throne, which was still unoccupied when Pizarro's troops landed at Túmbez.

Measles was the second epidemic disease. It probably broke out in the Caribbean in 1529, where it carried off the remaining Indian population. It reached Mexico in 1531 and then went on to Central America, from Honduras to Panamá.

A disease called *matlazáhuatl* by the Aztecs, which some think was typhus and others influenza (Álvarez Amézquita, 1960), devastated New Spain in 1545; within a year New Granada and Peru were affected. Cieza de León (1553) describes the disease thus: "At the time when the viceroy Blasco Núñez de Vela was involved in the disturbances caused by Gonzalo Pizarro and his companions, a general pestilence spread throughout the whole kingdom of Peru, beginning beyond Cuzco and spreading along the whole sierra, where countless people died. The disease caused headaches and very high temperatures, and then the pain moved to the left ear and became so bad that the victims only survived for two or three days." Referring to the area where the Quimbayas lived, he says: "The disease and earache so afflicted the inhabitants that the greater part of the population of the province perished, and the Spaniards lost their Indian housemaids, for very few survived."

It appears that the influenza epidemic experienced in the Old World in 1557 crossed the Atlantic and attacked the Indian population with extreme severity. The bubonic plague, only too well known in medieval Europe, also spread to America. There was also another disease, which the Aztecs called *cocolitzli*, a kind of fever. In 1563, smallpox claimed the lives of no less than thirty thousand people in the recently formed Jesuit settlements in the vicinity of Salvador (Bahia) in Brazil (Azevedo, 1955). At the beginning of the last quarter of the sixteenth century, *matlazáhuatl* wrought worse havoc than during its previous outbreak thirty years earlier. Father Dávila Padilla (1625) describes both episodes thus: "Throughout the whole land there are nearly always serious diseases assailing and killing people, and sometimes there are widespread plagues, which carry off many people at the same time. In 1545 there was a plague among them (the Indians) and eight hundred thousand people died. But this number was as nothing compared with the numbers that died in 1576 and 1577 when the disease struck throughout the whole country so rapidly that the living hardly had time to bury the dead: and in some villages we saw them dig great ditches into which they threw twenty, thirty, or forty bodies for shortage of space." The epidemic became engraved with letters of fire on the minds of the inhabitants of New Spain. Caracas, founded twelve years earlier in a healthy valley in Venezuela, was beset by measles and smallpox in the same year.

During the next decade, one epidemic followed another. Smallpox spread northward from Cuzco toward Lima and Quito. One in five of the inhabitants of the viceregal capital died at that time. Naturally it was the lower strata of society, the Indians, who were worst affected. Almost at the same time, Peru suffered yet another attack, which originated in Cartagena among a cargo of slaves. From the coast it went up to Bogotá, where the Indian inhabitants were literally decimated, and then went on to Quito, Lima, and Cuzco, all of which had already been seriously affected only four years earlier.

From the ancient Inca capital it moved into Upper Peru and ended up in Chile. The epidemic spread northward to New Spain in 1588. Another outbreak occurred in Mexico at the end of the century in 1595. Throughout the sixteenth century epidemics of virtual continental extent came at almost ten-year intervals (1519–24, 1529–35, 1545–46, 1558, 1576, 1588, and 1595). In the seventeenth century their occurrence was more irregular and their effects less widespread. This change can, perhaps, be explained by a new combination of factors. Depopulation isolated communities from one another and thus lessened the likelihood of contagion; or the Indians, after nearly three-quarters of a century, were developing their own antibodies and consequently were better prepared to meet infection. It is not impossible therefore that in some places the disease had become so endemic that the natives both developed a degree of immunity and themselves became carriers. Pestilences spread from such focal points and no longer required transmitting agents imported from overseas. The New World thus acquired a sinister self-sufficiency.

During the seventeenth century, numerous isolated outbreaks were reported. In 1602 Oruro experienced a deadly epidemic of "cold and measles," as a census of that time states. Mexico had epidemics in 1607, and Yucatán an outbreak of influenza at about the same time. In 1614 Cuzco was afflicted by diphtheria. Four years later smallpox raged along the Pacific coast, Upper Peru, and Chile. The epidemics of 1620–22, such as smallpox, measles, and chicken pox, have been described by Góngora (1970). Similar outbreaks were reported in Peru in 1628 and 1634. It was even reported that the far-off Jesuit missions in Paraguay did not escape in 1630. *Tabardillo*, typhus or typhoid fever, attacked Bogotá in 1633. A systematic review of sources is urgently needed.

The recurrence of epidemics at such short intervals caused an immediate drop in the native population and profoundly affected its reproductive capacity, thus also endangering its future. Each outbreak simultaneously attacked all ages. It pruned out the aged and the sick, but children and those of reproductive age were not spared. Before the children had reached marriageable age and had a chance to breed offspring of their own, it was more than likely that new epidemics would have thinned out the group. The new generation was thus affected twice, by the losses experienced by their parents and by the additional ones suffered in their own childhood. And so it went on, epidemic after epidemic, and generation after generation.

If only because their own interests were threatened, the ruling classes were disturbed by this drastic reduction in the native population. In 1594, Viceroy Velasco the Younger wrote to Philip II: "The Spanish population grows daily, and public works and secular and religious buildings become more numerous; meanwhile, the Indians are becoming so scarce that it is extremely difficult to maintain such works with so little labor available" (quoted by Chevalier, 1963).

Of course the Spaniards were by no means exempt from contagion, and they acquired native Indian diseases. Syphilis is claimed to be one of these. But nothing seriously threatened the stability of the dominant group. The Europeans either brought their immunity with them or, if they were born in the New World, inherited defense mechanisms from their parents. Their very social condition, moreover, rendered them less susceptible to any disease. It is well known that in European cities the plague spared the wealthy rather than the beggars. Whatever the reason may be, the fact that Europeans were less susceptible to disease than the Indians did not escape the notice of contemporaries. Even by 1665, more than one and a third centuries after the arrival of the Spaniards in Peru, the Indians had not yet adjusted to the changed environmental conditions while the Spaniards were more resistant. In the resolution approved by the Junta General on September 25 of that year one reads: "If the Indians who in summer come down to this city of Lima stay for long, the contrariness of the climate is such that the majority die, which situation applies only to them and not to Spaniards, as I have had occasion to observe. The same applies to people of other nationalities who, even if they come from cold climates, not only stay in this city, but many go to Panamá and Cartagena, where many stay with no evident danger to their lives, though some die."

It is as yet impossible to determine with any degree of certainty why the Indians of the tierras calientes died so much more easily than those living on the plateaus or in the mountains; on some islands they disappeared completely. Whatever the reason may have been, it was not long before they were replaced by Africans. Curtin (1968) states that the Africans' suitability for the hard work on the plantations was not due to any racial disposition. It is simply that the inherent immunity to disease they brought with them across the Atlantic allowed them to survive better than those who possessed no such immunity.

To sum up, one may say that the Conquest decimated the Indian population, but the decline did not occur everywhere simultaneously: first, the Caribbean and low-lying tropical coasts were affected; then the mountains and plateaus; and only later, the peripheral areas that were not conquered. In the latter area the Indians were able to retain their own way of life for a long time; domination and European customs only reached them when territorial expansion started again in the seventeenth and eighteenth centuries.

Diseases imported from Europe or Africa by the conquistadores or slaves, and against which the natives possessed no natural immunity, seem to have been the main cause of the catastrophic fall in the Indian population. The social and economic disturbance caused by European domination rendered the Indians even more susceptible to disease-carrying germs. The breakup of their cultural life deprived them of the vitality needed to preserve their ethnic identity. Nor, of course, can one omit the acts of violence to which they were subjected.

A clear understanding of this catastrophe takes one well beyond the strictly demographic point of view and bears on the whole significance of the colonization of America. The nature of the colonial regime, the fact of *mestizaje*, and the type of agricultural institutions so characteristic of Latin America together provide us with a key to the understanding of the situation, if not a full explanation of it. The numerical decline of the Indian population permitted the complete domination of the conquered people by a minority without the necessity of any intermediaries. In the long run the Spaniards did not need to make use of native institutions or the native nobility, contrary to what happened in Portuguese or British India, for example.

Leaving aside the fact that other empires discouraged interracial marriages, if the disastrous contraction of the native population had not occurred, *mestizaje* would not have come to play the part that it did in ethnic fusion. Latin America is proud of having achieved it when attempts in other colonial areas managed at best a superficial cultural assimilation.

Depopulation also left so much land unoccupied and so disrupted the encomiendas that it paved the way for the latifundia, which were to become such a typical feature of Latin America, with peons or slaves as the work force.

Hollingsworth (1969) has recently suggested that it would not be unreasonable to compare the Spanish conquest of Mexico with the Arab conquest of Egypt or the Moghul invasion of China, so far as the demographic effect was concerned. Apparently Egypt had a population of 30 million inhabitants in the sixth century, before the

Moslem invasion, that is, as many as it had in about 1966. At its lowest point, which ended around 1798, the population had apparently fallen to only 2.5 million. If the description of this demographic evolution can be considered correct, then the case of Egypt might well invalidate the theory that rules out the possibility that in places the pre-Columbian population of America could have reached numbers equal to those attained at the beginning of the present century. The parallel is, of course, an inviting one, but until the demographic history of Egypt is more reliably known it is unwise to let oneself be tempted by such analogies.

IBERIAN AND AFRICAN INFLUX

The first voyages of exploration and conquest brought to the New World a mere handful of sailors, soldiers, civil servants, and clerics, who had no intention of settling there permanently. They would have been astonished had anyone suggested that they were pioneering a route which, over the centuries, would be followed by millions of Europeans who would leave their homelands of their own free will to settle permanently in the New World with their families.

Once they were conquered, it was necessary to establish a European population in the new lands in order to ensure their continued subjection. In the interest of the mother country, the colonies could not rely on a flow of temporary migrants. A stable population of Europeans to counterbalance the Indians would create more permanent bonds and would provide the social and political elite necessary to maintain control. Young bachelors who came over in search of adventure or to preach the Gospel, not to mention married men whose families remained in Europe, did not constitute a suitable contingent. If they lived with Indian women on a permanent basis, then the links that tied them to their society of origin tended to weaken. Fear of this soon led the authorities to encourage the migration of women and whole families. For this reason the Portuguese crown even sent out to Brazil women whose moral reputations did not particularly recommend them as the basis of a secure family life.

The encouragement of female migration and that of whole families was only partially successful. In comparison with men, the number of women who migrated was very low. Of the 15,000 names listed in the *Catálogo de pasajeros a Indias* compiled by the Archivo General de Indias on the basis of the incomplete listings of migration permits granted, only 10 percent were women. Quite apart from the physical attraction which certain types of Indian women had for the conquistadores, a fact frequently mentioned in the chronicles, Spaniards and Portuguese were compelled to associate with Indian women for lack of any others. Lockhart (1968) estimates that about 1540 in Peru there were 7 or 8 Spanish men for every white woman. The 1514 census of Hispaniola lists 392 male Spanish inhabitants, of whom 92 had Spanish-born wives and 52 were married to Indian women (Sauer, 1969). It is not unreasonable to assume that the remaining three-fifths enjoyed relationships with Indian women that did not receive the blessing of the church.

The early bonds between Spaniards and Indian women were seldom stable, and even less frequently received the sanction of the church, since mixed marriages were frowned on by social convention. As a matter of political expediency, the crown initially encouraged the conquistadores to marry into the Aztec or Inca royal houses or into their nobility. The most distinguished offspring of such a marriage, that of a Spanish caballero with an Inca princess, was the Inca Garcilaso de la Vega, a famous writer. But these unions were naturally few in number. Later on pressure was occasionally brought to bear to legitimize consensual unions, but neither the authorities nor the church were overzealous in the matter. Instead of being the exception, as in Europe, concubinage became the rule. The rigid family structure of Europe became a respected aim, but was disregarded in the course of practical everyday life. Such dual standards still exist today. In nearly all the countries of Latin America one finds, alongside the ideal standard of the traditional family, a high proportion of free unions and illegitimate births (Mortara, 1961). If the contemporary Latin-American family does not exactly correspond to the European model, but exists in a variety of types, this is partially due to the fact that the free relationships established in the very early colonial days undermined the blind social acceptance of customs and prejudices imported from overseas. An additional factor is the slight acculturation of large segments of the Indian population, at least until recently.

The immediate result of the mixed unions was the appearance of a large group of mestizos often considered as whites. Initially, they integrated easily into the ruling class, whose privileges they enjoyed. Many *criollos* mentioned in the first censuses were not always pure white. Although they were the offspring of Indian mothers, they were socially accepted as Europeans.

For political and religious reasons only Spanish or Portuguese citizens were allowed to emigrate to the Indies, so migrants from other sources were very few in number. How many people did migrate? The Spanish *Catálogo de pasajeros a Indias*, already mentioned, lists the names of those who embarked during the half-century 1509–59. The record is incomplete, however, as the documents for several years are missing, and of course no one knows how many migrated without permission. The effort put into the compilation of the list by the staff of the Archivo de Indias was not so fruitful as one might wish, but it was by no means useless, as will be seen.

An investigation not associated with demographic studies has recently shed some light on the extent of migration. Philologists had been wondering for a long time whether the accents and dialectal turns of phrase noticeable in the Spanish spoken in America were features acquired in the New World or whether they had been imported from across the Atlantic. The most widely accepted theory suggested that certain basic elements had been introduced owing to the high proportion of colonists who came from Andalusia, where a form of Spanish is spoken that is somewhat similar to American Spanish. The characteristic speech introduced by these migrants would have come to predominate and would in time have become standard. Such an explanation was readily acceptable, since it was precisely from there that the ships and the fleets sailed for America.

A researcher of amazing perseverance decided to explore further the assumptions on which the former opinion is based, that is, that the majority of Spaniards living in the New World in the first century after the Conquest were from Andalusia. Dissatisfied with the coverage of the *Catálogo*, but using it as a starting point, Boyd-Bowman (1964 and 1968) collected the names of those who left behind some evidence of their stay in the Indies, in all known documents whether public or private. In this way he succeeded in raising the number of names recorded for the period 1520 to 1559 to some 40,000. His geo-biographical listing, though also incomplete, makes clear the extent of the gaps in the *Catálogo* and gives us a more realistic idea of the numbers migrating. Boyd-Bowman believes he has located only about 20 percent of the Spaniards who crossed the Atlantic during the century. The total must have been, then, about 200,000, or an average of 2,000 per year. On examination of their regional origin, a third did, in fact, come precisely from Andalusia, while about 28 percent came from the neighboring regions of Extremadura and New Castile. Of the remainder, a quarter came from Old Castile and León; the rest chiefly from the northern provinces. As one might expect, the majority went to Mexico.

At the beginning of the last quarter of the sixteenth century, the Spanish population settled in America must have numbered about 150,000. In 1574 the cosmographer and chronicler Juan López de Velasco completed his *Geografía y descripción universal de las Indias* as described in chapter one. According to his figures, there were 225 Spanish cities and towns in America containing 23,000 *vecinos* or legal residents, who at an average of six dependents to each householder, add up roughly to the above figure.

The ratio six, we used following Borah (1951), may seem high, but can be justified for several reasons. In the ideal patriarchal family, the vecino's household was not just a nucleus made up of parents and children, but generally included an admixture of relatives and other persons in some way associated with or in the charge of the head of the unit. Adding the servants, the household became extremely large, the size depending on the wealth and status of the head. Probably these extended families included more than six members, but one has to estimate an average that allows for the number of men who for a variety of reasons remained unmarried. Also some categories of persons did not show up in the family counts: the term *vecino* did not apply to clerics, to Spaniards living in Indian villages, or to hacienda managers.

Borah (1951) has found partial errors in the figures for New Spain. When these are corrected, the number of vecinos is raised from 6,114 to 10,061. There is so far no reason to suppose that the rest of Spanish America requires such a large readjustment as that necessary in Mexico, but even if it were needed, Spaniards resident in the New World would still add up to about 220,000 once the vecino count had been increased by 60 percent. This figure makes no significant difference in the relative proportion of whites to Indians. Whatever the exact figure may have been, the Europeans were always in a small minority, even making allowance for the few thousand Portuguese spread out along the coastline of Brazil. Furtado (1963) has estimated their number at about 30,000.

No more accurate figure could be provided for the number of Europeans living in the Portuguese colonies. As for their place of origin, a variety of political events provided for a more diversified stock than the one which went to Spanish America. Migrants came from every part of Portugal, though more were from the north than from the south. The northeast of Brazil received immigrants mainly from the area between the Minho and Douro rivers, especially from the vicinity of Viana do Castelo. It is well known that people from the Azores predominated in the Rio de Janeiro area. However, during the period that the Spanish and Portuguese crowns were united (1580–1640), many Spaniards went also to the disputed southern regions of Santa Catarina and Paraná, and even to São Paulo and the fortified towns on the northern coastline. The Dutch occupation also left traces in some of the present-day families in the northeast, and one should not forget that the French founded São Luiz de Maranhão.

The overall importance of Spaniards and Portuguese in America lies not so much in their numbers, which we have seen were small, but in their privileged position in the political, social, and economic fields. Demographically this white segment showed a strong tendency to increase, contrary to that of the Indians.

In the third decade of the seventeenth century, the *Compendio y descripción de las Indias Occidentales* recorded 77,600 vecinos in Spanish America, which figure, liberally interpreted, would give a population of almost half a million Spaniards, roughly three times the figure indicated by López de Velasco or twice the revised estimate. This book, unlike the *Geografía*, was not written from reports. Fray Antonio Vázquez de Espinosa, its author, traveled widely throughout America between 1612 and 1622 and in a decade came to know personally most of the areas he describes. There were few places he did not visit. In 1628 he finished writing up the notes he had been accumulating during his travels. Vázquez de Espinosa rounds off the figures and omits towns about which he lacks information. His predecessor committed as many, if not more, inaccuracies and omissions. Nevertheless, in order to view the changes that occurred, which a comparison of the two works makes possible, let us disregard such objections and suppose that the errors of the cosmographer and of the friar are of similar proportions. On this assumption, the estimates made by them both can, with some reservations, be taken as indicating a trend. From the comparison one can make at least some observations that accord with known socioeconomic developments. Even if part of the rapid population growth could be credited to the greater accuracy of Vázquez de Espinosa, there is no doubt that the Spanish population increased rapidly. This was due less to migration than to the extent of mestizaje and, above all, to a privileged fertility rate made possible by the excellent living conditions it enjoyed compared with those of the Indians.

Growth was not uniform everywhere. Some areas grew at a faster rate than the average, while others stagnated or saw their inhabitants move elsewhere (Hardoy and Aranovich, 1969). The audiencias of Charcas and Quito had the most rapid growth rate (6.09 and 5.05 percent per year, respectively); Charcas was due to the mining boom, and Quito to the flourishing plantations on the coast and the cattle industry in the sierra. In the viceroyalty of New Spain, the audiencia of Mexico increased rapidly (3.08 percent) but if we accept the corrections Borah made to the 1574 figures, then the increase would be only a modest one. The remaining audiencias show signs of stagnation: the growth rate in Guatemala was extremely slow (0.24 percent), and the audiencia of Guadalajara registered a figure of only 1.45 percent—an unimpressive rate in the Indies, although higher than that of any European country of the period. The average for the audiencia of Santo Domingo (1.88 percent) is not a true reflection of the decline of the population of the islands of the Caribbean since it is distorted by the size of towns in Venezuela. The low rate for Panamá (0.85 percent) confirms the relatively static situation in the Isthmus. Discouraged by the low profits in agricultural ventures, the inhabitants retreated to the city, hoping to make their fortunes as merchants, an occupation that flourished in the port of Panamá. In the viceroyalty of Peru, the growth rates of the audiencias of Bogotá and Lima were about the average for the region (2.24 and 2.38 percent respectively). In the far south, on the other hand, Chile experienced a net loss (−0.40 percent) as a result of the bloody encounters between the Spaniards and the Araucanian Indians, who were not brought under control for more than four decades.

This summary outline of mainly urban demographic trends reveals a general tendency during half a century for the dynamic elements in the population to drift toward the Andean regions of South America and toward the peripheral areas of Venezuela and the River Plate. In contrast, the tropical coastal lands, from which the conquering expeditions had set out and which had harbored the earliest Spanish settlements, stagnated. Mexico's population increased, but less in response to any reliable economic growth than because, perhaps, the cities and towns tended to attract a population that had previously been more widely spread and therefore less accurately recorded in statistics. Even the mining area of the audiencia of Guadalajara failed to grow at anything like the rate of the silver-mining area of Upper Peru. These changes were, of course, achieved by extensive internal migration.

Once the hemisphere's isolation from the continents to the east was broken, it was not long before another group from across the Atlantic was brought over among the servants of the conquistadores. African slaves were incorporated as auxiliaries in the early expeditions to the Spanish Main. Their first contacts with the Indians were consequently of a violent nature. However, their role in the Conquest was only occasional and ancillary; the real reason for their introduction was economic. And economics continued to control their importation for four centuries, even after independence, in fact, until the suppression of the slave trade and the abolition of slavery put an end to this forced migration.

Negroes had begun to replace Indian labor in the Antilles even before Bartolomé de las Casas recommended their introduction as part of his campaign to protect the Indians. For the natives were rapidly disappearing at a time when the colonists urgently needed a reliable, productive work force to develop their plantations. The Negroes adapted easily to the living conditions prevailing in the torrid climate of the Caribbean and eventually replaced the native population in the low-lying tropical lands of the hemisphere. In the temperate highlands, where the mines were located and where abundant Indian labor was available, the Negro was not so necessary. This did not prevent him from being found all over the continent, employed in a variety of occupations. He was used in the mines, where his labor proved costly, and on cattle ranches, where, of necessity, he was allowed more freedom. Since, however, he was a costly piece of merchandise, he was used mainly where his physical efforts could be profitably engaged. This economic factor only ceased to matter when his use as a house servant raised the social status of his master.

The Negro was, above all, an item of capital goods, and his importation was dictated by the commercial requirements and needs of the moment. As with other commercial enterprises, the state tried several methods of regularizing his importation. The first such import licenses granted to conquistadores, royal officials posted to the Indies, officials of the Consejo de Indias and the Casa de Contratación in Seville, were intended as a reward for outstanding services to the crown, or to provide compensation, without charge to the treasury, for expenses incurred by private individuals in the course of discovery or conquest. Such permission was granted, for example, to Hernán Cortés and Francisco Pizarro. But imports under these concessions were never numerous. As commercial interest in the operations grew, the acquisition of a license took on a more mercantile stamp and the business became more widespread. Instead of being bought in Seville, the slaves were transported direct from Africa to licensed ports in the New World, that is, those of the Antilles and Veracruz, Nombre de Dios, and Cartagena on the mainland.

Toward the end of the sixteenth century, in a state of acute financial embarrassment, the Spanish government preferred to set up a monopolistic system that would ensure it a substantial income in advance. The asiento granted to a company was for a specific period and stipulated a maximum number of slaves that could be transported. Despite fluctuations in demand, and so forth, the monopoly remained in force for the whole of the seventeenth century and into the eighteenth. The first people to profit from this new system were Portuguese businessmen, then subjects of the king of Spain, who had plenty of money to invest and who were, moreover, experienced in the trade, having dominated the traffic between the Portuguese Cape Verde Islands in the Atlantic and São Tomé in the Gulf of Guinea.

None of these islands on its own had a sufficiently large population to supply the large numbers required by the trade. From the depots set up on them, they forwarded slaves purchased or captured on the mainland. The stopover at the supply bases makes it hard to determine now ethnic or geographical origins. Slave traders themselves had no great knowledge either of the geography of Africa or of its tribes and their society, so that one can hardly trust their information. Apart from a few Muslim Berbers, who were not Negroes and whose importation into America was early prohibited lest they should proselytize there, during the sixteenth century the Africans came mainly from such West African areas as Senegal and Gambia, from the Gulf of Guinea coast, or from the mouth of the Congo. These are the Negroes known in the Indies as Mandingas, Minas, and Congos.

From a few somewhat fragmentary samples of the slave population of Mexico and Peru in the middle of the sixteenth century, it seems that more than four-fifths of the Africans living there then were from Senegal, Gambia, and Guinea (Curtin, 1969). This is very probable because until the last two decades of the century nearly all the licenses were granted to slave traders based on Cape Verde. For a while Guinea supplied the trade direct. In the third decade of the seventeenth century, Angola supplanted its rivals and almost monopolized the trade (Chaunu, 1955–60).

Before the "pieces" from Angola came to predominate in the slave markets of Spanish America, they had been taken regularly to the Portuguese settlements in Brazil opposite the southern coasts of

Africa. Some were then smuggled across the demarcation line between the two empires and on to Peru and the River Plate.

Pieza de Indias was the term used at the time to describe a male slave in the prime of life. Women, children, youths, and some men were only worth a fraction of the price of such a man. Consequently, any numerical estimate of the slave-population based on *piezas* is an underestimate of the real figure.

The largest landing of slaves authorized by the Spanish crown, 26,100, was recorded in the last five years of the sixteenth century. The numbers remained at about this figure during the following quarter of a century, when adverse economic conditions plunged the trade into a depression. Between 1641 and 1650, the trade was even officially suspended. In the period of greatest activity, an average of 3,500 *piezas* per year were imported into Spanish America, according to the asientos granted.

It is not easy to estimate, from the partial figures available, the number of Africans who came to the New World in the voyages that took place until the world economic crisis of the mid-seventeenth century. The licenses and asientos found and studied by Chaunu suggest that between 1551 and 1640 the Spanish crown authorized the transport from Africa of 170,000 *piezas*, of which about 100,-000 were granted during the first forty years of the seventeenth century. By the time they actually arrived in the New World, the cargoes had been considerably reduced by the high mortality rate at sea. None of these figures, however, records more than a fraction of the total transported, for they do not include the slaves brought in illegally, those brought in before 1551, who must have numbered about 20,000 or 30,000, or those sold in Brazil from 1538 onward. These latter were probably considerably more than those brought into Spanish America at the time. If we accept the conservative estimate of Curtin (1969) that Spanish America received some 75,000 slaves during the sixteenth century, and Brazil some 100,000 in the second half alone of that century, and we add the 125,000 and 200,-000 respectively that were imported between 1600 and 1650, we find that the total number of those who crossed the Atlantic during the first century and a half after the discovery must have been about half a million.

Consequently the number of involuntary African migrants was considerably greater than the Portuguese and Spaniards, who went of their own free will. It should be borne in mind that the slave figure is a net one, since there were no returns, while the number of *penin-*

sulares is gross, since it omits the not insignificant number who returned home.

Despite their greater numbers, the Negroes in the long run made less impression on the ethnic composition of America than did the whites. The slaves did not reproduce rapidly, because of the unequal distribution of the sexes in each shipment. Regulations aimed at correcting this imbalance were introduced later, requiring that a third of each cargo should be women, but even if the law had been implemented, the imbalance would still not have been righted. In addition to the lack of women, there was a high mortality resulting from the appalling conditions of health, nutrition, and work. Adverse conditions did not, however, prevent the Negro from contributing to the racial melting pot. From the union of white man and Negress there emerged the mulatto, while the Negroes' association with Indian women produced the zambo.

In purely demographic terms, the consequences for Africa of this draining off of its inhabitants were not particularly serious until the seventeenth century. The loss of a couple of thousand people per year until that date could not have meant a threat serious enough to upset the population balance in a continent with some 100 million inhabitants, menaced rather by regular food shortages and epidemics. Not even the population of the western coastal fringe, which was most directly affected by the slave trade, can have been seriously threatened. The undoubtedly profound harm that was done was of a social and moral nature.

With the conquest of the Philippines another source of migrants for the New World was opened up. The nature of their migration was no more voluntary than that of the Africans. After 1565, the date of Legazpi's voyage which established the centuries-long permanent link between the archipelago and New Spain—for the Philippines were administratively dependent on that viceroyalty and not on the mother country—Acapulco witnessed the arrival from across the Pacific of some thousands of Filipino slaves, as well as Chinese and Japanese and even some East Indian slaves. The union of Spain and Portugal, which occurred in 1581 as a result of the extinction of the Portuguese dynasty, favored the entry of the latter.

Most of the Asiatics remained, as may be expected, in Mexico (Aguirre Beltrán, 1946), but some were sent on to Peru in the entourage of important persons, or in some other way. The Lima census of 1613 indicates the presence in the city of 114 Orientals: 38 were Chinese or Filipinos, 20 were Japanese, and the remaining 56 were described as coming from the Portuguese Indies. This latter category included several Malays and one Cambodian (N. D. Cook, 1968). The majority were adult craftsmen or servants. There were never many Asiatics in the Indies, and the prohibition of the slave trade in Orientals in 1597 by Philip II soon cut off legal supplies from this source, and only an insignificant number of these highly valued people were smuggled in after that date.

TOWNS AND CITIES OF THE "TWO NATIONS"

An assembly of Franciscan theologians from the ecclesiastical province of Mexico declared in 1594 that "this State of New Spain is made up of two nations, Spaniards and Indians." Thus, one century after the discovery, two communities, subject to the same temporal and spiritual powers, existed side by side, but had not become integrated. The Franciscans purposely underlined this duality in the declaration they made on this occasion concerning the way in which Indians were shared out among the Spaniards by the repartimiento system. They argued quite logically that the mere juxtaposition of two races was no reason for the domination of one over the other, and consequently they rejected encomiendas and repartimientos. Concerning the Indians, they observed that "they are the natives, for they are in their own country," while they remarked of the Spaniards: "They are newcomers who have arrived to follow their fortune in these kingdoms or have been born here to Spanish parents, for neither by official station in life nor by their own free will do they belong to the Indians' commonwealth" (Galaviz de Capdevielle, 1967).

In practice the two groups did not live in complete isolation from each other. The Spaniards subjected and exploited the Indians, but there was no strict segregation. While only occasionally did a *peninsular* become assimilated into aboriginal life in a native village or, more frequently, live there as a royal officer or as a priest, the presence of Indians in Spanish cities, on the other hand, was not unusual but rather necessary. Cities were redesigned on the site of some pre-Columbian one, following a grid in the Renaissance manner, with streets at right angles to one another; their original inhabitants were removed from the center, but remained grouped together on the outskirts in their unplanned barrios, or villages. Every Spanish city always needed a liberal supply of Indian servants. We have already mentioned elsewhere the early appearance of *mestizaje*, which is proof of intercourse between the races.

The distinction made by the Franciscans, certainly following ideas widespread in the literature of the period, corresponded to clear reality. The natives were used to living apart in their own communities. They were governed there by their own authorities and according to their own customs, though their institutions became more and more infiltrated by Spanish norms. The Spaniards lived in their towns and capital cities, and only occasionally went to stay on their country properties.

When one adds the loss of their great political and religious centers to the population decline itself, the number of Indians living in cities in the early colonial period was probably less than previously, measured in absolute terms; in this sense aboriginal society became deurbanized. It would be rash to conclude, however, that the Conquest had a rural stamp or that it encouraged dispersion. The Spaniards themselves liked living in cities, and colonization itself did not force the Indians to disperse. On the contrary, the dynamic of domination compelled both the crown and the church to prefer to keep them grouped together. Rather, it was the pressures of social and economic evolution that led the Indians to become dispersed.

The present-day Indian towns and villages are seldom located on the sites they occupied before the arrival of Columbus. It was not the mobility of the Independence or contemporary periods that caused the abandoning of the original sites, for this had occurred much earlier. Nothing in recent centuries can compare with the chaotic shuffling around of men, institutions, and ideas that took place during the early days of Spanish domination. The subjugation of the Indians entailed the shifting of population, sometimes to far-distant lands, and large-scale movements to concentrate it. Many Indians left their primitive villages to live in towns built for them on new sites.

The abandonment of sites that had been inhabited for generations was also due to the high mortality rate of the time. If the life of a place was as seriously affected as we have seen, the survivors were scarcely in a condition to renew economic activity by their own unaided efforts. Assistance from other groups who had been similarly afflicted would, however, increase collective energy and so rebuild a community. It was thus that some new groupings occurred.

When Indian society had become seriously disorganized, Spanish landowners gathered together the remaining nuclei for the sake of convenience. By doing this they were doubly advantaged. First, they managed to assemble a pool of labor near their haciendas, and second, the shift of population left land vacant, which they could appropriate to increase the size of their properties.

If social and economic circumstances kept Indians from dispersing, the religious orders had earlier adopted a policy with the same aim in view, but for quite different reasons. The orders sought to evangelize them and, once they were converted, to endow their communities with institutions like the Spanish ones, which would ensure them of an independent existence away from the greed of the colonists. To this end it was convenient that they should live together under the fatherly care of the friars. To house these congregations many villages were built in which even the typically Spanish plan and architectural style were pressed into service in the attempted assimilation. Thus the roots with local religious practices were severed through removal to a new site, and the preaching of the new faith could be done much more efficiently.

The authorities for their part also pursued a policy of concentration for the sake of peace. In this way it was much easier to keep an eye on the Indians, and the Royal Treasury benefited through the simplification of tax collection. In the tribute records for the Tzeltal Indians of Chiapas, it was stated: "In order that the Indians may be better and more easily indoctrinated and suitably cared for and live in a Christian manner and in association with *hombres de razón* [rational human beings], it has been desired and an attempt has been made to 'reduce' [concentrate] them into settlements, since suitable care could not be taken of them dispersed around the countryside as they were" (Reyes García, 1962). The king himself was not indifferent to the lands thus left vacant, for he could grant them to loyal colonists as a reward.

The first legal expression of the concentration policy is to be found in the Laws of Burgos of 1512. Charles V adopted the policy, though recommending that violence should not be used. His decision was incorporated in the *Recopilación de Leyes de Indias* under Title III of Book VI. Viceroy Toledo was responsible for the large-scale implementation of this policy, as we have already seen. Mexico was more remiss in carrying out the royal instructions. In 1591 Philip II, impatient with the rate of progress there, decreed that compulsory *congregación* should be put into effect. Together with the measures taken during the previous rule of Monterrey, Viceroy Montesclaros finally carried it out between 1603 and 1605. Cline (1949) has estimated that the measure affected almost a quarter of a million people in New Spain; the majority were gathered together in villages containing four or five hundred tributarios or more, that is, a population of between one and three thousand inhabitants, figures which roughly coincide with those of Upper Peru. In New Granada, the visitador Luis Henríquez decided upon a drastic measure, the concentration of Indians into villages of three to four hundred tributarios, but local resistance condemned the experiment to failure (Colmenares, 1970). Forced concentration was opposed not only by the Indians, but even by the encomenderos because of the economic disturbances it caused.

It is quite natural that the Spaniards should have preferred to live in cities. Although most of them came from rural stock, the cultural legacy of Spain was saturated with urban elements. Besides, if the few thousand men who came to the Indies had spread themselves out over the continent they would have been extremely few and far between, and in the long run they would have been absorbed by Indian society. To retain their identity they had to stay together. Besides, they wanted to share power, language, tastes, and leisure with people of their own stock. Consequently, even if their business interests retained them for part of each year isolated on their landholdings, they endeavored to have a house available in the capital or in neighboring towns, according to their status as powerful *latifundistas* or lesser *hacendados*. They went to live there whenever circumstances permitted. Their fondness for the city was so strong that absenteeism from country properties became common once their possession of them became clearly established and they could leave the management to others. Finally, when that inclination was not strong enough, the authorities themselves compelled Spaniards to maintain their urban connections. Thus, in the north of Mexico, those who lived on estancias were required to acquire a house in town and live in it at least during the major religious festivals of the year.

The first stage of urban evolution in Spanish America began in the uncertain years of the precarious settlements, made as chance discovery dictated, on the islands of the Caribbean and the nearby mainland. One of the few cities of this period to survive until the present day is Santo Domingo, once the capital of the Indies. This instability was due both to the lack of experience of the colonists in a strange land and to the way in which they tended to spread out along the shoreline inhabited by seminomadic people. This tentative approach came to an end when Hernán Cortés found his way to Anáhuac; his entry into Mexico meant a firm commitment, which Cortés himself sensed when he burned his ships. The time for experiments was over. It was a matter of marching straight to the capture of cities, some of them most impressive, which had been built by highly urbanized societies. Permanent occupation of the political and religious centers was essential to make use of the symbolic value that such supplanting of traditional control would have over the natives. It was then that new Spanish cities were built on the site of, or alongside, the Indian city. Mexico City and Trujillo, respectively, are examples of these two different plans. The latter was built beside the ancient Chan Chan in northern Peru and the former on the ruins of the Aztec capital.

Once in control of all key points, later expansion required the establishment of another type of center, on sites never previously occupied by the Indians. These places were seldom more than encampments, subject to the fluctuating fortunes of colonization. In fact their only ground for getting a city coat of arms was the king's far-sighted generosity. Asunción in Paraguay is a typical case in point.

Finally, ports were established, whose function was not to exercise control over a given area but to link certain regions with other parts of the empire. Thus Veracruz in Mexico, Nombre de Dios and Panamá on either side of the Isthmus, Callao and later Buenos Aires in the viceroyalty of Peru grew up as a result of expanding commerce between one region and another, or between one area and the mother country.

The network of Spanish cities had already been established when López de Velasco wrote his *Geografía y descripción universal de las Indias*. Between then and the time when Vázquez de Espinosa put his travel notes in order, not much change took place despite the founding of some additional cities or the inclusion of marginal areas. Nor did the disappearance of some centers have much noticeable overall effect. The half-century that separated the two authors was a period in which cities generally became consolidated and flourished. Their main characteristic was one of overall expansion, and in this respect Peru had a slight lead. In Central America and the Caribbean, the only ports to prosper were those where the fleets on the Indies run tied up, and which had only just been founded when López de Velasco was writing; these flourished, while the rest languished.

The average number of vecinos in the centers for which the *Geografía* provides data was 121 in 1574, including the two great viceregal capitals. Even allowing for a generous figure to cover "the rabble of serving persons, Yanacona Indians, Negroes and mulattoes," or simply the people who did not rank as vecinos, this number is less than the minimum that present-day censuses would consider indicative of an urban population: they were little more than villages.

But in this case, a mere quantitative assessment is not entirely appropriate, since the political, administrative, economic, and religious functions fulfilled by those centers clearly endowed them with the status of cities (Hardoy and Aranovich, 1970). (See Map 1.)

Later on, the reservation we made above has less justification.

The average-sized town had attained a population of three thousand, statistically accepted as an urban nucleus. In the 1621 enumeration, the number of cities had gone up to 331, a hundred more than in 1574, though the number for which population data are available went down from 191 to 165. The average number of vecinos quoted for these 165 places increased nearly four times, from 121 to 470.

The most urbanized regions in 1625 were the same as half a century earlier, specifically those in which the viceregal capitals were situated. According to Vázquez de Espinosa, Mexico City—the most highly populated city on the continent—had fifteen thousand vecinos or at least ninety thousand inhabitants inclusive of Spaniards and their servants, but disregarding any Indians living there on their own account. This concentration is comparable with that of the largest cities in Europe at the time. Lima had approximately ten thousand vecinos.

Between 1574 and 1628, the average size of towns and cities in the audiencia of Mexico increased sixfold, while in the audiencia of Lima they did not increase even threefold. Contrary to what one might expect, the greater growth rate of Mexico is no proof of greater dynamism. With closed horizons to the north and palpably decadent Guatemala to the south—that is, with no new towns and no population increase—it was in no condition to encourage development. It tended, rather, to turn in upon itself. Lower Peru, on the other hand, looked toward the "frontiers" of Upper Peru, the River Plate, and Quito, which became the goals of many a fearless man who still preferred the mirage of adventure to the calm provincial life of the already settled coast. The most spectacular growth occurred, in fact, in Quito, where the number of population centers increased by about 50 percent, from sixteen to twenty-four, and the size of the population went up eightfold. In the audiencia of Charcas, which included the mountain ranges and plateau country of Upper Peru and the vast plains of the River Plate region, the number of centers increased from twelve to forty and the population fivefold.

Comparing the cities, it is evident that the greatest changes occurred in the ports, in the mining centers, especially in Upper Peru, and in the administrative capitals. Of all the towns in the Indies, Havana showed the greatest increase. From a population of 60 vecinos assigned to it by López de Velasco, it could boast 1,200 half a century later, thus displacing Santo Domingo from its leading position in the Caribbean. The galleons that anchored in its bay during the spring, waiting for the fleet to assemble and sail for Seville in the early summer, greatly enriched the new capital of Cuba. This boom, of course, continually attracted new inhabitants. Cartagena de Indias was another strategic point on the sea route that regularly linked Spain with her colonies. Its population rose from some 250 vecinos to 1,500, six times as many. The remaining terminals of the traditional sea route either modestly doubled their populations, as was the case with Veracruz, or were newly built as, for example, was Portobelo, which replaced the ruined harbor of Nombre de Dios in 1596. The only Pacific port that notably increased in size was Guayaquil. As it was the only outlet to the sea for the audiencia of Quito, its population increased fourfold, owing to the growing exports of cacao produced on the coastal haciendas and cloth manufactured in workshops up in the mountains. There was also Acapulco, which was of modest proportions having been founded fairly late as a result of the dispatch of the annual galleon to Manila.

Of the mining centers, Potosí and La Plata, both in Upper Peru, grew ten- and elevenfold respectively. The first increased from 400 to 4,000 vecinos in half a century, according to Vázquez de Espinosa. The last figure is below the one drawn from the census carried out by chief magistrate (*presidente*) Bejarano on the orders of the viceroy, the marquis of Montesclaros. In 1611, Bejarano apparently found there a European population three times that indicated by the Carmelite friar, and, in addition, 66,000 Indians of various sorts as well as 6,000 Negroes and mulattoes. The total comes to some 150,000 inhabitants. Even accepting the modest 4,000 vecinos mentioned in the *Descripción de las Indias*, Potosí stood out as the third city of the continent, surpassed only by Mexico City and Lima. The magnificent architecture of that century has caused the present provincial city to retain something of the majesty of its earlier days as the "Imperial City." As for La Plata, its population grew from 100 to 1,100 vecinos, thus displacing Asunción from its second position within the audiencia of Charcas. But the most surprising case was that of Oruro. The villa de San Felipe de Oruro was solemnly founded in November 1606 near the silver deposits discovered a few years previously. In no time at all, a veritable human avalanche descended on it so that it boasted 1,000 vecinos and became the third city of the audiencia.

New mining towns sprang up, scattered all over the map in other parts of America. In the audiencia of Guadalajara, to the northwest of Mexico City, were founded Cuencamé, Fresnillo, Saltillo, and Mapimí. The older Zacatecas trebled in size to attain a population of

1,000 vecinos. The gold mines attracted 300 new vecinos to Zaragoza in the audiencia of Bogotá. But none of these increases was nearly so impressive as those in Upper Peru.

Among administrative capitals, Mexico City and Lima, the viceregal government seats, increased fivefold. In the more northerly audiencias, the inhabitants of Valladolid (Morelia) and Durango increased thirteenfold, Tlaxcala tenfold, Mérida (Yucatán) and Puebla sixfold. In South America, Quito increased sevenfold, Caracas more than fivefold, and among the old cities, Cuzco fourfold.

There were few instances where the population decreased, and in every one this was due to a local economic crisis, especially in areas where the economy was dominated by a single product, or to natural events such as earthquakes or volcanic eruptions. From some mining camps and towns in the north of New Spain, in New Galicia, and in New Biscay (Durango, Chihuahua, and Coahuila), people went off in search of richer lodes. Guanajuato lost half of its inhabitants at this time. In Central America, San Miguel and Sonsonate (now in El Salvador) were destroyed by earthquakes and fires, and could not recover, because markets which had previously absorbed cacao from the audiencia of Guatemala were soon supplied from Guayaquil. In Peru, Huánuco and Arequipa also declined, the latter because of the volcanic eruptions of 1582 and 1600. Volcanic activity also forced the removal of the city of León de Nicaragua to a new site in 1609. Some Chilean cities were even completely abandoned. The uprising by the Araucanian Indians forced the evacuation of southern towns below the River Bío-Bío. This setback had a demoralizing effect on the remaining towns in the audiencia.

Not so much is known of the demographic history of Portuguese cities in the New World. Their beginnings were more modest. It must not be forgotten that twenty years elapsed between the start of the Spanish Conquest and effective Portuguese occupation of Brazil. At a time when the Spaniards had captured the Indian capital cities and had already reconstructed them, the Portuguese were just beginning to set up their precarious settlements among the tribes on the Atlantic shore. In addition to this chronological difference, a large Indian population and much wealth, such as existed among the Aztecs and Incas, simply did not exist in Brazil. The population centers of Olinda, Ilhéus, Espírito Santo, Rio de Janeiro, or São Paulo, all military or agricultural enclaves, were outranked by Spanish colonial cities. Salvador da Bahia, the regional economic capital and seat of the colonial administration, had a population of a mere eight hundred vecinos and a few thousand Negroes and baptized Indians at the end of the sixteenth century (Azevedo, 1955). In comparison with other parts of America, it was a very second-rate place. Then the temporary Dutch occupation of the northeast bestowed on Recife a more orderly plan than was to be found in other Brazilian population centers at that time. Its population was also greater than that of the capital. Thus began the instability of the urban network so characteristic of the history of the country. In contradistinction to the Spanish city, the shape of Portuguese towns in America was more spontaneous and irregular. They allowed topography to dictate the plan rather than accept the grid pattern (R. C. Smith, 1955).

Despite disquieting signs, the cities continued to grow throughout the seventeenth century. The decline of the Indian population caused alarm but did not retard progress. The economic recession after 1620, rather than harming the cities, on the whole favored them. As agricultural, cattle-raising, and mining activities offered no more good economic prospects, many preferred the salaries and safe jobs offered by the colonial administration. The sale of offices made available to them positions that had to be carried out in the capital cities. This is similar to what happened at the time in Europe, which was suffering from the same economic crisis. There, instead of disappearing, the centers of population that flourished thanks to the prosperity of the sixteenth century, became firmly established. People fled from the countryside to the city, which was a safer place to be in time of trouble.

IV

A New Course

FROM the beginning of the second third of the seventeenth century to the end of the first third of the twentieth, there extend three centuries of a new period in the history of the population of Latin America, a long stretch of time that embraces two very different political and economic regimes, for it includes two centuries of colonial status and one of independence. It may surprise some readers that we should leap over the established historical divisions. But it so happens that demographic changes occur at a slower pace than do political and economic ones, which are always more easily seen. Moreover, so far as population dynamic is concerned, the movement occurring in this period was very different from both the preceding and the succeeding periods. These three centuries are, in fact, as different from the decline of the Conquest phase as they are from the dizzy speed of the present population explosion.

The increase that occurred between the second half of the eighteenth century and the beginning of the twentieth was greater than that of any other region in the world except North America. According to recent estimates by Durand (1967*a*), Central and South America together recorded an average growth rate of 0.8 percent between 1750 and 1800, 0.9 percent between 1800 and 1850, 1.3 percent between 1850 and 1900, and 1.6 percent between 1900 and 1950. Western and Central Europe, on the other hand, recorded 0.4, 0.6, 0.7, and 0.6 percent during the same intervals of time.

Latin America's population consequently grew more rapidly than that of Europe, even though the restraints holding back the Old World's expansion had been removed. The New World, meanwhile, did not experience comparable demographic changes. In fact, apart from immigration, which only affected certain limited areas, Latin America's population was still expanding under exclusively *ancien régime* conditions. It was only much later, in the twentieth century, that the present phase of demographic modernization began. To use an expression in vogue among social scientists, let us call those three centuries the period of "traditional society."

By stressing the unity of this period, no uniformity throughout it is implied. Subperiods could be distinguished, in fact, three of them. The first was a time of stabilization, during which the native Indian population slowly reached a new equilibrium after the disastrous setbacks it had experienced during the Conquest; this subperiod acted also as a kind of preamble to the general population expansion that was to occur during the second stage, that is the second half of the eighteenth and early nineteenth centuries. The third subdivision was somehow the antithesis; while the colonial society continued to prevail, new forces were sapping it, foreshadowing the present situation.

The discrepancy between the first and second subperiods is, above all, quantitative. A slow growth rate was followed by one which was, on the whole, quite rapid. Between the second subperiod and the third, the acceleration observed is not as significant as the qualitative factors that distinguish them. Ethnically, the phases of stabilization and expansion coincide, for both acted as a melting pot for the three racial elements which the Conquest brought together: the Indian, the African, and the Spaniard or Portuguese. Finally, during the third period, the continent opened up still further to receive migrants from other countries, thus producing an even richer ethnic mixture.

During the whole period, for the majority, the joys of childbirth and the sorrows of death followed with monotonous, frequent, and foreseeable regularity; this span, however, is too long and complex to be described in a few words. Consequently, without impairing the conception of unity expounded above, it has been found helpful to divide the description up into two chapters. The first follows the course of the stabilization and expansion processes for over two centuries. The second, shorter chapter deals with just over three-quarters of a century, starting from the middle of the nineteenth century. The dates are purposely vague.

STABILIZATION

No large, fresco-like surveys such as those of López de Velasco and Vázquez de Espinosa are to be found dealing with the following period, of which little is known in any field. Simpson appropriately calls it "the forgotten century."

No modern scholar has taken up the challenge of filling in this knowledge vacuum. The period lacks the fascination of the Conquest or the luster of the last days of the colonial era. Researchers avoid it, because of alleged shortage of documents. The adjective "stingy," used by Miranda to describe the seventeenth century, is not at all inappropriate; but it is nevertheless true that a variety of primary demographic sources do exist, awaiting a patient, imaginative researcher, as he himself has shown in a work that we will now examine.

The records of the half-*real* tax that the Indians of the *alcaldías mayores* or *corregimientos* paid annually to maintain the cathedrals were discovered in the Mexican national archive. Miranda (1963) set about to exercise his ingenuity in an attempt to calculate the increase in the number of *tributarios* recorded in three bishoprics, those of Mexico, Puebla, and Michoacán, between the middle and the end of the seventeenth century. The data obviously do not include those tributarios who managed to avoid the counts by a variety of means; the author calculates this evasion rate as having been one-fifth of the total. In the three areas concerned, there was an average increase of 28 percent which, when broken down, amounts to 32 percent for Mexico, 19 percent for Puebla, and 53 percent for Michoacán. Allowing for five dependents for each adult Indian tributario and tax evader, the 170,476 tributarios at the end of the century would amount to one million Indian inhabitants. This is the number that Borah assigned, not to these three areas, but to the whole of Mexico in 1605.

The noticeable difference in growth rates between the three regions gives some idea of the drift of population from some areas to other more attractive ones. The Bajío, where the nomadic Chichimecas had hitherto camped at will, was occupied by sedentary Indians attracted from areas that were most disturbed by Spanish occupation. In nearly half a century, between 1644 and 1696, the area of Celaya, Acámbaro, Jilotepec, Querétaro, Orizaba, and Huatusco showed an increase in the number of tributarios from two thousand to nine thousand, an increase of four and a half times. The number of towns raised to the status of *cabecera*, the appearance of newly founded ones, and the dismemberment of earlier centers confirms this migration.

This investigation was immediately followed by others: Gibson (1964), Miranda (1966) once again, and Cook and Borah (1968 and 1971). Gibson studied the Aztecs of the valley of Mexico; Miranda, the Otomí Indians of the district of Ixmiquilpan; and Cook and Borah, the Mixteca Alta (1968), and recently the northwest, an area comprising New Galicia and adjacent parts of New Spain, that is, the present-day states of Jalisco, Nayarit, Colima, and Aguascalientes. These works all confirm the above tendency. If we restrict ourselves to the examination of the following places listed by Gibson: Chalco, Citlatepec, Coyoacán, Cuauhtitlán, Ecatepec, Mexicalcingo, Otumba, Tacuba, Texcoco, and Xochimilco, it appears that the number of tributarios went up from 15,028 to 27,767 between 1644 and 1742. This alteration is equivalent to an annual increase of six per thousand throughout the course of almost a century. Expressed in inhabitants, the increase could have been greater, since it is probable that the coefficient applicable to the tributarios went up. In Ixmiquilpan, on the other hand, the rate went up to ten per thousand between 1643 and 1746, and to twelve per thousand among the Indian inhabitants of New Galicia between 1644 and 1760. All of these examples are indicative of a rural population well on the way to recovery.

A further indication that the Indian population had become stabilized, or slightly increased, is provided by the tribute records of the *alcaldía mayor* of Sonsonate, which covered the territory of the two western districts of the present-day republic of El Salvador (Barón Castro, 1942). Counts made between 1672 and 1681 were incorporated in the *Razón* of the audiencia of Guatemala in 1682. The Indians then numbered 4,964, a few more than the 4,673 counted in 1549–51. After more than a century the population was tenaciously holding its own. However, it would be more accurate to say that it had started to grow again, since after 1551 it must certainly have lost ground, for reasons which affected all Indians and which we have examined at length in the previous chapter. In the case of Sonsonate, moreover, it is clear that earthquakes and the cacao crisis reduced the Spanish urban population at the beginning of that century. It would be very surprising if such disasters spared the Indians.

In the same area, in 1713–14, a census was taken by the governor, Lacayo de Briones, in ten Indian villages in Costa Rica. This records that, of 263 married couples out of a total population of one thousand, 31.4 percent had had no children, 17.4 percent only one, 22.7 percent two children, and the remainder three or more. The situation described proved to Bishop Thiel (1951) the high sterility rate among the Indians. Yet despite the truth of his observation, these figures do not seem as disastrous as those already quoted concerning the Indian population of Colombia.

Moreover, it was precisely in New Granada that the number of Indian tributarios continued to decline, according to recent studies. In the province of Tunja, they lost 44 percent between the Valcarce census of 1636 and that taken 120 years later by the *visitador* Verdugo de Oquendo (Friede, 1965). Both in 1755 and in 1778, when a new population census was carried out by Moreno Escandón and Campuzano, there now appeared alongside the Indian population proper a considerable number of Spaniards and mestizos, whose presence suggests not so much a population decrease as a sociological change brought about by mestizaje or mere acculturation. In fact, in eight *corregimientos* in Tunja (Turmeque, Sachica, Paipa, Sogamoso, Chivata, Duitama, Gameza, and Tenza), alongside an Indian population of 20,697, Verdugo de Oquendo found 28,243 whites and mestizos (Colmenares, 1970). Thus by the middle of the eighteenth century the Indians accounted for only 42 percent of the population, not the near totality which had been the case in 1636. It is interesting to note that the 42,930 inhabitants were only slightly less numerous than the Indian population of the previous century.

When did the majority of the Indians of New Granada react to avoid an extinction which at times seemed unavoidable? When did they recover the life force they had earlier lost and succeed in making up their numbers, either within their own community or by transferring them to the mixed-blood society? If we examine the case of Pamplona, also studied by Colmenares (1969), the change may well have started fairly early in the seventeenth century, although it was hardly perceptible at first. In 1602, 43 percent of the families had no children, 27 percent had one, and 19 percent had two. In view of this, it is astonishing that the Indians did not disappear. Twenty years later, in 1623, only 30 percent had no children, 27 percent one, and 22 percent two; the gain was slight, but as in Costa Rica, the worst, happily, seemed to be past.

The letters that the *presidente* and the *fiscal* of the audiencia of Quito sent to the king at the beginning of the seventeenth century both agree that, far from declining, the population of the cordillera was then increasing (Phelan, 1967). Those *relaciones* (reports), sent in the quarter century after the foundation of Quito and published by Jiménez de la Espada (1965), show that this was no subjective impression on the part of complacent civil servants, but that the trend had started earlier. In the *Relación* of Sancho de Paz Ponce de León concerning the Indians of the *partido* of Otavalo, the children of fifteen years and under formed 46 percent of the total population; in that written by Miguel de Cantos concerning the corregimiento of Chimbo, there were three places in which boys of up to seventeen years of age constituted a quarter of the total. Both of these fractions are indicative of a youthful population not untypical of our day. In the *Relación* of the city and province of Cuenca, written in 1582, an explanation is advanced for this unusual situation: "Thus it appears that the above mentioned [Indians] are increasing and not declining; for in the time of Atahualpa and Huáscar with the wars and rebellions that occurred in the province, all the Cañares died, for of the 50,000 that there had been, only 3,000 were left when the Spaniards arrived; since then they have increased to twelve thousand souls, for they are very contented and free and not so oppressed as they were in the time when the Inca was their lord and master."

The case of Quito is exceptional, both on account of the extent of the disaster it experienced during the last years of Inca rule, and the beneficial results paradoxically brought about by the Conquest. Be that as it may, demographic recovery was under way by the end of the sixteenth century.

Farther south, in Peru, the decline seems to have continued until much later. If one compares the 598,026 Indians which N. D. Cook (1970) estimates to have been the population of the area about 1620, with 401,111, which is the number recorded in the census carried out by the Viceroy Superunda in 1754 (Vollmer, 1967), it would appear that the Indian population went down by one-third. But if no population contraction seems to have happened in Tunja, where there was an even sharper fall in Indian numbers during almost the same period, then surely the same might also apply in Peru. Could not the growth of a large mestizo population compensate for or cancel out the reduction of pure-blooded Indians? An ethnic transference rather than a demographic fall is possible in some regions: it certainly took place in some intendencies which, according to the census of Viceroy Gil de Taboada, had large numbers of mixed-bloods at the end of the eighteenth century; it is also possible in some of the eastern parts of the intendency of Cochabamba in Upper Peru, according to the information provided by its governor, Francisco de Viedma. Nevertheless, as the Indians never ceased to predominate in the "Indian patch"—southern Peru and the altiplano—it is difficult to attribute their numerical decline there to a massive transfer from one group classification to another. Some explanations will be suggested here.

In the last quarter of the seventeenth and the first half of the following century, the disappearance of the Indian was a constant source of concern to the colonial authorities. When ordering a new census of the Indians in 1683, the viceroy, the duke de la Palata, made the following statement in a written proclamation: "For many years now we have been aware of the serious depopulation experienced by all the villages in these vast provinces of Peru, and of the grave results ensuing if no remedy is found for so widespread a disaster, for the major cities alone cannot support the kingdom if the remaining parts of it become weakened and depopulated, as is presently the case." The duke attributed this phenomenon to "the ease with which the Indians can move their homes, withdrawing from the cities and hiding where news from their chiefs and government officers cannot reach them . . . to thus free themselves from their vassal status and the payment of taxes." Nor was the representative of the Spanish king entirely wrong in this. Physical evasion frequently occurred to avoid taxation. The Indians used to disappear in the rugged mountains or among the hitherto unconquered tribes, or they would hide in the outskirts of the cities, or else end up hiring themselves out as laborers on haciendas far from their ayllus, where it was in the interests of the Spanish landowners to conceal them, as they provided him with scarce yet cheap labor. The priest at Limatambo, distressed by the state of his parish, complained thus in 1744: "In order to flee from such outrageous tyranny, whole families have left their houses here, some for the distant mountains to live among the heathen, thereby endangering the Holy Faith . . . and the remainder to different places where they may live with the consolation of being sons of God" (Colin, 1966).

The disturbance must have been very great, and the tracks of those who departed must have become lost in the multitude of paths open to them. The Indians were thus hidden from the sight of chiefs and census takers, but they certainly remained alive and thus ensured the continuity of future generations. From a demographic point of view, flight and isolation did not favor reproduction to the same extent as life in a stable society.

While the Indian ayllu shrank and the ancient encomiendas tended to disappear, the Indian reappeared occasionally as a *forastero* ("stranger"). The contraction of the original Indian population and its gradual substitution by other classes of Indians is suggested in table 4.1. The statistics are taken from the tribute recounts for the

TABLE 4.1 Changes in the Indigenous Population in Three Repartimientos of Chayanta, 1695–1754

	1695		1734		1754	
	Original inhabi-tants	Forasteros	Original inhabi-tants	Forasteros	Original inhabi-tants	Forasteros
San Juan Bautista de Pocoata	482	—	414	13	634	309
Santiago de Moscarí	163	34	115	69	120	224
San Luis de Sacaca and adjoining areas	592	15	387	191	369	498

SOURCE: Achivo General de la Nación, Buenos Aires.

province of Chayanta, in present-day Bolivia. Between the *revisita* carried out in 1695 by Antonio de Garramuño, and the one made by Simón de Amezaga in 1734, the Indian population declined in the three parishes considered in the table. The 482 tributarios of Pocoata became 427, the 197 of Moscarí, 184, and the 607 of Sacaca, 578. The influx of forasteros partially compensated for the fall; otherwise, the absolute losses would have been greater. The migrant group was the one which then showed greater dynamism and brought about the demographic recovery. In 1754, the forasteros had succeeded in out-numbering the original inhabitants in two of the three repartimientos. The tributarios then numbered 943, 344, and 867 respectively.

The economic and social causes of the breakup of the Indian communities affected the declining population until well into the eighteenth century. Epidemic diseases also continued to exact a high toll until very late in Peru and in Upper Peru. Another report on census revisions, in the province of Carangas, states: "Fleeing from such piteous epidemics, the Indians moved away to far-off, remote places, thus suffering from numerical loss and decline." Fear of epidemics was responsible for the Indians' flight, but it was by this action that they spread the disease even more rapidly throughout the country. The widespread epidemic of 1719, to which the above text refers, took such a toll of Indian lives in the sierra and on the altiplano that the authorities had to take rapid measures lest the few survivors be overwhelmed by the weight of taxation. To this end they carried out a new census of tributarios which allowed the local tax assessment to be adjusted to the actual number of tributarios. The 1719 epidemic, together with later, localized outbreaks, reduced the Indian population to the minimum as shown by the contemporary documents.

The Norte Chico of Chile, on the other hand, provides a perfect example of a different tendency: the social, rather than the ethnic transference from the Indian to the mestizo or even the white community. Many Indians left estancias, haciendas, or mines, and when, for some reason or other, they wanted to be associated once more with the society they had left on a sudden impulse, they returned— not, as in Upper Peru, as forasteros—but as peons, free Indians, "ranking as alleged mestizos." According to the register of baptisms and deaths in the parish of Quillota, the Indian population remained steady between 1700 and 1729, showing no sign of increase; meanwhile the whites and mestizos increased by 18 percent each decade (Carmagnani, 1963). Why the Chilean Indian who had fled became, upon his return, a mestizo, while the Indian from Upper Peru merely turned into a forastero, is an interesting sociological point, but one which is beyond the scope of a purely demographic study.

Another way of considering the dynamics of population is to examine the size of families. This is a very broad research field; therefore we provide only a few examples, extracted from the records of the Jesuit missions in Paraguay, which abound in the Archivo General de la Nación in Buenos Aires. In fact, four general censuses are preserved there. The first, dating from 1657, was carried out by Blázquez de Valverde; the second, from 1676, was the work of Ibáñez de Faría. The remaining two date from 1735 and 1772, the latter being after the expulsion of the Jesuits; these were the censuses of Vázquez de Agüero and Larrazábal respectively. According to them, the population of the missions rose from 41,508 Indians to 73,762 between 1657 and 1735, a considerable increase, due more to successful evangelization than to natural growth.

In the first census, the *reducción* of San Carlos had 815 families totaling 3,229 individuals. The Indian tributarios there numbered only 619. The first coefficient was 1:3.9; that of the tributarios 1:5.2. Thus four people made up the typical nuclear family, a number sufficient to ensure the steady replacement of the generations. With their fervent policy of defending family life, the Jesuits had thus stabilized the population. The higher coefficient of the tributarios compared with the others is due to the fact that each head of household had as his dependents only his own immediate family, whereas the tributario's dependents included not only his own family but the numerous Indians who were exempt from taxation. These were the males over fifty, chiefs and their first and second sons, the *alcaldes regidores* and *pajes*, as well as some officials, singers, majordomos, and sacristans.

Nearly eighty years later, in 1735, Vázquez de Agüero recorded the following figures concerning the missions of La Candelaria and La Concepción. The first had 2,990 souls, 692 families and 550 tributarios, while the corresponding figures in the second were 5,320, 1,273, and 1,052. Dividing persons by families, one gets the coefficients 4.7 and 4.1, while in the case of the tributarios they are 5.4 and 5. Between 1657 and 1735 the ratio of population and tributarios did not change, but that of the families did slightly. The fact that the average number per family was over four may indicate some limited advance.

In the areas between the Spanish and Portuguese empires, on the borders of Chile, the mountain valleys of Tucumán, the *sertões* of the interior of Brazil, the Amazon jungle, the plains of Venezuela, and the plateaus in the north of New Spain—all of which were unconquered or only recently occupied areas—the disruption of Indian communities continued owing to slave-hunting raids, called either *malocas, bandeiras,* or *congregas.*

In the middle of the seventeenth century, the *malocas* provided the Chilean colonists with an abundance of slaves. On the other side of the Andes, in the neighboring *gobernación* of Tucumán, Indian resistance amounted to a regular war, as a result of which the Indians declined in numbers until the first quarter of the following century. The two uprisings of the Calchaquíes in 1630 and 1665 laid waste extensive areas in the valleys, and when finally conquered they were banished. Entire tribes were carried off to the vicinity of Catamarca, La Rioja, or the eastern slopes of Aconquija, and others were even driven as far as the borders of Buenos Aires and Santa Fe, more than a thousand kilometers from their native mountains. There are a few records of the people who were thus transported, and they reveal family units so incredibly small that quick recovery was out of the question.

In Brazil, the expeditions of the *bandeirantes* in search of slave labor wrought havoc with the Indian tribes of the *sertões.* Hundreds of thousands of Indians were roped together and hauled off to the plantations or the cattle ranches. The damage caused in this way cannot be measured by counting only the enormous number of those captured "pieces"; one must also consider the progressive disintegration of the economy and the family life of the Indians caused by continual harassment. Even the Jesuit reductions were not safe from attack. On most occasions they were ravaged by the colonists, but on others the fathers armed the Indians and with their assistance repelled *bandeirante* raids. Yet, thanks to these expeditions, Brazil expanded its territory widely.

The discovery of mineral deposits was responsible for the later raids. The hazardous, decidedly dreary, and even miserable life led by the mamelucos at the end of the century was suddenly enlivened by the news that their century-old hopes were realized at last. The coveted precious metals had finally been found on the northeastern route to the *sertão*. Instead of the silver that the mountains of the Andes hid, the rivers of the Minas Gerais plateau contained gold-bearing alluvium. At the vaguest rumor hordes of people from all points of the compass rushed to that inhospitable land empty-handed, with no means of support. The first to arrive were the Paulistas (people of São Paulo), who are said to have been responsible for the discovery. After them, following the São Francisco river upstream, came people from Bahia and Pernambuco, and even from the coasts of Piauí. As soon as the sensational news reached the mother country, thousands of Portuguese fought for space on the decks and in the holds of ships.

The Paulistas tried to hold the new El Dorado for themselves and did their best to keep outsiders away. In 1701, the authorities demanded a passport to enter the mining area, and this was only granted to persons of some means. The access routes from north and east were closed, and the only one allowed was the one connecting the area with the coast of São Paulo. But it was all in vain. It is estimated that in 1709 there must already have been some thirty thousand settlers in the district, a fair proportion of whom were outsiders. The locals harassed those they regarded as interlopers, until a real armed struggle broke out, the so-called Guerra das Emboabas (1709), *emboabas* being a name which the Paulistas used contemptuously to indicate both Brazilians from the northeast and Portuguese. Emigration from Portugal was so great that in 1720 the government of the mother country, disturbed by the effects at home, prohibited the departure of Portuguese citizens for the colonies.

As is usual in mining camps, the sex and age distribution was very disproportionate, the death rate high and marriages few, while free and interracial unions abounded. Thus demographic growth depended for a long time on the influx of migrants. In any case, a little-known, sparsely inhabited region saw numerous villages and even urban centers spring up overnight. In less than two decades, Vila Rica de Ouro Prêto acquired a population of over a hundred thousand. Though the figure may be slightly exaggerated, it is nevertheless true that for a few years its population ranked third in the New World, surpassed only by Mexico City and Lima. Its name and that of Minas Gerais perpetuate the memory of the mining boom during which the city and the captaincy were created.

The only outsiders the Paulistas were prepared to allow in were Negro slaves, with whom there was no risk of having to share the benefit of their finds. Moreover, they provided the manual labor for washing the sands and later for digging mining shafts. According to the register made to put into effect a head tax, in the first half of 1736 the slaves in Minas Gerais numbered 98,730, and free Negroes 1,384 (Boxer, 1969). The real figures must have been somewhat higher, since presumably some tax evasion took place. By districts, the slave population was distributed as follows: Mariana, formerly Ribeirão do Carmo and bishopric of the captaincy of Minas Gerais, 26,752; Sabará, 24,284; Vila Rica, 20,904; Rio das Mortes, 14,471; Serro Frio, 8,988; and the interior, 3,331. The half-yearly registers continued until 1749, and recorded numbers show a gradual tendency to decline.

Gold-bearing deposits were also discovered later well inland: first in Cuiabá in 1719, then in Goiás in 1725, and lastly around Guaporé, in Mato Grosso, in 1734. Their discovery led to the well-known gold rushes. The discovery of diamonds, on the other hand, aroused little interest. From an early date, the crown forbade private exploitation and created a mining monopoly for itself. The continual discovery of new deposits, together with the high death rate at the mines, made a regular, plentiful supply of slaves necessary, and an attempt was made to meet this demand without detriment to the work force available on the coastal plantations. This, of course, meant an increase in the number of slaves imported.

Large numbers of Africans entered Brazil during the first half of the eighteenth century. The figures, if not absolutely exact, seem reasonably reliable. Between 1701 and 1760, nearly a million slaves must have disembarked (Curtin, 1969). Arranged in ten-year periods, the importation figures read as follows: 1701–10, 153,700; 1711–20, 139,000; 1721–30, 146,300; 1731–40, 166,100; 1741–50, 185,100; and 1751–60, 169,400. The variation between the maximum and the minimum figure for these decades is relatively small. The average, 16,000 per year, is four and a half times the annual average during the second half of the seventeenth century. They came from a variety of places. The Sudanese, at least initially, were preferred on account of their greater stamina. Nevertheless, the Bantu gradually replaced the men from the Costa de Mina (Ghana). Between 1741 and 1750, in fact, the slavers brought in 130,000 from Angola, and only 55,000 from Guinea.

In Spanish America, once the prohibition order effective between 1640 and 1651 had been revoked, the various commercial experiments carried out during the second half of the seventeenth century did not succeed in providing a regular and plentiful supply of slave labor. The failure of both direct administration and contractors, the frequent change of suppliers in search of higher profits, indicate not only inefficiency but also slight demand. Not even the Royal French Company in the Gulf of Guinea, which acquired the privilege of slave trading after the détente between the crowns of France and Spain, proved any more successful. Of the 600 "pieces" it undertook to deliver to Buenos Aires each year, it brought, in fact, only an average of 215 (Studer, 1958). In view of the above, the figure of 163,000 Africans quoted by Curtin (1969) as having been imported into Spanish America between 1651 and 1700 seems excessive. It would mean an average of 3,200 per annum, a figure as high as that prevailing at the beginning of the century when the slave trade was flourishing.

With the signing of the Peace of Utrecht in 1713, England succeeded in legally eliminating its competitors on the Spanish American market. From Spain it obtained the slave trade monopoly, with the right to have agents in Campeche, Veracruz, Havana, Cartagena, Portobelo, Panamá, Caracas, and Buenos Aires. The British crown, in turn, ceded its privilege to the South Sea Company. With the assistance of another British company operating in Africa, it provided the Spanish Indies with slave labor, the demand for which rose as the economy improved. It was then the turn of the English to feel the effects of contraband activity by French and Dutch, especially on the Venezuelan coast. Illicit Portuguese trade with the River Plate was based at the colony of Sacramento, located within sight of Buenos Aires, the new legal entry point for "pieces" destined for Upper Peru and Chile.

Despite the abuses of agents and the difficulties created by the colonial authorities, the contract lasted for thirty-seven years, until

1750, with a few brief interruptions caused by the outbreak of hostilities. From then on, Spain reverted to the former system of limited concessions. Curtin (1969) calculates that between 1701 and 1760, 181,000 slaves entered Spanish America. This figure is slightly higher than the 144,000 "pieces" which the South Sea Company promised to deliver during the period that its privilege lasted, at the rate of 4,800 per year. The average for the period was 3,000 slaves, a lesser quantity than that suggested by Curtin for the previous half-century, which was a period of economic stagnation. The figures are thus in need of revision.

Future studies of the Portuguese and Spanish sources will be able to provide a more accurate estimate of the influx of slaves, but the extent of European migration seems more difficult to assess. The Portuguese who emigrated to Brazil at the time cannot have been more than 200,000, that is, a fifth of the number of slaves who crossed the Atlantic in the same sixty years of the eighteenth century. The only migration of any significance as far as Spanish America is concerned was that of laborers from the Canaries to Cuba, or that of the few who went to Montevideo in 1726.

Borah (1951) established the growth rates of the cities of Mexico by comparing the works of Díez de la Calle and O'Crouley (table 4.2a). Between 1646 and 1774, the number of Spanish *vecinos* in Durango multiplied twenty-nine times, in Puebla thirteen, in Valladolid ten, in San Bartolomé and Oaxaca about seven. The other places recorded at least a doubling of population in 128 years. Admittedly, Culiacán remained stationary and Acapulco declined, but these are only two cases out of the eleven examined.

TABLE 4.2a Spanish Vecinos in the Cities of Mexico, 1646–1774

Cities	1646 (Díez de la Calle)	1774 (O'Crouley)
Acapulco	150	8
Culiacán	80	80
Durango	120	3,500
Oaxaca	600	4,100
Parral	250	300
Puebla	1,000	13,000
San Bartolomé	40	300
Tlaxcala	200	400
Valladolid	250	2,500
Veracruz	500	1,300
Zacatecas	500	2,800

SOURCE: Borah, 1951.

TABLE 4.2*b* Spanish Vecinos and Inhabitants in Peruvian cities, 1628–1764

Cities	Vecinos in 1628 (Vázquez de Espinosa)	Inhabitants in 1764 (Bueno)
Lima	9,500	54,000
Cuzco	3,500	26,000
La Paz	200	20,000
Trujillo	400	9,000
Piura	100	5,000
Chachapoyas	200	3,500
Huamanga	400	2,500
Camaná	70	1,500

In imitation of Borah, we have constructed table 4.2*b* in which the numbers of vecinos given by Vázquez de Espinosa are contrasted with the inhabitants of the few Peruvian cities for which Cosme Bueno quotes a figure. The time lapse—1628 to 1764—is similar to that covered for Mexico. In comparing one column with another, it should not be forgotten that the population in each case is calculated on a different basis. One must multiply the 1628 figure of vecinos by the coefficient 6 or divide the 1764 inhabitants figure by the same number. The resulting comparison shows the capital cities of Lima and Cuzco as having a stationary population; the same applies to a less important place such as Huamanga. The greatest growth rate was recorded in La Paz, where the population increased sixteenfold, while Piura's went up eight times. The three remaining cities more or less trebled their population in about one century. Whatever the merit of the comparison, it is evident that urban growth in Peru was not nearly so rapid as in Mexico; nor had the population of Peru as a whole recovered as much as that of New Spain by that time.

Before population historians paid the attention they now do to registers of baptisms and death, Besio Moreno (1939) had endeavored to trace the ups and downs in the vital statistics of the city of Buenos Aires during the seventeenth century by making an examination of parish registers. Thanks to this initiative, the Argentine capital is the only one on the continent which can provide a series of such records from such an early date. These figures supplement the census data, which are usually easier to obtain, and help to establish the invariable overall tendency of the population of the urban nucleus to increase, despite understandable fluctuations. An additional advantage of the book is that it provides a wealth of information about local epidemics. The date and the diagnosis of each disease are provided primarily by the *actas capitulares* (city council records), but the burial registers also provide substantial supplementary information. These records, in fact, enable one to discover surprisingly sudden high death rates not revealed by the city council records and which are obviously attributable to epidemics. Such disasters occurred, for example, in 1652–53 and 1670. During the first outbreak, 446 and 224 burials were recorded in the years concerned, compared with an average of 132 per year over the previous seven years, that is, two and a half times the usual rate. The second outbreak, which was not as severe, was responsible for a figure of 176 burials compared with an average of 149 per annum over the previous decade, that is, an increase of one-fifth.

As will be seen, the extent and the frequency of the epidemics made the conditions of life in Latin American cities comparable to those in European cities during the Old Regime. Basio Moreno established the following dates for Buenos Aires as those of peak mortality rates: 1642–43, 1652–53, 1670, 1675, 1687, 1694, 1700–1705, 1717–20, 1734, and 1742. Valparaíso figures provided by Thayer Ojeda (1934) on the basis of burial records, show similar peaks in 1687, 1694, 1706, 1713, and 1718. It is well known, on the other hand, that Caracas suffered from the plague in 1658 and from an attack of smallpox in 1667 (Gasparini, 1969). The mere enumeration of these facts makes clear the permanent hazards to which urban populations were subject, and the chronological coincidences give an indication of how widespread such epidemics were.

The epidemics of 1687, 1694, and 1717–20 were on a vast scale and were extremely widespread. The 1694 outbreak, for example, was an epidemic of measles which affected the whole of Peru, having started in Quito two years earlier, and its effects were felt as far south as the River Plate (Dobyns, 1963). It seems that typhus was the epidemic that seriously affected Mexico in the same year (Álvarez Amézquita, 1960). The 1717–20 epidemic, referred to a few pages back, was an outbreak of bubonic plague, which started aboard a slave ship at Buenos Aires. From there it spread upriver to the remote missions of Paraguay, where it killed one-fifth of the inhabitants, and then, without pausing, on to the "upper provinces," whence it progressed into Peru. At that time, the Tribunal de la Santa Cruzada in Lima promptly informed the king of the seriousness of the outbreak: "The universal calamity that has affected twenty-five provinces of this kingdom has been caused by the plague, one of the worst experienced since the discovery [of Peru], for . . . it caused villages, towns, and cities to be set ablaze, leaving them in ruins and deserted by their original inhabitants. According to the reports received from priests and *corregidores*, the number of dead comes to four hundred thousand, and in many places only the walls are left standing to bear mute testimony to the severity with which God has chastised us for our sins." Then, referring specifically to the city of Cuzco, the Tribunal reported: "Sixty thousand have perished, there being daily in the streets a bloody scene of corpses torn to pieces by dogs, for the living are without strength to bury the dead." Once again, the level of society worst affected was "the lower class and those low in the social scale, who are the persons most likely to suffer from such a disaster," as the *protomédico* of Lima and professor of medicine in the university wrote to the viceroy. "The Spaniards," he went on, "who feed themselves properly and eat foods that we call *multe virtutis et pauce molis* in these regions, have seldom been affected by the disease and few have died" (Colin, 1966).

Besides measles, the bubonic plague, and other diseases of the Old World, there was a disease of African origin, which found suitable conditions for its propagation on the low-lying tropical coastlines. Before 1648, the yellow-fever-carrying mosquito spread along the coasts of Cuba, Veracruz, and Yucatán and then became so firmly established that only systematic health campaigns carried out at government level about half a century ago managed to eradicate it. This deadly insect soon spread southward also. In 1685, it appeared in northeastern Brazil, and two years later the disease took a firm hold in the city of Caracas for sixteen consecutive months. The *peste da bicha*, as it was known in Brazil, the black vomit, mainly affected urban areas and had a particular partiality for the higher strata of society, including Europeans of all kinds. A contemporary observer wrote: "It was a matter worthy of note that this disease did not attack Negroes, Mulattoes, Indians, or mixed-bloods, either in Bahia or Pernambuco. Consequently there was no shortage of persons to look after those afflicted; nevertheless food supplies were short, since those who usually brought them would rather lose any possible profit than risk their own lives by entering places where so furious a disease was rampant" (Azevedo, 1955). A century later, Alcedo, author of a *Diccionario geográfico-histórico de las Indias Occidentales* (1786–89), also confirmed the observation by the *Bahiano* observer concerning the discriminatory nature of the disease. He pointed out that the black vomit was "an endemic disease in the seaports and warm climatic regions of America and regularly attacked newly arrived Europeans and had wrought such havoc that it has happened at Portobelo that the galleons had to winter there, as nearly all their crews had died, and the situation was much the same in Veracruz, Caracas, and Cartagena, since it was very seldom that a patient ever recovered."

So far, there is little information available about famines in the seventeenth century. In a lively account, Simpson (1966) has rescued from oblivion the disturbances resulting from the food shortages in Mexico City in 1624 and 1692, similar to the bread riots on the other side of the Atlantic; but these chance reports do not indicate the effect of the shortages on the population. As for the eighteenth century, Florescano (1969) has clearly established the relationship existing between agriculture and population crises by applying on this side of the Atlantic a technique well known in Europe. In America it is the price of maize, rather than of wheat, which indicates a bad harvest and the consequential shortages and famine. His study shows that periodic shortages regularly preceded the epidemics mentioned above. Human defense mechanisms were weakened by hunger, thus favoring the spread of disease. But bad harvests alone did not affect population trends by facilitating the spread of epidemics. It is high time that parish records were examined to establish the correlation between meteorological disasters and the death rate. Local crises, when added together, were as responsible for checking population growth as more widespread phenomena.

Numerous earthquakes and volcanic eruptions also restricted population growth, especially in cities. Populous capital cities collapsed, and their inhabitants, resigned to their fate, as with the torture of Tantalus, immediately mobilized their energies to rebuild buildings or monuments, which would not survive the next tremor. Of such disasters we will only recall the cruel earthquakes of 1678, 1687, 1725, and 1746, which devastated the Pacific coast of South America, about which Barriga (1951) has rescued extensive evidence concerning the much afflicted city of Arequipa.

To sum up, one may say that the process of stabilization, little known until now, followed a complex and sometimes contradictory course. Mexico appears to have reacted early against the long decline. The steady increase of the Indian population made possible the growth of its cities and the northward territorial expansion of the viceroyalty in the direction of Texas and New Mexico. A spectacular increase occurred in the interior of Brazil. At the expense of the nomadic Indian tribes, there grew up a wealthy and extravagant society which attracted the get-rich-quick and encouraged the importation of a large African slave population. In Spanish South

America, excluding the equatorial regions, the Indian population continued its disastrous decline until the beginning of the eighteenth century. Excessive labor, oppressive taxation, and inadequate or unsuitable food maintained their disruptive course, while the virulence of epidemics remained unabated. However, depopulation for which there is a large amount of evidence was less than census records would suggest, since no one will ever know how many Indians fled beyond the reach of encomenderos and corregidores, thus saving not merely their own lives, but also those of their descendants. In time, the offspring of those fugitives were to reappear in demographic records, suggesting a rate of increase which after all was not perhaps so great. We do not know how many then forgot their Indian ancestry to swell the ranks of the mestizos. In any case, the unhurried growth of Spanish cities does not lead us to suppose that the Indians were increasing very rapidly.

EXPANSION

From the last third of the eighteenth century onward, the whole world witnessed a simultaneous development of productive capacity and population. The relationship between the two phenomena is not very clear. Was the economy or the population responsible for initiating the change? The question is still being debated. On previous occasions a new ceiling was soon reached, but it did not happen this time; on the contrary, the population of the Western world leapt beyond the bounds supposed to limit its growth, for, contrary to the fears of Malthus, the supply of food managed to keep pace with the number of mouths. When any country ceased to be self-supporting, another one appeared overseas which was able to provide the necessary supplies in exchange for money or other goods. The expansion of domestic and international trade and the cultivation of virgin lands guaranteed sustained population growth.

Not only did the size of the population grow, but the way in which it grew altered. The increase did not necessitate any greater biological urge. It did not mean that women had more children. When the death rate fell, enormous numbers of people survived who would previously have died in their early childhood; later, when the conception rate went down, the simultaneous but more rapid decline in the death rate more than compensated for the decreased birthrate. For the first time in history the population increased steadily despite a decrease in the birthrate.

The peripheral regions felt the effect of that change but, contrary to what was happening in the countries which both pioneered it and dictated world economic policy, the traditional patterns scarcely altered. Thus during the latter part of the eighteenth century and throughout the whole of the nineteenth, Latin America accompanied the European nations in their growth, though the nature of the growth was different.

First of all, the increase in the population of America was not always the result of domestic factors. External pressures had an influence on the situation. The fact that the New World's demographic structure and dynamic continued to follow previous patterns does not by any means imply that it was isolated in terms of the human, social, or economic points of view. European countries were then experiencing a growing demand for primary products, and this, in turn, led to the acquisition of more land or the more intensive cultivation of crops needing a large work force. Even toward the end of the nineteenth century, the Old World supplied the New with labor when a shortage threatened to hold up the development of some parts of Latin America. This mobilization effected by Europe was not always clearly or directly felt, nor was it equally intense in all parts of Latin America. Naturally the coastal fringes or urban centers, more regularly linked with the advanced nations, were more vulnerable to outside influences. These areas were the ones to which the modernizing demographic patterns arrived, and it was from them that they were disseminated. But it was to be a long time before they had any significant effect; the cities and the coastal areas did not as yet have much influence throughout Latin America as a whole. For a long time the pattern in the area continued to be the traditional one.

The rural population, considerably superior numerically, reacted in accordance with trends dictated by the type of agriculture predominating in each area—subsistence in some places, cash crops for export in others. By subsistence we do not, of course, mean to imply an entirely self-sufficient economy. Taxation, the compulsory purchase of European merchandise, which corregidores enforced on Indians in Peru until the 1780 revolt, and many other measures brought the country people, to a varying extent, within the market economy. They bought some goods from outside their own communities and consequently had to sell in order to obtain the wherewithal to make their purchases. However, the extent of production and consumption that was involved in the commercial economy was very small indeed. In practice, they produced more or less what was necessary to survive. The majority of the Indian farmers in the Andes, in a large part of Mexico, and in Central America lived in this rudimentary manner.

On the other hand, there were also the tropical crops and cattle raising both destined for export to world markets. Lack of transport prevented all suitable land from being put to the most profitable use. Some hacienda land was often set aside for the production of food crops, or subsistence agriculture was allowed in areas bordering on land producing cash crops, in order that the plantation workers should be self-supporting in food.

In the first case, what growth there was came about within the framework of an agrarian society aiming at self-sufficiency. It was limited in an almost Malthusian manner by the availability of food supplies. But since the demographic tragedy of the sixteenth century had left vast areas of land unoccupied, there was plenty of opportunity for future reoccupation of the land.

The export economy, however, depended on the world market. Accordingly, the ability of the land to support a given population increased or decreased with world market fluctuations, which were also responsible for attracting or turning away migrants. Despite these vicissitudes it was in these areas that population expansion was greatest, and eventually the growing importance of these zones tipped the demographic balance of the continent toward the Atlantic coast. As the densely populated areas at the time of the Conquest were on the western slopes of the continent and for a long time were to keep to an almost self-sufficient economy, the ancient state of population imbalance was partially righted as the previously nearly deserted eastern coasts expanded. The Atlantic region gained in importance.

According to the overall estimate made by Durand (1967a), which has already been referred to, South and Central America must have grown between 1750 and 1850 at quite a significant rate, slightly over 0.8 percent per annum. As with all averages, this does not reveal the very distinctive variations.

The best known rapid advances are illustrated in figure 3, which records the figures concerning four roughly comparable areas. Over the same period of time, all four increased their initial population (about 100,000) four or five times. The regions concerned are Cuba, the Antioquia-Cauca region of present-day Colombia, the bishopric of Santiago de Chile, and the captaincy of São Paulo in Brazil. Two are in the Northern Hemisphere, two in the Southern. The geography of the four has nothing in common: one is a tropical island in the Caribbean, another is in the high mountain valleys of the northern

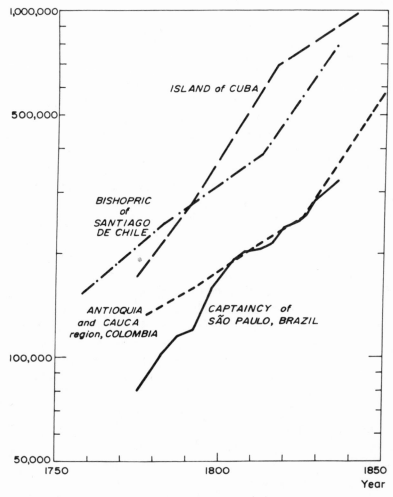

FIGURE 3. Trends of population growth in four areas: Cuba, central Chile, São Paulo, and Antioquia-Cauca, 1750–1850. (Sources: for Cuba, Guerra y Sánchez, 1958; for Chile, Carmagnani, 1967; for São Paulo, Lisanti, 1962–63; for Antioquia-Cauca, Vergara y Velasco, 1891.)

Andes, the third is on the temperate western slopes overlooking the South Pacific Ocean, and the fourth includes the plateau and coastline overlooking the South Atlantic Ocean. Nor is their historic or demographic evolution similar: one was a land of plantation economy made possible by slave labor. The second was an isolated, declining region, which began to expand southward (Parsons, 1968). The third sheltered a population which, after long years of uncertainty, lived quietly by its own efforts. The last was an area open on all sides, with *mato* country ripe for expansion to the west and north, active colonization in progress to the south, and maritime links with Europe along the eastern coast. Of the four areas, two are on the Pacific side of the continent, and two face the Atlantic. Cuba and São Paulo, but especially the former, received a considerable and regular influx of migrants from overseas, while Chile and Antioquia-Cauca did not. Cuba, the best documented case so far as census data are concerned and also the area that received the greatest benefit from immigration, increased its population more rapidly than the other three, doubling it every twenty-five years. Antioquia-Cauca, the most inward-looking area, had a slower growth rate: it took half a century to double its population, stopped abruptly, and then in quarter of a century—or half the time—doubled it again. The situations are different, but all show a bigger increase than the average given by Durand. The lines are steep even though the semilogarithmic ordinates tend to lessen the visual impact of the graph.

The above examples are neither unique nor unusual, as can be seen from the following cases. Though of greater territorial extent than the regions examined above, the River Plate area and Venezuela had similar population increases; the first followed the Colombian pattern, while the second, if figures are reliable, increased even more rapidly than Puerto Rico (Janer, 1945), Haiti (Young, 1949), and Cuba itself. Costa Rica shows a similar increase, but within a shorter space of time. It should be noted that the highland on the isthmus of Central America attracted migrants, not merely because of its own inherent advantages, but because it also provided a refuge for the population of the Caribbean coast of Nicaragua (the Mosquito Coast) where the zambo Mosquito tribe regularly raided the cacao plantations (Jiménez Castro, 1956). Finally, it should be pointed out that between the colonial census of 1778 and the Gran Colombia census of 1825, the audiencia of Quito, which was populated mainly by Indian rural communities, experienced what one can rate as a mediocre increase, doubling in sixty years; yet even this was faster than the continental average (Paz y Miño, 1936).

Wherever the great bulk of the Indian population continued farming by their exhausting, rudimentary methods of traditional agricultural practice, their numbers did not increase rapidly. López Sarre-langue (1963) has estimated that the Indians of Mexico increased in the second half of the eighteenth century by 44 percent, and by less in the center of the country than in the peripheral areas. In a

study already referred to, Miranda examined in detail a district occupied by Otomí Indians. The increase he observed was greater than
the average quoted above, but it was nevertheless seen to fall off as
the century advanced. Ixmiquilpan, in fact, had a population of 13,-
750 Otomíes according to the census of Viceroy Fuenclara, 18,011
according to that of Revillagigedo, and only 22,534 in the 1804
census preserved in the Archivo Municipal. Cook and Borah (1968)
investigated the Mixteca Alta, and west central Mexico—New Galicia, part of Jalisco, Ávalos, Colima, and Motines—(1971); the
demographic curve in these recently studied areas generally coincides with that of Ixmiquilpan, though it is a little out of phase, since
the rapid rate of growth continued until the end of the eighteenth
century. However, at the beginning of the new century the population
did decline; and this happened before the necessarily disruptive forces
of the independence movement brought a brief demographic recession in the early nineteenth century.

  Even at the time of the José de Gálvez census in El Salvador—
a country that enjoys the rare privilege of having a continuous, well-
documented demographic history, thanks to the efforts of Barón
Castro (1942)—three-fifths of its inhabitants were Indians and only
one-sixth of pure European descent. From then on the region seemed
to show signs of activity, but the growth rate was so slow that it took
three-quarters of a century to double its population.

  The various studies carried out on the population of Peru have
not so far clearly established the growth rate during the late colonial
and early independence periods. Kubler (1952) discovered and
analyzed the periodic rolls by which the republican administration
regulated the *contribución* payable by Indians; the term was but a
new one to designate what in colonial days was referred to as *tributo*.
The Spanish Cortes generously abolished the latter tax in 1811, but
it was reintroduced with the restoration of the Bourbon dynasty.
Later on, when the republic was in financial difficulty and found it
could not do without the income from that source, it merely changed
the hated title to one more in accord with the political aims of the
new state. The *contribución* was not abolished finally until the time
of Marshal Castilla in 1854, when the income from the export levy
on guano made it possible to do without it. Between 1826 and 1854
the treasury officials responsible for keeping the records up to date
continued to revise the rolls every five years, just as required in the
instructions issued in 1778 by the *visitador* Areche. Colonial prac-

tices continued to be followed, and consequently the sequence of register revisions was kept up with no break except during the disturbed period preceding independence.

Kubler's main object was to discover what had been the population trends for the categories known as Indian and mestizo. The American professor took for granted that, at the beginning of the nineteenth century, both terms no longer indicated any biological significance and that they expressed rather the social attitudes toward race that were shared both by the governing classes and, tacitly, by the governed. Kubler summarized the statistics found in the Archivo Nacional and in the Archivo Histórico del Ministerio de Hacienda, both in Lima, and compared them with those contained in the last colonial census and with the national censuses of 1876 and 1940. Because of the loose interpretation of the term *Indian*, he was unable to determine demographic growth and could only gauge how far acculturation had progressed in some areas or had been held back in others. Kubler's estimates for the total population are likewise invalid, for his figures relating to the Indian population have recently been proved to be underestimates (Vollmer, 1967).

This German historian delved into the records of the Archivo de Indias in Seville and has clearly achieved the object indicated in the title of his book: to investigate demographic policy and structure during the administrative term of the last viceroy. However, despite the vast compass of the source material he so carefully handles, it is still difficult to make out from Vollmer's work any clear trend of demographic progression. After a study of the demographic and fiscal policy of the colonial government, which students of Peru and other historians will find very valuable, the work goes on to analyze the ethnic structure of the viceroyalty as recorded in the census taken by Gil de Taboada in 1792.

To the data provided by Kubler and Vollmer will be added the information that Professor Macera will publish shortly and which he has been kind enough to let me examine in proof stage. His data are based on records and accounts of colonial taxes of which Kubler was not aware. Little of this material duplicates that examined by Vollmer in the Archivo de Indias.

Thus the amount of demographic information has increased, thanks to successive discoveries, but it is nevertheless not as satisfactory as one could wish. In future it is to be hoped that one-sided investigations will be avoided, now that the existence of useful data on both sides of the Atlantic is known; the sources in Lima and Seville must both be taken into account. For lack, as yet, of any work of synthesis in this regard, the following two tables are provided, compiled from data contained in Macera's forthcoming book. The observations will suggest, rather than assert, an evolutionary trend.

Table 4.3 assembles the demographic information provided in the statistical tables of population, wealth and *contribuciones* in the various provinces, as published in *La Prensa Peruana* between 1828 and 1829. These tables provide figures concerning the size of the population under the headings Indians and *castas*. The term *castas* is used to indicate non-Indians, and thus includes mestizos, whites, and slaves. In addition to a column indicating the sum of the two

TABLE 4.3 Population of Some Provinces in Peru, 1792–1827

	1827			1792	Variation		Indigenous population as a % of the total population
	Indians	Castas	Total	Total	Absolute	Percentage	
	(1)	(2)	(3)	(4)	(5)	(6)	(7)
Lima							
Lima	—	—	58,326	62,910	-4,584	-7.3	—
Cañete	10,243	3,649	13,892	12,616	1,276	10.1	74
Chancay	10,791	7,921	18,712	13,945	4,766	34.2	58
Yauyos	10,981	1,295	12,276	9,574	2,702	28.2	89
Huarochirí	16,140	409	16,549	14,024	2,525	18.0	98
Canta	12,368	1,564	13,932	12,133	1,799	14.8	89
				125,202	8,484	6.8	
Trujillo							
Piura	30,946	22,872	53,818	44,491	9,327	21.0	58
Cajamarca	21,787	20,206	41,993	62,196	-20,203	-32.5	52
Chachapoyas	10,275	4,233	14,508	25,398	-10,890	-42.9	71
				132,085	-21,766	-16.5	
Tarma							
Pasco	19,380	17,670	37,050	34,911	2,139	6.1	52
Jauja	37,854	23,169	61,023	52,286	8,737	16.7	62
Cajatambo	11,321	7,143	18,464	16,872	1,592	9.4	61
Huaylas	25,409	24,258	49,667	40,822	8,845	21.7	51
Huamalies	7,121	6,051	13,172	14,234	-1,602	-7.5	54
Huánuco	9,048	5,486	14,534	16,826	-2,292	-13.6	62
				175,951	17,959	10.2	
Cuzco							
Abancay	34,654	4,884	39,538	25,259	14,279	56.5	88
Urubamba	9,530	5,388	14,918	9,250	5,668	61.3	64
Paruro	9,760	2,366	12,126	20,236	-8,110	-40.1	80
Quispicanchis	23,033	3,832	26,865	24,337	2,528	10.4	86
				79,082	14,365	18.2	
Arequipa							
Arica	10,545	9,640	20,185	18,776	1,409	7.5	52

SOURCE: Macera, n.d.

previous ones—Indians and *castas*—there is one recording the total population according to the 1792 census; as a logical consequence, the figures are also given to indicate the plus or minus variation that occurred during the thirty-five years concerned. Column 6 gives this variation as a percentage increase or decrease, while column 7 expresses the Indian population as a percentage of the whole. By consulting the last column, one can thus determine in which areas there was a net predominance of Indians at the beginning of the Republic, and in which the mestizos and other ethnic groups equaled or outnumbered the Indians. The provinces are grouped by intendencies. The selection is geographically unequal; thus figures are given for six of the seven provinces in the intendency of Tarma, while there are only six out of the eight in the intendency of Lima. Similarly, only four out of eleven in Cuzco and three out of seven in Trujillo are shown. Only one province of Arequipa is listed, and none at all for the two remaining intendencies, Huancavelica and Huamanga. Some of the areas are omitted for lack of data, while others do not appear because of some inherent anomalies. The four provinces of Cuzco only increased by 18 percent in thirty-five years, but this figure is nevertheless higher than that of any other region. Tarma recorded only a modest increase of 10.2 percent, while in Trujillo, the mountain and Amazon areas, rather than the coast around Piura, experienced a high degree of depopulation.

In addition to the bare facts recorded in the table, one may make the following observation concerning Lima. From 1812, when a census was taken by Viceroy Abascal, the city, its suburbs, and the surrounding valleys persistently lost inhabitants until in 1827 it had only as many as in the days of Viceroy Superunda in the middle of the previous century. Thus Lima had no population progress to record after the passage of three-quarters of a century. The urban crisis, however, did not affect the country districts of the intendency; but the modest 6 percent average increase is far from the vigorous growth rates of Chile, São Paulo, Antioquia, or Cuba.

Districts not included in the table, but for which Indian population figures exist, show trends similar to those recorded in the table. For what they are worth, we have extracted from the welter of information available the figures relating to the number of *tributarios* recorded in each quinquennial *visita*. This material is to be found in table 4.4. Not every quinquennial figure is available. Ica, Condesuyos, Conchucos, Chumbivilcas, and Calca y Lares provide figures with conscientious regularity. The remaining three districts leave

TABLE 4.4 *Tributarios* or *Contribuyentes* in Some Provinces in Peru according to *Revisitas* of Indians

Ica		Humachuco		Condesuyos		Conchucos	
1778–79	1,747	1778	4,325	1795	1,989	1783	3,585
1785–86	1,771	1781	3,848	1800	2,109	1793	4,132
1790	1,661	1786	4,951	1805	1,969	1798	4,474
1801	1,868	1808	5,104	1810	2,078	1803	4,875
1806	1,996			1815	1,974	1809	5,241
						1815	5,289
Castrovirreina		Chumbivilcas		Tinta		Calca y Lares	
1731	1,173	1786	2,780	1774–75	4,207	1796	2,518
1754	1,338	1791	2,822	1783	5,307	1801	2,660
1768	1,894	1796	2,992	1785	6,564	1806	2,684
1789	2,140	1801	3,181	1791	7,014	1811	2,767
1794	2,239	1806	3,387	1796	7,950	1815	3,073
1799	2,269	1811	3,095	1811	7,715		
1802	2,229	1815	2,530	1815	8,030		
1809	2,538	1817	3,001	1821	10,367		
1818	2,764						

SOURCE: Macera, n.d.

long gaps: Huamachuco has one of twenty-two years, Tinta one of fifteen, and Castrovirreina one between 1768 and 1789, though the latter makes up for this in some manner, since its series of recordings begin nearly half a century before the others. Despite the lack of continuity and other disadvantages inherent in the manner in which the records were made, there is an undoubted population increase, but it is by no means rapid. In Castrovirreina, for example, the population took three-quarters of a century to double from 1731 onward.

In its way, table 4.4 complements the picture provided by table 4.3. The case of Ica on the coast confirms the remarks made concerning the intendency of Lima. Huamachuco and Condesuyos make up for the fall recorded in Cajamarca farther north. Castrovirreina indicates that there was an increase in the intendency of Huancavelica. The figures for Condesuyos confirm the situation in Arequipa. Chumbivilcas, Tinta, and Calca y Lares all show an increase comparable with that recorded for Cuzco. The information we are examining covers both coastal valleys (Lima, Cañete, Ica, Arica, Chancay, and Piura), and the northern, central, and southern sierras (the provinces of Yauyos, Huarochirí, Canta, and Cajamarca and the intendencies of Huancavelica, Huamanga, and Cuzco). As for the composition of the population, there are included provinces of the central cordillera or Cuzco in which nearly the whole population is Indian, others in which there are many mestizos (Tarma, for example), and lastly, those in which whites and Negroes together form the second minority after the omnipresent Indians.

The population of a territory and of a society which is so fragmented could hardly be expected to follow any uniform trend. Whichever of the two methods is used to trace the upward movement of population—either the increase between censuses or the series of tributario counts—it is patently obvious that increase was painfully slow. The seven intendencies of Lower Peru (the present Republic of Peru) which, owing to their wealth and population had previously been worthy of heading a vast viceroyalty, were lagging behind. Though more than one growing European nation was moving then at a similar pace to that of the Pacific coastal areas of South America, by New World standards, this was, however, a modest increase, a rate which condemned the country to fall behind other areas. The River Plate, Cuba, and Venezuela, which eighty years previously, one must remember, had only between a fifth and a third of Peru's population, had increased their populations to two-thirds that of Peru by the middle of the nineteenth century because of the difference in their growth rates.

What was the reason for this general population increase, evident everywhere, though at varying rates? What is known of the fertility and the death rates, of the demographic factors that brought about the increase at this particular time? The best information on this subject is that concerning the area now called Argentina. Three examples taken from this area illustrate, in our view, three situations typical of America. Despite the complexity of existing social patterns in Latin America as a whole, these few samples may reasonably be considered fairly representative. The greatest difficulty is that the samples have not all been analyzed using the same categories.

The three geographical areas concerned are first, Jujuy in 1778, an inland, mountain region, fairly well populated by an Indian peasantry similar to that of Peru; second, the city of Buenos Aires, macrocephalic capital of a cattle-raising plain, thinly populated, cosmopolitan, and in some degree typical of any urban area on the American coastline; third, the province of Córdoba in 1813, in a situation midway between the other two, inland, but bordering on the open pampa zone.

In Jujuy, the parishes in the country in 1778 have regular age pyramids, with a broader base than those of the local capital cities, and with a very prominent indentation in the group aged ten to nineteen, indicative of the high child mortality rate (Rasini, 1965).

Despite this, throughout the whole area, town and country, children and young people of both sexes up to the age of twenty form 49 percent of the total population, while only 4.5 percent survived beyond the age of sixty. This is obviously a young population. But this optimistic impression is somewhat altered when one examines the state of the family. One can see that 23 percent of the young women got married between the ages of fifteen and nineteen, and nearly half the total did so between twenty and twenty-nine. A tenth were still unmarried after the age of forty, when they mingled with the widows, who at that age already formed one-fifth of the group. More than half of the males did not get married until after the age of thirty. It is hardly surprising that couples composed of thirty-year-old men and women nearly ten years younger produced families averaging only 2.7 children, if one excludes those who had no children at all, or 2.5 if one includes them. The nuclear family type, disregarding those individuals who figured on the census but had no family, was made up of 4.1 persons. Whites and Negroes had a slightly higher average number of children, and their nuclear family was consequently slightly larger than that of the Indians.

In the city of Buenos Aires, the age pyramid shows a similar wide base, followed by a similar narrowing (Moreno, 1965). The proportion of old people is also small. The average number of children per family goes up to 3.2 in a very wide social spectrum from the great landed proprietors at one extreme to the peons, day-wage laborers, and domestic servants at the other. The larger families were those of the wealthy; the first group had twice as many children as the second.

The province of Córdoba has the most youthful appearance of the three areas considered. With only 4.2 percent of old people over sixty, the young people constituted over 50 percent of the total population (Instituto de Estudios Americanistas). Considering fertility next, if we examine the ratio of children under the age of four born to every thousand women between the ages of fifteen and forty-four (the upper and lower limits of their childbearing period), it is obvious that the Spanish women of Córdoba were the most prolific female group of all. With their 602 children they even outclassed their peers in Buenos Aires, who had 538. The colored women of Córdoba likewise had more children than their peers in Buenos Aires, 542 as against 453. Within the colored group, Negro women of Córdoba recorded the lowest number, 313 per thousand, while the Indian women—and there were, admittedly, few of them—recorded the astonishingly high figure of 671 per thousand. From this comparison between the country area of Córdoba and the urban area of Buenos Aires, is it legitimate to maintain that urban groups already had a lower fertility rate?

Returning to the theme of the distribution of children per ethnic group, let us mention a nearby example, that of São Paulo, studied by Marcilio (1968). Expressed in more detailed ratios than those used for Córdoba, every thousand nonslave women between twenty and forty-nine had, in 1798, 349 girls under the age of four who could be relied upon to maintain their population in the future, whereas slave women had only 273.

Thus there are differences depending on regions, ethnic groups, and class. If the Indian is tied to the land and exploited, he behaves like a starving peasant; if the Negro is a slave, he behaves like one. Only a few years ago the Brazilian Negress had 6 percent fewer children surviving to adulthood than white Brazilian women, according to the 1950 census (Mortara, 1957). There are many similar studies of differential fertility rates in the Mississippi delta (T. L. Smith, 1959). It is therefore hardly surprising that this should also be the case in the eighteenth century. In the northwestern Andes, the country Indians did not increase as rapidly as did the Spaniards, who, needless to say, formed the upper strata of society. The same applies in the port of Buenos Aires when we compare Negro slaves and their white owners, who were at less of a social disadvantage. After this situation had gone on for centuries, it is hardly surprising that the Iberian nucleus should have succeeded in lightening the color of the population as a whole. Latin America passes as white, or at least as mestizo, although the human influx from the Iberian peninsula was necessarily limited. The above facts could surely explain the ethnic alteration. It is certain that many so-called descendants of Europeans acquired that distinction purely and simply by crossing the color line.

High fertility rates, and an age distribution in which youth predominates, are both characteristics of Old Regime demography. Vital statistics confirm these traditional features. That kind of society was characterized by death at an early age, and this was compensated for by a high birthrate, which flooded society with children and young people. The best example we have of consecutive data concerning this so far is provided in table 4.5, dealing with the captaincy of São Paulo and covering a period of half a century. The birthrates quoted, expressed per thousand inhabitants, should cause no surprise; the figures are consistently high, and are also typical of present-day de-

TABLE 4.5 Vital Statistics of the Captaincy of São Paulo, 1777–1836

Year	Birth	Death	Marriage	Natural growth
1777	43.3	27.7	—	15.4
1782	41.6	25.9	—	15.7
1797	46.9	25.9	—	21.0
1803	27.8	25.1	14.9	22.7
1813	43.1	21.2	11.7	21.9
1815	47.0	21.5	14.5	25.5
1829	43.6	25.6	12.8	18.0
1836	52.6 (?)	28.9	9.7	23.7

SOURCE: Lisanti, 1962–63.

veloping nations. The death rate, however, seems somewhat low. The high positive figure shown in the natural increase column, resulting from the difference between the birth and death rate columns, readily explains the rapid rate of population growth in that part of Brazil. Between 1765 and 1797 the increase is rapid, about 3 percent per annum; thereafter, from 1797 to 1836, it is slightly slower, 2.6 percent. The São Paulo figures are by no means exceptional. In 1826, Ecuador recorded a figure of 49.7 per thousand births and 22.5 for deaths, resulting in an even higher natural increase of 27.2 per thousand.

If the relationships established by Mortara between life expectancy and general mortality apply to past centuries, the death rate in São Paulo would represent a life expectancy at birth of thirty-eight, a very reasonable figure for the time, since recent calculations by Arriaga (1968a) suggest that Brazil as a whole did not achieve this figure until 1940.

To determine such a rate, one has to compare census figures with the vital movement of that precise year. If there is no civil register, then the baptismal, marriage, and burial registers kept by the parish can provide a useful substitute, especially in countries of proven religious unity such as those of Latin America, where failure to go to church might be due to carelessness or latent hostility, but did not imply belonging to another church. Even if no census figures are available, parish registers allow one to establish the extent of population growth by merely noting the increased number of entries. Let us look at the Chilean Norte Chico as recorded in an inexplicably unpublished study quoted by Carmagnani (1963). The number of baptisms in the period 1690–99 was 435. Half a century later, between 1740 and 1749, it had more than doubled to 926. Half a century later, 1790–99, the number was four times greater, 2,301.

Another Chilean example is that of Valparaíso (Thayer Ojeda,

1934). The average number of children baptized in the parish went up from 201 to 319 between 1797–1801 and 1817–21. It went up again in 1836–40 to reach 1,455. This means that there was a 58 percent increase during the first interval of time, and no less than 356 percent during the second. Even though the total population figure is not known, we are quite certain that the population of Valparaíso went up very rapidly after independence. The greater proportionate increase of burials, from 102 percent to 461 percent during the two time intervals concerned, is indicative of the fact that many migrants arrived in the port.

The parish registers also enable one to detect the seasonal movement of marriages and conceptions, which are very expressive of the beliefs or motivations of the married couples, and also the seasonal variation in the death rate. For lack of further details, a study of the latter can throw some light on the causes of death at the time. Weddings followed the regular cycle in Christian countries. During the religious festivals of Advent and Lent, fewer engaged couples came to be married. So far as conceptions were concerned, the concentration on spring months characteristic of Europe did not apply. Over a period of nearly a century and a half (1710–1850), couples in the city of Mogi das Cruzes preferred to conceive in summer, that is, from December to February. São Paulo couples, however, spread their conceptions out over the whole year (Marcilio, 1968). As for deaths, they reached their peak in summer in São Paulo, and this feature is even more noticeable in Valparaíso, where the burials of children were concentrated in the period from November to March, thus evincing the predisposition to contract summer gastric diseases. These were not so evident in São Paulo, despite the very high infant mortality rate (about 288 per thousand in 1798) and the puerperal fever rate, which accounted for 154 per thousand deaths among the nonslave population. The most noteworthy causes of death there were fever and worms.

If we look more fully at the subject of death, we see that the specter of epidemics continually shows its horrific face. Smallpox, measles, dysentery, and typhoid fever were the common scourges, not to mention influenza. In addition, there were those of tropical origin— cholera and yellow fever—which struck hard and often in the warmer countries.

We have a deep and detailed study of five epidemics that afflicted the city of Mexico (Cooper, 1965): the typhus epidemic of 1761, which coincided with an outbreak of smallpox; smallpox again in

1779–1780; another epidemic not definitely identified, but which may have been diphtheria and which had disastrous effects in 1784–87, especially when added to the famine affecting the area at the same time; the return of smallpox in 1797–98; and, lastly, the fevers of 1813. Despite their virulence, neither the 1761–62 outbreak, nor that of 1813, bears comparison with the outbreak of *matlazahuatl* in the last quarter of the sixteenth century, and still less with the epidemics of the Conquest period.

In Buenos Aires, the records consulted by Besio Moreno (1939) revealed a series of epidemics in the following years: 1796, 1799, 1803, 1809, 1817, 1823, 1829, 1843, and 1847. Although they were not as widespread, they were more frequent. Córdoba, in the interior of Argentina, had its worst epidemic of smallpox in 1823, and Valparaíso, farther west on the Pacific coast, had outbreaks in 1783, 1803, 1822, 1832–33, 1840, and 1846. The coincidences are significant.

Little is known of what happened between Mexico and the far south. Was the smallpox outbreak in Caracas in 1766 in any way connected with the epidemic that hit Mexico some years earlier? On this occasion, the vigorous Venezuelan city lost a quarter of its population.

Smallpox began to be less of a menace after the introduction of inoculation, which was first used in 1779–80 and then on a wider scale in 1797–98. But these were no more than tentative first steps. Although it did not completely solve the problem, the expedition of Francisco Javier de Balmis was very much more significant, since it distributed vaccine throughout North and South America. Balmis sailed from Galicia in the autumn of 1803, at the head of a team of doctors and nurses. He took with him twenty-two children inoculated with the virus. From the pustules that formed on their arms, he extracted the fluid, which was immediately used on those who wanted to be vaccinated. After a voyage of several weeks, including a stop in the Canaries, he arrived at Puerto Rico. From there he went on to Puerto Cabello and Caracas in Venezuela. Wherever he stopped, he spent several days vaccinating and carefully looking after the cultures, since their destruction would have meant the failure of the project. After dealing with the Cumaná and Maracaibo areas, he set off for Barranquilla, from where a separate team was sent southward under the charge of Salvany. Meanwhile the expedition leader himself continued his journey, vaccinating in Havana and Mérida. From Yucatán another team was dispatched to Guatemala. Balmis himself eventually arrived at Veracruz and, leaving the Gulf of Mexico, went inland into New Spain. He went up to the capital, to Puebla, and then northward to Zacatecas and Durango. Once back in Mexico City he set off for Acapulco, where he embarked for the Philippines, arriving in Manila in April 1805 to continue his work there. Finally he returned to Cádiz in Spain, having circumnavigated the world on a philanthropic mission. Meanwhile Salvany sent a team off to Panamá from Barranquilla, while he went to Lima via Santa Fe de Bogotá, Quito, Cuenca, Piura, and Trujillo. Having finished its task in the viceregal capital, one team went off to Huánuco and then turned south to Chile. The main body went via Arequipa, Puno, and La Paz and, after crossing the altiplano, ended up in Buenos Aires, five years after setting out from La Coruña (Díaz de Yraola, 1947).

This prodigious health campaign, of continental dimensions, had only limited immediate effects. It is obvious that, however long the expedition stayed and however hard they tried not to leave out important centers, they could not hope to vaccinate the whole population of Spanish America. S. F. Cook (1941–1942) believes the expedition concentrated its efforts on saving children, vaccinating a hundred thousand in Mexico between July 1804 and January 1806, that is, one in five. The effects felt were to be long-lasting, however. The efforts of Balmis and his colleagues spread medical knowledge to both doctors and the general public, and tipped the balance in favor of zealous public servants and the most progressive medical practitioners by giving them official backing.

The ports and large cities were naturally the first to benefit from the vaccine, and within them, the most enlightened sectors of society. It was a slower and more difficult process to sell the idea of immunization to the lower classes. Even though vaccination was given free, it was inevitably regarded with suspicion. But the greatest stumbling block was the lack of education and health precautions among the rural masses. Smallpox therefore continued to take its toll of lives throughout the nineteenth century, although it gradually became less deadly. As late as 1842, the Peruvian treasury official responsible for taking the Indian census in the province of Huaylas, Marcos Dextre, could write: "The deadly effects of smallpox are continually experienced because of inadequate vaccine distribution in the province, since complete families recorded in the 1836 census have now been wiped out as a result of the very virulent outbreak experienced in recent years in the districts of Pamparonas, Quillo, and other neighboring ones along the coast, which affected not merely children but adults as well." Nevertheless, in the *visita* carried out in 1848, Dextre's successor, Matías P. Mejía, was then able to declare: "The distribution of vaccine by itinerant vaccinators, a measure introduced by the last Congress, and its storage in this city by the head medical officer, and by venerable priests and local authorities in other population centers, saved from death a considerable number of people who would previously have fallen victim to smallpox." The report of his colleague in Santa shares Mejía's enthusiasm for the work of the itinerant vaccinators. In Peru, at least, the decisive turning point was reached in the middle of the nineteenth century. With the lowering of the death rate peaks, population expansion could proceed without any fertility increase.

Local circumstances sometimes compromised such increase. The Indians on the Jesuit missions in the province of Paraguay were freed from any restraints on their movements when the order was expelled from the American colonies on the orders of Charles III. They then passed from the care of the Jesuits to become subject to civil administration under the name of *temporalidades*. In 1772, five years after the expulsion of the Jesuits, the *visitador* Larrazábal counted 80,352 Indians in thirty settlements; in 1797, a further survey recorded only 54,388. The breakup of the mission settlements had not eliminated them but displaced them. They found food and employment in distant towns or on far off *estancias*, when they did not find refuge in the forests. From then on, the missions declined. The traditionally stable family and community life was disrupted, thus adversely affecting the trend toward an increasing population.

Independence brought with it serious population losses in those areas where violent confrontations occurred, as in Haiti, Mexico, Venezuela, and the Banda Oriental (Uruguay). The racial strife in Haiti, which accompanied the first independence revolution to succeed in Latin America, caused loss of life, population shrinkage through emigration, and changes in the ethnic composition of the country. The slaughter of the slave owners had little demographic effect, but was enough to frighten the whites who fled elsewhere. They returned to France or sought asylum in other places in the Caribbean, especially Cuba. The census carried out after the Napoleonic attempt to reconquer the island showed that in 1804 the new nation of African stock had been reduced to half a million people. The small white element, which had previously dominated the colony, had disappeared, and the island was left in the possession of the former slaves and the mulattoes. To the toll taken by the war of independence, and the killing and later emigration of the French, was added that caused by the yellow fever epidemic (Young, 1949). This wrought havoc upon the expeditionary army dispatched by Napoleon under the command of General Leclerc, who himself succumbed; it thus contributed to the consolidation of the republic, but it spared neither soldiers nor Haitian civilians, countless numbers of whom also died.

According to the statements of a royalist journalist, the "war to the death" cost Venezuela no less than 221,741 lives. This includes those killed in combat and those who would have been born had hostilities not interrupted the steady upward trend of the population. In 1822, the urban population age pyramids, and in particular that of Caracas, show a deficit in the age group twenty-five to twenty-nine, as well as an excess of women over men, facts attributable to the wars of the preceding decade (Brito Figueroa, 1966).

It seems evident from the study which Cook and Borah (1968) carried out in the Mixteca Alta that, while Hidalgo's military operations in the Bajío and Michoacán did not cause many deaths, Morelos' campaign, which extended over many years, had a more significant effect on population figures in the south of Mexico. However, not even that was comparable with the losses inflicted on the Banda Oriental by the famous *Redota* (rout) of 1811. About a fifth of the civil population of the country, according to the records of the Banda Oriental families who emigrated to Entre Ríos, crossed the River Uruguay with the troops of Artigas from fear of royalist reprisals or Portuguese exactions. Terrible sufferings were experienced by the soldiers and civilians, who stolidly accepted the price they had to pay for adhering to their revolutionary principles.

The history of this period records other internal population movements, which were less violent and spectacular than those brought about by the military campaigns of the armies of liberation. From the last third of the eighteenth century, Cuba experienced a displacement of population in precisely the opposite direction to that which it had known in the preceding century. The coast was recolonized from the center to the periphery. There was, in addition, the influx of French colonists from the island of Santo Domingo and Louisiana, and of *gachupines* (Spaniards) from Mexico and many other parts of the disintegrating Spanish empire. The last remaining colony in the area became the safe haven for refugees from revolution.

Movement in the opposite direction, that is, centripetal migration, occurred in Costa Rica. The coasts were abandoned in favor of the plateau, which offered a pleasanter climate and better economic opportunities. In 1815, 84 percent of the forty-six thousand inhabitants of the territory lived on the plateau, according to Bishop Garza Jerez. San José, the capital, which had been founded only a few decades earlier in 1755, contained one-quarter of the total (Jiménez Castro, 1956).

Once the gold mines were worked out in the west of present-day Colombia, Antioquia also experienced a transition from a mining to an agricultural economy. Early marriages and large families favored population expansion, but the agrarian economy was unable to support this growth. Population pressure caused migration southward into the temperate regions of the cordillera slopes, where the pioneers occupied new lands made available by the Real Cédula of 1789. This decree entrusted *jueces-pobladores* with the task of establishing agricultural colonies and distributing land to those who arrived wishing to settle. In 1764 the colonists crossed the River Arma and set foot in Caldas. Independence held up the advance for a while and the war destroyed some places where royalist strongholds existed, such as Anserma. Once calm returned, the government of the republic continued the policy of granting concessions, as a result of which emigrants from Antioquia entered the Cauca Valley and Cauca itself (Parsons, 1968).

In the eighteenth century, it was cattle that brought men back to the deserted countryside, contrary to what happened before when animals drove the natives from their land. In the wake of the cattle, there came those who were to become *llaneros* from Aragua to Barinas north of the Orinoco, or gauchos in the River Plate basin, from Viamão in Rio Grande do Sul to the Buenos Aires pampa. We know of no studies on the spread of population over the llanos of Venezuela. In the River Plate region a vast plain, almost deserted in places, received a heterogeneous population, which constructed towns in suitable places to serve the pastoral community. Evidence suggests that it was the excess population from Santiago del Estero, Córdoba, Cuyo, and the former Jesuit missions which settled in this area to do the really rough work. Meanwhile, the Paulistas came south from the Campos Gerais in search of mules, the sale of which was to make the Sorocaba livestock fairs so famous. Not only did the breeding of mules lead to the establishment of *estancias*, which assured Portuguese control over Rio Grande do Sul, but they also made it possible to transport men and goods into Mato Grosso, with similar territorial results.

The pioneers of the cattle country in southern Brazil made good use of the wild cattle, which provided leather and meat, for toward the end of the eighteenth century they learned how to make industrial and commercial use of the meat by the preparation of charqui, or jerked beef. Even before this, the interior of Bahia, the valleys of the Parnaíba in Piauí, and the Jaguaribe in Ceará had been opened up. The origin of several present-day cities in the area can be traced straight back to the haciendas that flourished there as a result of the trade in dried meat. But the disastrous droughts of 1791 to 1793 devastated the northeastern cattle regions, while their Paulista competitors prospered. With the destruction of seven-eighths of the breeding stock in the northern *sertão*, contrary to what happened in Rio Grande do Sul, men lost their jobs and left the land, except for those who took refuge in the hill country of Ceará and there developed a modest agricultural economy.

In the latter days of the colonial period, and during the early days of independence, there was a spontaneous flow of Portuguese and Spaniards who continued to migrate to their respective possessions or former colonies. After independence, Europeans from countries other than Spain and Portugal openly arrived for the first time, although there had always been a few in seaports and capital cities. Involuntary African immigration also reached its peak at this time until the infamous slave trade was eventually abolished.

Celso Furtado (1963) has estimated the overall number of Portuguese who came to America in the eighteenth century to be between three hundred thousand and a half-million, though he is not very precise about time limits. Although a fair proportion of them must have come to Brazil when the discovery of gold and diamonds acted as powerful magnets, the prosperity of the latter part of the century attracted just as many. When the royal family left Portugal and took refuge in Rio de Janeiro in 1808, after fleeing from Napoleon's invasion, numerous civil servants and people of all classes accompanied them. Fifty thousand people came over between then and 1817, when the court went back to Lisbon; the majority remained in the New World. Rio de Janeiro, the new capital of the Portuguese empire, doubled its population almost overnight.

An unreliable estimate of the number of Spaniards who crossed the Atlantic in the eighteenth century is fifty-three thousand (Hernández y Sánchez Barba, 1954). Whatever the figure, it was less than the number of Portuguese and less than the number of African slaves. People from the Canaries, Andalusia, the Basque country, and Castile continued to arrive at the usual ports of entry in connection with trade or colonial administration. One should add to them the Catalans who, as subjects of the crown of Aragon, had not previously been allowed to emigrate. Nor had they been overenthusiastic about the Indies; but the economic recovery of Catalonia and the declaration of free trade in the late eighteenth century, caused them to seek outlets for their agricultural and industrial products. Any list of merchants' surnames in the major ports shows evidence of the arrival of Catalans.

The crown also wanted to extend to its overseas domains the population policy which reforming ministers had tried out in the mother country, adding to it a political coloring it did not possess in Spain: the desire to ensure effective control over areas to which the king had legal title and which, consequently, might be tempting to other European powers. The unsuccessful settlements founded in inhospitable Patagonia in 1779 and 1786 were in pursuit of this policy.

As for other Europeans, Brazil proclaimed an open-door policy shortly after the court was established in Rio de Janeiro. The triumvirate governing the United Provinces of the River Plate did the same four years later. Foreigners had not always waited for the formalization of their legal right of entry, of course, since events during the uncertain years of the early nineteenth century provided a favorable opportunity for them to move in. Within a few years of independence, a considerable proportion of Latin America's trade had fallen into the hands of British merchants. Their presence had little demographic effect, however, for most of them stayed only as long as there was profitable business to be carried on.

In view of the scarcity of skilled labor, some countries proposed a policy of colonization, as, for example, the Province of Buenos Aires did in 1821 when Rivadavia was minister. None of these experiments were successful, but they are worth remembering because the attempts provided governments with the experience necessary for the planning of future immigration policy. The later influx of migrants, because of its massive scale, could not help but have a decisive influence upon the demographic, social, and economic growth of large areas of the continent.

The influx of Africans during the period now being discussed was very considerable. Referring to Curtin (1969) once again, imports of slaves into Brazil were constantly increasing, and table 4.6 summarizes the numbers brought in between 1761 and 1810. The figures are based mainly on the import registration archives in Bahia. The corresponding yearly average is 18,636, approximately one-sixth more than during the six preceding decades and, of these, 78 percent came from Angola. On the other hand, Spanish America received only a third as many slaves as the number imported into Brazil, and most of these were taken to Cuba. Brazil and Spanish America together imported only 40 percent of the total number of Africans transported to the continent. The rest obviously landed up in the British, French, and Dutch colonies in the Caribbean and in the newly independent United States of America.

TABLE 4.6 Slaves Imported into Brazil and Spanish America, 1761–1860
(in thousands)

	1761–70	1771–80	1781–90	1791–1800	1801–10	Totals
Brazil	164.6	161.3	178.1	221.6	206.2	931.8
Spanish America	121.9			185.5		307.4
Totals	447.8			791.3		1,239.2

	1811–20	1821–30	1831–40	1841–50	1851–60	Totals
Brazil	266.8	325.0	212.0	338.3	3.3	1,145.4
Cuba	79.9	112.5	126.1	47.6	123.3	489.4
Puerto Rico	6.4	12.1	14.1	10.6	7.2	50.4
Totals	353.1	449.6	352.2	396.5	133.8	1,685.2

SOURCE: Curtin, 1969.

When England suppressed the slave trade, she tried to get other nations to do the same and actively harassed those who were slow in implementing the policy. As the former Spanish colonies also abolished slavery shortly after gaining their independence, this meant that Brazil and the remnants of the Spanish empire became the main recipients of slaves. These two areas together absorbed ninety-two percent of the Negroes who set foot on the continent between 1811 and 1860. The estimates made by Curtin (1969) for these years are based on figures reported in the British parliament. The distribution by decades is also shown in table 4.6. It should be noted that Cuba and Puerto Rico received their highest numbers in 1831–40, while Brazil's maximum was reached in 1841–50. The annual average for Brazil was nearly twenty-three thousand, and that of the Spanish Caribbean nearly ten thousand.

The cities were no exception to this general growth of population. Did they grow more rapidly than the rest of the population and become a magnet attracting the rural masses, or did they increase more slowly, thus postponing urbanization? Little is known, and still less in any systematic way, about the development of Latin-American cities at this time, but the impression prevailing so far is one of balanced growth, in which both the smaller and the larger urban centers grew and consolidated, but without causing a serious drift from the land or depriving the countryside of the services to which it quite rightly aspired. Consequently, there appears to have been no colossal increase nor yet a shortage of urban population; nor, as one might expect, was the growth rate identical in every city.

The Spanish city, which, during the Conquest period, seemed to have been superimposed on Indian society, had already come to a less violent relationship with its surroundings. Rather than fulfilling the requirements of an imperial system in which all the demands were imposed from outside, the urban complex became better adapted to local needs. Developing areas rapidly spawned rural centers which, with luck, would become the nuclei of future cities; such is the case in Brazil, for dozens of *vilas* were founded at that time in the captaincy of São Paulo (Morse, 1965).

The incorporation of the Atlantic coastline within world commercial currents favored the development of real urban nuclei. Thus, Havana, Caracas, and Buenos Aires, trading centers in developing export zones, grew phenomenally. According to the Las Casas census of 1791, Havana's population was then 51,037; by the time the 1817 census was taken by Cienfuegos it had increased to 84,075. Caracas jumped from 24,187 in 1772 to approximately 42,000 in 1812, despite the considerable losses incurred as a result of the earthquake of that year. As for Buenos Aires, Vértiz recorded a population of 24,363 in 1778, and this had become 55,416 by 1822 when the census ordered by Rivadavia was taken.

Of all the east coast cities, Rio de Janeiro was probably the city with the most rapid increase, but this growth was due rather to two lucky political circumstances than to growing economic significance. In fact its importance as a mining port declined, and shipments of coffee were not sufficient to make up for the ground lost. In 1763, Rio de Janeiro became the capital of Brazil, a distinction it lost only when Brasília replaced it some two centuries later in 1960. Until then Salvador da Bahia had been the seat of Portuguese colonial government in the New World. The arrival of the Portuguese court in 1808 confirmed Rio de Janeiro in its political role. According to Humboldt, Rio de Janeiro had a by no means insignificant population of 135,000 when Brazil declared its independence in 1822.

The expansion of Buenos Aires, Caracas, and Havana was also partially due to administrative considerations, but these were less important than in the case of Rio de Janeiro. The creation of a viceroyalty centered on Buenos Aires gave a stimulus to the old commercial port, and the building and town-planning improvements introduced by Viceroy Vértiz were to transform it into a city more in keeping with its manifold responsibilities. The same could be said of Caracas, which had been the seat of a new captaincy-general since 1777, or of Havana, which was gradually taking over the functions formerly carried out by Santo Domingo and which was to be much improved under the enlightened administration of Las Casas and the marquis of Someruelos. These cities were growing continuously as block after block was added; not only did they expand outward, as successive town plans show, but the original central areas became more closely packed with houses, and population density increased.

In backward areas, the cities of long standing progressed at a much slower rate than some of the modern ones. Lima, the capital of a mutilated viceroyalty turned away from the most active trade currents in the world, stagnated. From the 52,627 inhabitants recorded by Viceroy Gil de Fagoaga in 1792 there was an insignificant increase to 56,284 recorded in the census ordered by Viceroy Abascal in 1813. Mexico City was not in quite the same position, but a rise of 50 percent in thirty years was hardly as striking as that of other cities in the continent. In fact, the 112,926 inhabitants recorded by Revillagigedo in 1790 had increased to only 168,846 in 1820, according to Humboldt's estimate on the eve of Mexico's independence.

The following is a list of the major cities of Latin America in order of size, on the achievement of independence: Mexico City still in the lead, but with Rio de Janeiro not far behind; Havana; a little farther down the list, Lima, Buenos Aires, Caracas, Santiago de Chile, with about 50,000 inhabitants, together with some regional capital cities of similar size, such as Puebla (52,000) and Salvador da Bahia. Next come the majority of the regional centers, such as Guatemala (23,434 inhabitants in 1776), Quito (28,451 in 1778), Cuzco (32,000 in 1792), Potosí (22,000 in 1779), Oropesa, now called Cochabamba (22,000), and La Paz (21,000), both figures for 1796, Santa Fe de Bogotá (21,394), Recife (about 30,000),

São Luíz de Maranhão (22,000), Guanajuato (32,000), Zacatecas (25,000), and Mérida (28,000), the last three figures for 1793. Lastly come the typical provincial capitals, such as Durango (11,027 in 1790), San Salvador (12,054 in 1807), and Córdoba (10,587 in 1813), to name but a few.

RACE MIXTURE

Two and a half centuries of persistent contact, forcible in most cases, affectionate in others, had brought about the mingling of the three racial stocks that had met in the New World. *Mestizaje* (race mixture) had not at first aroused any angry opposition in the Spanish and Portuguese empires. The first mestizos benefited from the sentiments which their first-degree relationship with their Iberian fathers naturally aroused and, in addition, they acted as intermediaries and assistants in carrying out the imperative task of breaking down Indian society. That original task had been fulfilled by the middle of the eighteenth century when the Indians had been conquered and decimated, and now it was the mestizos themselves, with their rapid increase in numbers, who posed a quite natural threat to the dominant position of the whites. It is understandable that those in such privileged positions should put up some resistance, reinforcing social distinctions based on economic standing by psychological means, such as prejudice based on color.

To this typical reaction of a privileged class, there was added the classifying tendency characteristic of the orderly, rationalizing mentality of the century which could produce someone like Linnaeus. The classifying of men seemed a natural corollary to the classification of plants and animals. There was to spread throughout Spanish America an extremely complicated nomenclature to classify *castas de mezcla* (degrees of color admixture), which the Puebla artists Ignacio de Castro and José Joaquín Magón illustrated in frequently reproduced pictures. Every mixture possible, starting from the three pure original racial types, received its individual name. The terms *mestizo, mulato,* and *zambo* were of long standing, and need no further clarification. *Tercerón, cuarterón* (quadroon), and *quinterón* (quintroon) are self-explanatory. Peruvian Spanish of today still retains the terms *cholo* and *chino.* But who nowadays remembers the significance of such names as *castizo, morisco, lobo, jíbaro, albarazado, cambujo, barcino, puchuel, coyote, chamiso, gálfarro, genízaro, grifo, jarocho,* and *sambahigo,* or the more picturesque *salta atrás, tente en el aire, no te entiendo, ahí estés,* and so forth? To make matters even more complicated, there were regional differences as well: *chino* was more widely used in Peru and New Spain, while Venezuela preferred *zambo*. In Brazil, the offspring of Portuguese men and Indian women were known, from north to south, as *curiboca, caboclo,* and *mameluco*.

Time has blurred the distinctions between various shades of color, but even contemporaries did not use these terms currently and accurately. They were more legalistic jargon than anything else or, as Mörner (1967) says, "an entertaining genre of art, characteristic rather of eighteenth-century exoticism and rococo than a serious effort to depict the social reality of the Indies." In popular speech, vaguer, euphemistic expressions such as *moreno* (colored) and *pardo* (darkie) were used for Negroes and mulattoes. The term *pardo* was sometimes used for Negroes and sometimes for mestizos. Greater attention was paid to such differences in the large cities, as one can see in the famous description of the color castes of the port of Cartagena by Antonio de Ulloa.

The blurring of color distinctions was more likely to endanger social stratification in urban centers than in the countryside, where the predominance of the feudal lord was taken for granted. And it was precisely when this nomenclature was becoming increasingly academic that the identification of any individual's color heritage became more and more difficult to detect. Illegitimacy tended to make it more difficult to identify the preceding generation's color, and features only provided a rough-and-ready guide. All contemporary documents point out the frequency of illegitimate births in both Spanish America and Brazil, and recent studies based on baptismal records are making the extent of this clearer. About one-fifth of those baptized in the cathedrals of Guadalajara and Mexico City in 1821 were stated to have unknown fathers, or were piously classified as orphans (González Navarro, 1970).

Table 4.7 shows the number of free (nonslave) children who were baptized in the urban cathedral parish of São Paulo throughout one century. The data are grouped in periods of fifteen years. The percentage of children who were illegitimate or of unknown parentage are shown in separate columns. The percentage figures would certainly be higher if other socio-juridical categories were included. Between 1741 and 1845, the average of illegitimate births in the parish was 23 percent, and the average of foundlings was no less than 16 percent. Thus, legally speaking, 39 out of every 100 children were bastards. At no time during the hundred years covered was the

TABLE 4.7 Baptismal Records of Illegitimate Free (Nonslave) Children in the
Cathedral Parish of São Paulo, 1741–1845

	Total of baptisms	Percentage of illegitimate children	Percentage of foundlings	Total percentage
1741–1755	2,148	10.24	14.85	25.09
1756–1770	2,248	18.28	14.72	33.00
1771–1785	2,226	20.97	21.42	42.39
1786–1800	5,396	21.08	10.74	31.82
1801–1815	3,964	26.26	15.64	41.90
1816–1830	2,968	30.15	18.83	48.98
1831–1845	2,731	31.49	14.75	46.24
Totals	21,681	23.20	15.99	39.19

SOURCE: Marcilio, 1968.

proportion below one-quarter. Far from diminishing with the passage of time, the proportion actually increased: toward the end of the period it was nearly 50 percent. Since the proportion of foundlings remained almost constant, the increase must have been due to the figures recorded in the other column.

Such an increase in the illegitimacy rate can be observed in the middle of the seventeenth century and in the eighteenth and nineteenth centuries. Carmagnani (1970) has studied some examples of this during the earlier period in northern Mexico. In two mining centers, Charcas and San Luis Potosí, the number of illegitimate mestizo and mulatto births came to a peak in the middle of the seventeenth century. Three parishes in the French colony of Saint Domingue (Houdaille, 1963) and the parish of Quillota in the Chilean Norte Chico (Carmagnani, 1963) show a similar rise in the following century. In Quillota, for example, a third of those baptized between 1690 and 1729 were illegitimate. This proportion then went up to a peak of 37.9 percent between 1740 and 1749. Another rural parish, that of Santa María, in the Argentine province of Catamarca, provides a glimpse of the situation in the nineteenth century. The study we made of this pre-Andean valley remains unpublished, but the following details are extracted from it: one out of every four children baptized there between 1813 and 1818 was illegitimate; a quarter of a century later, 1834–44, the proportion was nearly one-half.

Having reached a ceiling, the illegitimacy rate started to go down again. In the case of Charcas, quoted above, it went down from 28.7 percent to 17.8 percent in 1720–24. In Quillota, it reduced to 25.8 percent in the middle of the eighteenth century. Only systematic investigations of local history will provide an explanation of these fluctuations, but for the moment it would appear that the period during which it increased was one in which miscegenation was unleashed. This hypothesis is supported by the manner in which the illegitimacy rate varied between the different racial groupings. To the brief comments above, one may now add a concrete example from South America.

The rural parish of Pelarco, near Talca in Central Chile, clearly reveals how sexual behavior differed in the various racial groups. According to table 4.8, the whites—here constituting an overall majority of the population—acted as their fellows in Quillota did. More than half of all the Indians and mulattoes (adding illegitimate and foundlings) were either bastards or born to common law unions. The group in which the situation was most pronounced was that of the mestizos, three-quarters of whom were born out of wedlock.

TABLE 4.8 Illegitimacy in Pelarco, Chile, 1786–1796 (in percentages)

	Racial group	Legitimate children	Illegitimate children	Father unknown
Spaniards	87.6	74.0	20.4	5.5
Indians	3.6	47.8	39.1	13.0
Mestizos	4.7	25.5	63.0	8.4
Mulattoes	4.0	46.0	48.0	6.0

SOURCE: Aranguiz Donoso, 1969.

Pelarco was inhabited by a small, mixed Spanish-Indian community whose sexual relationships came up against the well-known barriers of prejudice and social discrimination; but the group was primarily one of free men with a dual Spanish and Indian cultural background, as in the case of Charcas and San Luis Potosí studied by Carmagnani. The bastards served to bridge the gap between the racial extremes, at least on some social levels.

In a Portuguese African society where slavery was very widespread, such as in Minas Gerais, illegitimacy is indicative of a different situation. The whites record the highest baptismal legitimacy rates, but the other pure racial group does not come second, as in the above table. Instead of the Negro, there comes the hybrid, the free mulatto. Then come the free Negro, the Negro slave, and lastly the mulatto slave. In the latter category, no less than three-fifths were bastards (table 4.9). Thus here illegitimacy was organized following a vertical stratification appropriate to a class society. The peak is represented by the whites, and the other groups are arranged in order of their greater or lesser degree of racial proximity to the peak group,

TABLE 4.9 Legitimacy According to Sex, Color, and Social Status among Children Baptized in 110 of the 173 Parishes of Minas Gerais, 1844 (expressed as percentages)

	Legitimate	Illegitimate	Foundlings	Total
Whites				
male	87.8	9.5	2.5	2,461
female	84.5	13.3	2.0	2,442
Free Mulattoes				
male	69.5	28.8	1.6	3,641
female	66.4	32.5	1.0	3,784
Free Negroes				
male	61.7	37.7	0.4	839
female	60.4	39.4	0.1	763
Mulatto slaves				
male	41.1	58.8	—	471
female	38.7	61.2	—	490
Negro slaves				
male	48.0	51.7	0.1	1,840
female	40.8	59.1	—	1,860
Totals	66.1	32.6	1.1	18,591

SOURCE: Klein, 1969. ("0 1971" by Peter N. Stearns. Reprinted from the *Journal of Social History*, vol. IV, no. 4, pp. 333–356, by permission of the editor.)

except in the case of the mixed-blood slaves, who occupy the bottom of the ladder. Greater illegitimacy rates correspond to the lowest degree of assimilation to the dominant class, contrary to what happened among mestizos produced by the crossing of Indian and Spanish stock.

In 1778 the Spanish crown regulated marriage in the Indies, a matter in which civil authority had customarily been guided by canon law. The state then decided to intervene. This secularizing move was brought about by the very conservative desire to maintain the social status quo. The law required parental consent for the marriage of partners under the age of twenty-five. However, mestizos, mulattoes, and Negroes were relieved of this requirement because it was considered that they would find it difficult to locate their parents (Mörner, 1967), thus demonstrating how race and illegitimacy were associated in the legal mind. In the matrimonial law there certainly operated the conviction that, whatever the law might say, men and women of that class would not wait to receive the blessing of the church and official or family approval in order to pair up and have children. The consensual union and illegitimacy were the people's response to legal restrictions and the prejudice held by a rigorously stratified society which sought to perpetuate itself.

Classification in one group or another had far-reaching legal and social implications. The priest noted down the birth either in the baptismal register reserved for Spaniards, or in that for the Indians, or for the *castas*. The classification then assigned to a child stayed with him for life and was even passed on to his children, entitling them to privileges or marking them with a social stigma. However, this offensive system did have safety valves. Konetzke (1946) quotes a royal decree of November 26, 1814, in which the Spanish crown took note of the custom of parish priests to record baptisms in their registers as they thought fit. In view of the slackness of priests in this matter, it became necessary for the law to take over the determination of a person's class. Time had turned a racial distinction into a legal one. A financial contribution to the treasury enabled one to rise on the social ladder; thus a wealthy Negro could, by means of a *gracias a sacar* certificate, acquire from the crown the status of a white person.

The caste system was bound to disappear despite certain measures and attitudes endeavoring to preserve it. After independence the legal barriers were gradually broken down, but more subtle forms of discrimination were not so easy to remove and in some cases they continue to this day.

While racial classification corresponds roughly to the stratification of society, the racial variable shows differential behavior similar to that in data concerning occupation and profession. We have already seen how women belonging to differing racial groups had different fertility rates in the River Plate area, and how each group had very different illegitimacy rates. It would seem worthwhile, therefore, to have a brief look at how the original racial stocks and *castas* were distributed throughout Latin America toward the end of the colonial period, for that is the last moment at which such a survey can be attempted.

The River Plate basin in its widest sense was the largest and most markedly white area. This extended from Rio Grande do Sul in the north to the Buenos Aires plains in the south and Córdoba in the west and, including the Indian mission area, constituted some one million square kilometers. In 1778, three-quarters of the inhabitants of the pampa south of Buenos Aires were *peninsulares* or *criollos*, who stood out against the darker background provided by the few Indians and newly imported Africans who lived there. The plains of the Banda Oriental of Uruguay in 1781 had a population that was 72 percent of Iberian descent. In both cases the proportion was lower in the capital cities, the ports of Buenos Aires and Montevideo (68 percent and 70 percent respectively), on account of the presence of a greater concentration of Negroes there. But inland, Córdoba, which had a white population of 48 percent in 1778, had 57 percent white in 1813, which proves an influx of people from outside (Endrek, 1966). Both in Buenos Aires and in the Banda Oriental and Córdoba, the Negroes were the second most numerous group. On the other hand, in Corrientes, the whites predominated over a minority of Indian origin. The whites there constituted between 65 percent and 75 percent of the population in 1814, depending on the areas (Maeder, 1963).

Another region which, on paper at least, seems to have had a predominance of Europeans over Indians was Chile. The census carried out in the bishopric of Santiago in 1778 records a 69 percent white population, with even higher proportions in the northern *coregimientos* of Quillota and Aconcagua and in the southern ones of Colchagua and Maule (Carmagnani and Klein, 1965). The people there must have been culturally Spanish, but whether they were of Spanish descent seems less certain. Carmagnani (1963) is therefore right to overcome this difficulty by grouping whites and mestizos in the Chilean Norte Chico under one heading.

In the rest of Spanish and Portuguese America, pockets of whites appeared occasionally: in the south of Peru, between Arequipa in the mountains and Camaná on the coast, in the human oasis of Nuevo León in the north of New Spain, in Central America high up on the plateau of Costa Rica, here and there in Cuba, and, according to the 1772 *visita* of Bishop Martí, in the present state of Trujillo in western Venezuela, where seven tenths of the inhabitants were *criollos*.

The cities also attracted or held the Spaniards because of the wealth in circulation there, or on account of the administrative functions they were there to carry out. Thus Quito in 1781 had nearly 63 percent whites as against 32 percent Indians, and 5 percent *castas* and Negro slaves. In the surrounding countryside, however, there were 68 percent Indians, 5 percent *castas* and Negroes as against 27 percent of *peninsulares* and *criollos* (Paz y Miño, 1936). The city was like a white island in a sea of Indian peasants. The capital of New Spain was somewhat similar. Mexico City was, in fact, half Spanish and half Indian and mestizo, with few Negroes and mulattoes. Indians predominated throughout the rest of the viceroyalty.

The Indians, the earliest inhabitants of America, even though they declined extensively as a result of the Conquest, continued to prevail throughout vast areas of the continent. Frontier regions were still controlled by the Indians, since colonization had caused only very few, if any, Europeans to penetrate that far. These areas were poorly pacified and even unexplored. They extended from Texas to California in the north of the viceroyalty of New Spain, throughout the breadth of the so-called internal provinces. There were also groups of Indians spread throughout the Chaco and Amazonia, in the interior of South America, as well as over the endless plains of the pampa and the cold steppes of Patagonia. In all these isolated areas the Indians predominated, but their future was not a promising one. Neither the size of their communities nor their primitive cultures would enable them to retain their position when thousands of migrants suddenly descended on them.

The Indians were in a different position throughout the length of the mountainous backbone of the continent. The Spaniards had imposed their presence there for centuries, but owing to their high prehistoric population density and the cohesive nature of their culture, the Indians succeeded in retaining their numerical superiority despite the calamities that befell them and the temptations of *mestizaje*. In Mexico and Central America, the Indians maintained their clear lead over all the other racial groups combined, both pure and all the various mixed-blood groups, until the nineteenth century when *"ladinización"* or *mestizaje* became so extensive as to partially dilute their identity.

In 1810, Navarro Noriega estimated that three-fifths of the inhabitants of the viceroyalty of New Spain were still Indians. The next largest group was that of the *castas* (Lerner, 1968). The situation was the same in Guatemala, but there the proportion of mestizos was higher than that in Mexico (31 percent as against 21 percent). The captaincy had thus attracted fewer Spaniards.

In South America, the high, cold lands of the presidency of Quito, of the viceroyalty of Peru, and of the audiencia of Charcas stood out as bastions of Indian numerical superiority. The overall average for Peru, which was itself very high—two-thirds—does not, however, reveal the fact that occasionally there were areas where the proportion was even higher. In the intendency of Cuzco, a stronghold of Indian civilization, Indians formed three-quarters of the population, and here and there the proportion was even higher—92 percent, for example, in Cotabambas. Much more than today, the countryside then was essentially Indian. Similarly, on the altiplano, three out of every four people considered themselves Indian. Even in the cities, which were preferred by the whites, the Indians were extremely numerous. In Potosí 58 percent were Indians, while 22 percent were mestizos (Chao, 1965). The Indians spread from the altiplano over to the intendency of Salta in present-day Argentina, where they formed a large majority. The 1778 enumeration of the Jujuy district records that 57 percent of the population was Indian, about a fifth mestizo, and about one-seventh white, besides a high proportion of people of indeterminate parentage whom one could legitimately classify as Indian or mestizo (Rasini, 1965). In the eastern valleys of the intendency of Cochabamba, however, the Indians formed but a modest 40 percent of the population. In the capital, Oropesa, they were only 5 percent.

According to cultural rather than strictly racial distinctions, since the whites were decidedly few in number, *mestizaje* was extensive north of Peru and in New Granada where the Andes divide into two branches. In Peru, the Santa coastline, the mountains to the east of Trujillo (Huamachuco and Pataz), and the provinces of Conchucos and Tarma showed a high proportion of mestizos. The *cholos*—as the loose terminology of the census takers called them—formed more than half the total population (Vollmer, 1967). In the eastern and western Andean plateaus of New Granada, whose combined area made up two-thirds of the territory of that viceroyalty, about 45 percent were of mixed descent. This fact is to be found in the census taken by Viceroy Flórez in 1778 (Vergara y Velasco, 1891). In the east, the mixture resulted, perhaps, from a real interbreeding of Spaniards and Indians such as occurred in Chile, since the whites formed 37 percent of the racial composition of the area. In the west, the situation was different, for the European element did not constitute even a fifth of the total population.

Despite its numerical insignificance, another area where immigration from the Iberian Peninsula left a profound mark was in the north of New Spain, in the intendencies of Zacatecas, Durango, and Guadalajara. Since there were not many Indians before, both groups started off on an equal footing. On the dissolution of the viceroyalty, mestizos dominated in this zone.

The Negro lived along the coasts or in the islands. He seldom went inland, except to swell the ranks of the servant classes in the cities. There were Negroes working in the mines in the interior of Mexico and Peru, but they were few in number. Negroes extracted minerals and precious stones from the soil of Minas Gerais, Goiás, and Mato Grosso; they sowed the plantations of Tucumán; and drove herds across the llanos of Venezuela. In Guárico and Apure, for example, 50 percent of the population was Negro or mulatto, and on the western llanos of Barinas, Guanare, and Cojedes the proportion was only slightly lower (Brito Figueroa, 1966). It might be possible to add one or two more to the examples drawn from Brazil, the River Plate region, and Venezuela, but not many, for if the Negro was very numerous in those areas it was because the population there was scanty. The Negro was significant in sparsely populated areas. The vast expanse of the llanos had a population of only 74,000 people at the end of the eighteenth century. In the densely populated areas of the continental mainland, such as Mexico and Peru, inhabitants of African origin were necessarily a minority.

Contrary to the situation prevailing with their fellows in North America, the Negroes in Spanish and Portuguese America were permitted to live in cities and were attracted by life in them. The cities acted as a magnet for Negro slaves, who were needed to perform the multitude of domestic tasks there, but it also attracted many free Negroes, mulattoes, and zambos of all kinds whom necessity and discrimination compelled to act as a pool of unskilled labor. The city, nevertheless, probably offered them their best chances of improving their lot. Africans abounded not only in cities such as Havana, Caracas, Salvador da Bahia, and Rio de Janeiro. These were, after all, economic and political centers of Atlantic coastal regions specializing in the cultivation of sugar, cacao, and cotton, which always needed slave labor. In these areas, at least two-thirds of the population were colored, Negro or mulatto. The Negroes also congregated in the capitals of viceroyalties and *gobernaciones* within whose borders, as in Peru and Chile, there was a limited number of Africans. In 1792, for example, the city of Lima had a population of no less than 44.6 percent Negroes and mulattoes, while four parishes of Santiago de Chile, according to a census carried out in the archbishopric of Chile in 1778, had exactly 25 percent.

The highest percentages of Africans were to be found in the islands and coastline of the so-called American Mediterranean, the northeastern coasts of South America, and the northern Pacific coastline of South America, from Trujillo to Chocó. According to the report sent by the captains-general and governors to the king of Portugal in 1818, Brazil had a population of a mere 3,617,900 inhabitants. Of that number 1,728,000 were Negro slaves and 159,500 free Negroes, together making 52 percent of the total; in addition, there were 202,000 mulatto slaves and 426,000 free mestizos, mamelucos, and mulattoes. This brings the total of coloreds, excluding Indians, to nearly three-quarters of the whole (Rosenblat, 1954).

During the half-century prior to this report, Brazil had imported vast numbers of slaves for work on the plantations. The cultivation of the monocultural export crops of the area expanded at this time in response to growing European demand, and they, of course, needed more labor. The wealth then accumulated by the landowners provided them with sufficient financial resources to purchase the necessary work force. The regions of Brazil which had the highest number of slaves were precisely the cotton- and sugar-producing ones. Thus two-thirds of the inhabitants of Maranhão, a typical cotton-growing area, were slaves; Alagoas, where both cotton and sugar were produced, had a 38 percent African slave population. Similar proportions prevailed in Pernambuco, Bahia, Rio de Janeiro, and São Paulo.

The island of Cuba was another place where Negro blood was introduced on such a scale as eventually to predominate. The 1774 census carried out by La Torre shows a clear white majority, as can be seen in table 4.10, but this situation was not to last long. The in-

TABLE 4.10 Population of Cuba
(a) Racial composition (population figures expressed in thousands)

Year	Whites	Slaves	Negroes % increase between censuses	Free	Free and slave mulattoes	Total of coloreds	Total of Cuba	Color % in Cuba
1774	96.5	41.6	—	11.6	22.8	76.0	172.6	44.0
1792	133.5	72.4	3.7	20.2	46.0	138.7	272.3	50.9
1817	239.7	166.8	3.4	54.3	91.9	313.2	533.0	56.6
1827	311.0	286.9a	3.7	48.9	57.5	393.4	704.4	55.8
1841	418.2	436.5	3.0		152.9	589.3	1007.6	58.5

aIncludes mulatto slaves.
SOURCE: Guerra y Sánchez, 1958.

(b) Proportion of males in the slave population (PMSP) and proportion of the Negro and mulatto elements (NM) in relation to the total population in the three principal regions of the island

	1772		1817		1841	
	PMSP	NM% of total	PMSP	NM% of total	PMSP	NM% of total
West	65.3	41.5	68.4	54.8	64.7	61.4
Center	55.2	36.0	57.4	41.9	68.0	41.8
East	65.8	57.1	50.2	75.9	50.9	67.2

SOURCE: W. Zelinsky, 1949.

creasing volume of the slave trade, caused by the sugar boom, altered the relationship between the two racial groups within the following decade, so that by about 1791 Negroes and mulattoes were in a majority. Increasing at the colossal rate indicated in the same table, it is not surprising that the Negroes were to outnumber the whites, even if one leaves the mulattoes out of the count. This was imminent throughout the island when the captain general, Cienfuegos, and the *intendente*, Ramírez, carried out the census of 1817. The predominance of Negroes had already come about in some areas before this. In the department of Oriente, three-quarters of the inhabitants were of part-African stock. Alarmed by the state of affairs revealed in the new census, the authorities founded the *Junta de Población Blanca* (Board for White Population) aiming to encourage white immigration to counter the stream of Africans entering the country. The attempt failed, however, since the only people to immigrate there were Spaniards who were reluctant to remain in the newly independent Spanish American republics, or those who preferred to leave Louisiana and Florida rather than become subjects of the United States.

From 1817 onward, the proportion between the groups remained fairly constant until 1861, when the whites again took the lead; the census of that year showed 57 percent whites. The turn of the tide was foreseeable, for in the 1840s the entry of slaves into the country became difficult and the slave population had to rely on its own natural increase. The analysis of the 1841 census shows how unfavorable was the proportion of males in the colored population. Only in the eastern area were the sexes numerically equal; in the central and western areas there was only one female for every two colored male slaves (table 4.10). Children and adolescents under the age of fifteen, on whom the future of the following generation depended, formed only 21 percent of the group, whereas among whites the proportion was 41 percent. The sex ratio and the age structure did not allow Cuban Africans to reproduce normally, and this adversely affected the population growth rate on the island. As Spaniards were not attracted to emigrate to Cuba, the population growth rate began to slow down. Between 1841 and 1861, it went down to 1.7 percent per year, a figure which, although considerable, was very much lower than Cuba had known in the past.

On the nearby island of Puerto Rico, the continued influx of slaves brought a correspondingly rapid increase in the colored population. Until the end of the eighteenth century, only one-ninth of the population of the Spanish colony had consisted of Negro slaves. Then suddenly, between 1802 and 1865, some sixty thousand slaves were brought in (Curtin, 1969). The 1860 census consequently recorded a 48 percent Negro population, but once this peak was reached, the proportion of Puerto Ricans of African origin tended to decline.

In Santo Domingo, a country concerning which little numerical information of any kind is available, the proportion of Negroes and mulattoes also went up during the same period, though for different reasons. Here the cattle industry was not restricted by the encroachment of sugar plantations, as it was on other islands. There was consequently no significant increase in the number of slaves, and they formed only a very small proportion of the population. At the beginning of the nineteenth century, they constituted only 3 percent of a total population of 104,000. What did influence the racial composition of the whole island was the large-scale departure of Europeans and the later influx of Haitians. The first to be expelled when Spain reconquered her colony were the French, who had arrived there under cover of the Napoleonic expedition; but soon it was the *peninsulares* themselves who fled from the invading Haitian army. The whole island became depopulated, not only through successive waves of emigration but also because of war. According to British consuls in Haiti, the aggressive policy of the self-created monarch Dessalines cost Santo Domingo 70 percent of its population, and the reduction in Haiti itself was not much less.

The island tried to compensate in part for these enormous losses by receiving freed Negroes from the southern U.S.A., some of whom for awhile regarded Santo Domingo as a sort of promised land in the same way that others regarded Liberia. One can still identify on the Samaná peninsula descendants of those who took part in that unsuccessful attempt at colonization (Hoetink, 1970). The numbers involved, however, were very small. On the other hand, throughout the nineteenth and twentieth centuries, Negroes have not ceased to move to and fro across the forever shifting frontier between the former French and Spanish possessions.

In Colombia and Venezuela, on the southern shore of the Caribbean, Negroes and mulattoes were not numerically superior in the east—in Barcelona and Cumaná, which were more Indian—but in the central valleys and on the central coastline, particularly in the Maracaibo valley, they numbered between 45 and 60 percent of the total population. Two out of every three people there were mulattoes. Similarly high concentrations were also to be found dotted along the

Atlantic coastline of Colombia, forming as much as 50 percent of the population in some places. Thus, in 1778, African blood was to be found in half the inhabitants of Medellín (Parsons, 1968).

Unhealthy, isolated coastal regions provided safe refuge for runaway slaves, who for centuries led free but miserable lives there. The Colombian Pacific coastline of Chocó was one of these Negro enclaves. The zambos, descendants of runaway slaves, drove the Cuna Indians away to the north and established themselves on their territory, regardless of colonial and republican governments. Those fleeing from the mines in the province of Nóvita continually brought in new blood to swell their numbers and revitalize them. The zambos of the Mosquito Coast of Nicaragua were more aggressive and, not content with imposing their rule on the *tierra caliente* area there, continually attacked the cacao haciendas on the Caribbean coast of Costa Rica, until they succeeded in depopulating the Matina valley (Jiménez Castro, 1956).

African penetration of the New World was most widespread and intense in the period from the last third of the eighteenth century to the first half of the nineteenth. More than at any previous time, Negroes expanded the areas where their race already predominated. But from a certain given moment, however, the situation began to change, the exact time varying from one region to another. Traces of Negro blood began to disappear in certain areas, such as the River Plate region, while in others their proportion of the total population declined, as indicated in the case of Cuba. Thus in Brazil, the first national census in 1872 revealed that three-fifths of the inhabitants of the empire were Negroes or of mixed blood, a considerably lower proportion than at the beginning of the century.

With the abolition of the slave trade and later of slavery itself, the source of African slaves dried up. Once the Negroes were freed and left on their own, their mortality rate increased because of the appalling living conditions to which they were subject, and their reproductive capacity was lowered because of the disproportionate distribution of the sexes inherited from the days of the slave trade (Stein, 1970). The temptations of *mestizaje*, or the mere crossing of the color barrier similarly reduced their numbers.

At the beginning of the new century, in 1801, Toussaint l'Ouverture, the Jacobin Negro champion of the independence of Haiti, was the first in the New World to declare the abolition of slavery, thus confirming the achievement of former slaves who had won their freedom through force of arms. In Spanish America and in Brazil, emancipation was achieved more slowly, and in a less chaotic manner. It was not gained by violence, although in some places it was precipitated by political pressures.

The first concession consisted in reducing the regular influx of slaves. The Junta Suprema of Caracas has the honor of being the leader in this field, suppressing the slave trade in August 1810. This was followed by similar declarations by the Chilean Congress in 1811 and by the triumvirate governing the River Plate region in 1812. It was also enshrined in the constitution of the state of Cartagena in the same year. Five years later, Ferdinand VII of Spain agreed with England to end the trade after May 1820 in those parts of the Spanish empire that were still in royalist hands. When the time actually arrived, the agreement was not honored and a new treaty was signed in 1835. In fact, it was only in 1845, with the promulgation of a penal law inflicting heavy punishment on slave traffickers, that the infamous trade was brought to an end in the Spanish West Indies. The republics that had thrown off the yoke of Ferdinand VII after 1820 also promulgated laws to abolish the slave trade. In 1821, the Congress of Cúcuta confirmed what had already been resolved two years earlier at the Congress of Angostura. In the same year, San Martín also declared its abolition, after he had liberated Peru.

It was not easy to implement the laws very effectively, and the situation varied with the changes of political fortune. In the time of Gamarra, the Congress of Huancayo annulled the Peruvian legislation of 1821 and again permitted the trade. During the administration of Rosas, the River Plate again became a centre of the slave trade, and the Uruguayan flag was used temporarily to cover the slave trade to Cuba, Brazil, and Montevideo itself (Curtin, 1969). Such manifest infractions of Uruguayan law caused Great Britain to exert heavy pressure to secure the effective elimination of the trade, which she herself had renounced some time earlier, in 1807. The Argentine dictator Rosas finally bowed to British demands by subscribing to the treaty of 1839. Meanwhile the *colorado* caudillo of the Banda Oriental (Uruguay), Rivera, also concurred. After protracted negotiations, the republican governments of Mexico, Venezuela, Colombia, Ecuador, Bolivia, and Chile signed similar agreements about the same time, granting Great Britain the right to patrol the high seas in pursuit of slaving ships (King, 1944).

The Portuguese monarchy, and later the Brazilian empire, also signed similar agreements with Great Britain before the above-mentioned countries, but these were of little effect. The influx of slaves continued to be enormous until the fifth decade of the century, until finally the Eusébio de Queiroz law put an end to it (Bethell, 1970). Not daunted by the ending of the trade, the south of Brazil found itself compelled to pay very high prices to persuade owners in the agriculturally depressed areas, such as the northeast, to sell their surplus slaves for work on the flourishing coffee plantations. In the 1870s, nature itself took a hand in swelling the tide of migration from the north to Rio de Janeiro and São Paulo; prolonged droughts laid waste the land and compelled the planters in the northeast to sell off their slaves (Stein, 1970). The abolition of the slave trade thus caused enormous internal migrations in Brazil—some calculate that about two hundred thousand individuals were moved by sea alone (Klein, 1970). This meant that by 1880, two-thirds of the slaves in the Brazilian empire were concentrated in states to the south of Espíritu Santo, thereby inverting the previous regional distribution pattern.

A second way in which the institution of slavery was gradually and prudently done away with was the introduction of "free womb" legislation, by which the child of a slave mother would be declared free at birth. Once again, Chile and the United Provinces of the River Plate took the first step in this direction, introducing it in 1811 and 1813. San Martín carried the principle to Peru, and the Congress of Cúcuta decreed its application to Gran Colombia in 1821. The República Oriental de Uruguay followed suit in 1825. Eventually such a law was introduced in Brazil by Rio Branco, but it was passed only with difficulty, in order to avoid other, more drastic measures that were being demanded.

Tutelary obligations had provided loopholes whereby slave owners could avoid compliance with redemptive legislation, until the proclamation of complete abolition made this impossible. Even when some government was prepared to proclaim the solemn abolition of slavery, the implementation of the resolution was a more difficult task, for it was constantly being opposed by powerful vested interests. Admittedly, abolition was implemented without great difficulty in those countries which had not relied on slave labor as a work force, and where the amount of capital involved was not great. Chile freed its last slaves in 1823, and the Central American Federation and Mexico passed appropriate legislation and implemented it in 1824 and 1829 respectively. Argentina, which still had a large number of slaves, reaffirmed a previous declaration in 1840, and Uruguay finally abolished slavery six years later in 1846. It was, however, civil strife and new prospects of economic development in the following decade which put an end to the institution in those countries with the strongest tradition of slavery, such as Venezuela, Colombia, Ecuador, and Peru. Two politicians in search of popular favor, J. T. Monagas and Marshal R. Castilla, decreed its abolition almost simultaneously in 1854. The former did so in Venezuela, where there were still twenty thousand slaves, and the latter in Peru, where there were about twelve thousand.

From then on, the only remaining strongholds of slavery were the Spanish West Indian colonies, Brazil, and Paraguay. The latter finally abolished it after being defeated in the War of the Triple Alliance in 1870. That same year, spurred by the devastating war of liberation it had been confronted with in Cuba, and at the insistence of the newly installed liberal regime, Spain began to accept the inevitability of the situation. The Spanish Cortes then promulgated a preparatory law for the gradual abolition of slavery, and in 1873 the first Spanish republic implemented the measure in Puerto Rico. Vested interests succeeded in postponing the inevitable for another seven years in Cuba. The law was not really fully enforced until 1886, when the disguised form of slavery known as *patronato* was abolished (Corwin, 1967). Brazil, for its part, could no longer continue to entertain public opinion by delaying tactics, such as the law freeing sexagenarian slaves. In 1888, amid great public excitement, both chambers of the Brazilian parliament approved the final abolition of slavery without any indemnity being paid to owners. The Golden Law, as it is called, put an end to slavery in the New World.

V

"To Govern Is to Populate"

AFTER a pause of several decades, the faith in its brilliant future which Latin America forged for itself in the struggle for independence began to reemerge. Civil strife, territorial disputes, and persistent economic depression had clouded that vision in the early years of independence. But by the middle of the last century the new states had achieved stable frontiers, with some minor exceptions, and politics had entered a more constructive phase, although occasional upheavals still occurred. Attempts at political union such as Gran Colombia, the Central American and Bolivia-Peru federations, and the union of Haiti and Santo Domingo had definitively failed. Uruguay and Paraguay resolutely defended their independence from the United Provinces of the River Plate. Mexico had finally and irretrievably been shorn of its northern provinces. A precarious form of political stability was at last achieved through a combination of weariness and yet further illusions.

The international situation also favored political and social consolidation. At the time, the European countries were rapidly expanding and required growing quantities and varieties of raw materials as well as assured markets for their manufactures. Latin America itself was eager to find markets for its agricultural products and minerals. Besides, the prospect of getting manufactured goods it had wanted for so long was a dazzling one. As world trade brought prosperity to these countries, it lessened their internal tensions, and their political situation became more stable. Thus, Latin America was being brought into the world trading community at the price of relegation to a subordinate position. A more subtle form of dependence than that from which it had just freed itself was gradually imposed on it. The term neocolonial defines the close link thus created by this expansion of trade relationships. Latin America suddenly discovered a desperate need for labor to set to work on real or imaginary development projects. The gradual population increase that had taken place during the previous century was too little to supply the demand. It had to be speeded up or, at least, not allowed to slow down.

This goal was not new. At the beginning of the independence era, Latin America was still under the influence of the Bourbon population policy, suited for the period when men and economic activity were slack and a whipping proved an effective stimulant. It was also at this time endeavoring to assert legal title to vast unoccupied areas by colonization. For the agrarian republics which took over the administration of the Spanish empire, a plethora of citizens continued to symbolize greatness: the larger the number of inhabitants, the greater the power and the greater the wealth. "Since population is the basis of industry and the corner stone of the happiness of States," read the decree issued by the triumvirate on September 4, 1812, opening the River Plate area to immigration. Because of the increases that had occurred in the later colonial period, Latin America as a whole had overcome the former population shortage. In some places, men even started overflowing into more fertile areas, though in others meagerness of material resources held up development. Although there was no real overall lack of population it was not distributed to best advantage. Underemployed labor would not necessarily have gone where it was needed had transport been easier. Occasionally some population movement did occur spontaneously along certain specific routes, and sometimes this was brought about by disruptions occasioned by the wars of independence or civil strife. But inadequate communications and reluctance to move still prevented internal migrations that were on a sufficiently large scale or fast enough. Rather than encouraging them, as the colonial authorities had done, it was easier to disregard local labor. It was better, and perhaps more economical, to import a Chinese coolie than to try to bring natives down from the mountains. Thus Spanish and Portuguese America opened their doors to migrants from overseas.

The decision was based not on economic grounds alone but also to a great extent on prejudice. People were sought not only for their muscle power but also for know-how. Latin America was seeking to benefit both from the influx of the workers themselves and from the capital and technology they would bring with them, whether they were German or Italian peasants. Internal migration might well have provided the muscles, but not the know-how. The training of local manpower would have been a slow process and an expensive investment when time was of the essence. By saving the educational and training cost for millions of immigrants who came, the recipient countries turned to account an invisible huge capital inflow; its amount is by no means easy to estimate, as has been pointed out by Mortara (1946).

Unfortunately, this relatively valid reasoning became tainted by bias, as if technical progress were associated with the color of a person's skin. Not only was the native bypassed to save time, but he came to be regarded as a hindrance and was condemned to backwardness. L. Ayarragaray (1910) was to become the bluntest exponent of this attitude. And racist arguments did not stop there. Differentiation was made between various European groups. Thus immigrants from northern Europe were definitely preferred. Most, if not all, of the new nations sought to attract qualified agricultural migrants from the Nordic countries. It so happened that Germany, Switzerland, Ireland, and the Scandinavian countries were experiencing a considerable population growth, which their internal development was incapable of absorbing. Emigration was thus a safety valve for them. The surplus population had already started going to the U.S.A. in large numbers, but there were always some who were dazzled by the more exotic prospects offered by countries farther south. Thus the Latin-American preference for such migrants happened to coincide with a considerable, ready supply from those sources.

Potential migrants could not be attracted to the newly independent Spanish-speaking states and Brazil merely by reversing the restrictive policies of colonial days and allowing foreigners in, or even by promising them religious freedom in order to avoid trouble on that score. The few who came of their own accord were merchants, artisans, or soldiers of fortune, and a handful of farmers. Material conditions were not such as to enable them to establish themselves without assistance, and governments had to adopt a much more active policy, negotiating with promoters for the setting up of colonies.

Brazil attracted the greatest number of immigrants at the time.

In 1818, not far from Rio de Janeiro, there was founded the Swiss colony of Nova Friburgo. Six years later, São Leopoldo was settled. These first attempts, although successful, were not followed up. There was a pause in immigration until Senator Vergueiro set the process in motion again. In this second stage, starting in 1847, there were founded São Pedro de Alcântara in Paraná, Petrópolis in Rio de Janeiro, and Blumenau in Santa Catarina. But even this experiment was not going to last (Carneiro, 1948). Slavery, which still existed under the empire, tended to discourage the influx of free migrants. The foreigners who arrived during that exploratory, trial period numbered several tens of thousands.

If Brazil attracted the greatest number of immigrants; the greatest impact was felt in Uruguay. The social and national composition of the new wave of migrants was also different from that received by Brazil. Between 1835 and 1842, 33,138 migrants arrived in Montevideo from overseas; 60 percent were French and 25 percent were Spaniards. The majority tried their luck in the capital itself, so that the 1843 census showed that for every 100 Uruguayan nationals living in Montevideo there were no less than 168 foreigners (Oddone, 1966a).

Across the River Plate estuary, in the state of Buenos Aires, once Rivadavia's immigration plans were over, the only significant influx was a thousand Irishmen who were needed to start a sheep-rearing industry. Later on, the Argentine Confederation encouraged Swiss and German settlements in the province of Santa Fe, such as that at Esperanza. Smaller groups came to Entre Ríos. By that time, in 1862, a group of Welsh settlers arrived in the remote, harsh, lower valley of the Chubut River in Patagonia. On the other side of the Andes, at approximately the same latitude, the Chilean government installed a colony of Germans on the wooded Pacific slopes during Montt's presidency, and their mark was soon firmly imprinted on the countryside formerly occupied by the Araucanian Indians. Further contingents of German migrants arrived later, and to this day the rural and urban areas of Valdivia, Osorno, La Unión, and Puerto Montt are markedly German in character. In Peru, President Gamarra in 1832 granted land to any foreigners who came to settle, but the measure was of little effect. During the presidency of Marshal Castilla, a law passed in 1849 attracted a limited number of Irish, Italian, and German migrants (Río, 1929). Three hundred of the latter, for example, went to Pozuzo in 1857. Germans also arrived in Nicaragua and Venezuela, but the Nicaraguan colony of Karlsruhe did not last long. On the other hand, Tovar, not far from Caracas (Venezuela), proved to be a success.

Despite the good intentions of governments and the sums invested in these experiments, the results were somewhat disappointing. The migrants were never numerous—not even if one adds to the number of colonists the artisans and merchants. Some thousands of them came spontaneously in search of fortune or as political refugees and they were soon lost sight of in the urban populations. In the countryside, isolation made integration difficult. Pockets of population retained their ethnic traits and are still identifiable despite the high degree of integration that has now occurred. The government's expectations of social and economic changes resulting from such migration were disappointed. The fact that millions of migrants left Europe over a period of some fifty years, but did not go to Latin America, proves that the appropriate conditions for their reception did not exist at that time. The United States, on the other hand, received and absorbed them without difficulty. When more favorable conditions arose at a later date, Latin America found no difficulty in bringing in a massive second wave of European migrants.

The exhausting labor on tropical plantations was hardly likely to prove attractive to free workers from Europe, and the planters were not prepared to pay them adequate wages to compensate for the work involved; so the shortage of labor had to be tackled by the use of slaves. The abolition, first of the slave trade itself, and then of the very institution of slavery, was initially postponed for as long as possible. And even before total abolition was implemented, labor became scarce. Cuba then tried to alleviate the situation for a while by buying, as slaves, Indians from the Yucatán peninsula who had been imprisoned there after a period of interracial warfare. Polynesians and Hawaiians were even tricked into coming to Peru (Río, 1929). But the most common practice, in Cuba, Peru, and Mexico, was to introduce contract Chinese labor to work under conditions hardly distinguishable from slavery. In 1847, the first shipment of Chinese coolies left the Far East for the Caribbean. Between 1853 and 1873, and particularly after the treaty concluded between the Spanish and Manchu governments in 1864, 132,435 emigrants were taken on board at Shanghai and Canton; some 13 percent of these died during the voyage. It was thus that the 1877 census in Cuba could record 43,811 Asiatics as being resident in the island, that is, 3 percent of the total population; because of their very high mortality rate, these numbers had been reduced to 14,863 by the 1899 census (Chang-Rodríguez, 1958).

Local agents in Chinese ports recruited the most miserable of the inhabitants or scoured the countryside in search of unwary people who would allow themselves to be inveigled into signing labor contracts by specious promises. Once in America, they were set to work cutting cane, laying railway tracks, or harvesting coffee beans. When they discovered how they had been fooled, they fled from the countryside by any available means as soon as the opportunity presented itself, and ended up swelling the ranks of the itinerant street traders. It was in this way that some Spanish American cities acquired the Oriental population whose idioms and culinary tastes have become so characteristic of them. Lima is a case in point.

In 1849 Peru opened its frontiers to Asiatic immigration, a measure which allowed President Castilla to abolish the Negro slave trade. As a result of this, some 87,000 Chinese entered the country between 1859 and 1874, and most of them went to work on the sugar plantations in the north. This traffic in human beings was later the subject of a treaty between Peru and the Chinese empire in 1874, but the War of the Pacific put an end to this influx of migrants shortly after the treaty was signed. The Oriental workers rapidly moved into Trujillo from the sugar plantations and, from there, to the capital (Stewart, 1951). The Asiatic content of Peru's population in 1876 amounted to 1.9 percent of the total.

Smaller numbers also went to Chile and Colombia. In the former, Peruvian Chinese arrived to work in the nitrate mines before the War of the Pacific, and stayed there when the territory changed hands (Segall, 1968). Those who went to Colombia were contracted primarily to work on the excavation of the future Panama Canal.

THE FLOOD OF MIGRANTS

"To govern is to populate," theorized Juan Bautista Alberdi, in his work entitled *Bases*, published in 1853, almost four decades after the United Provinces of the River Plate proclaimed their independence from Spain. The concise, catchy formula was to make fortunes and raise its author to the stature of a visionary. From that corner of Latin America most sensitive to population questions, arose a voice proclaiming the very need for labor and skills to which we alluded at the beginning of this chapter. The Argentine thinker had the satisfaction of seeing his ideas incorporated in the Magna Carta of his country, which the constitutional assembly was drafting at that time. Article 28 of the 1853 Constitution expressly states: "The federal government will encourage European immigration." But however good were the provisions adopted and however great the incentives offered by migration agents or the information offices opened in Europe by some countries, the immigrants were not forthcoming, to the despair of the governments concerned.

Migration theories had less influence on intercontinental migration than one would imagine. During the long rule of Porfirio Díaz in Mexico, fervent efforts were made to settle Europeans in the northern frontier areas, along the Gulf of Mexico and the south Pacific coast in Chiapas; but the Italian migrants almost immediately abandoned the settlement begun in 1881. In order to save the project from complete failure, the government eventually let Mexican nationals occupy the area. In 1908, of the 1,665 colonists left, only 271 were Italians (González Navarro, 1960). A vast amount of migration legislation passed at the time was to remain a dead letter for lack of the appropriate economic climate. Ecuador passed an immigration law in 1889, but it had no noticeable effect on the then very slow rate of population increase. Peru introduced another law in 1893; Venezuela one, in 1894; Costa Rica, in 1896; Paraguay, in 1903; Bolivia, in 1905; Honduras, in 1906; and finally Guatemala, in 1909. In no case did the legislation have the desired result.

But not only did ideologists and governments not get the numbers they desired. Argentina in the 1880s would have liked to see the pampa swarming with fair-haired Germans, and if they were Protestants, so much the better. But the successors of Alberdi and Sarmiento had to be content with fair-skinned Roman Catholics from Piedmont and the Basque country, or—even less favorably regarded —olive-skinned Sicilians or Murcians. Then there were to follow the "Turks" from the Middle East and the "Russians" from southern Poland or the Jewish communities in the Ukraine. In retrospect, and somewhat reluctantly, it was recognized and appreciated that there was some racial and cultural affinity between the migrants and the native population of the receiving country. This awareness of a common heritage was constantly stimulated by the immoderate use of the term *Latinity*. But the truth about the origin of these migrants is more prosaic.

It is impossible to guess all the individual reasons that moved people to cross the "pond," as Spanish migrants referred to the Atlantic Ocean with a mixture of humor and affectation. In each case it was a personal decision made for a variety of motives. But analysis of social and economic conditions in the home countries clearly indicates that there were pressures driving people to leave their homelands in search of better opportunities. After the 1880s, the whole of Europe experienced population pressure resulting from a decline in the death rate without a corresponding and simultaneous decrease in the fertility rate. The industrialized nations managed to absorb the resultant surplus population, but among the latecomers economic development did not keep pace with the demographic increase. Far from it, for the virgin soil overseas was competing with agricultural produce in Europe to the latter's disadvantage; the consequent agrarian depression made surplus hundreds of thousands of farm laborers. The incipient industrialization in the Mediterranean and Eastern European countries could not provide sufficient opportunities for employment in the cities. Thus, the only way out for these people was mass migration to North and South America. But this time South America was in better condition to compete for them. The second wave of migrants, which continued for fifty years until the Great Depression of 1930, was necessarily of a different racial composition from that of the smaller exodus of the mid-nineteenth century.

If this explains why migrants came from where they did rather than from elsewhere, and also the scale of the migration, it is nevertheless not the complete explanation. Whether few or many migrants went to Uruguay, for example, at any given time, depended also on the economic opportunities available there. Mexico, rightly or wrongly, wanted to get migrants from abroad, but did not get them, because it already had a surplus of unskilled labor. Quite rightly, Luis Siliceo wrote: "How much more humane and patriotic it would be to settle first the thousands of our own homeless, starving Indians than rely upon a few handfuls of foreigners brought in at great expense to the national exchequer, and who do not always turn out to be a profitable investment to the country" (González Navarro, 1960). The Mexican census of 1900 recorded 57,507 foreigners, of whom 16,000 were Spaniards and 15,000 were from North America, that is, an insignificant proportion of the whole population, only 0.5 percent. The countries of Central America, as well as Colombia, Venezuela, and Peru, had ambitions similar to those of Mexico, but natural barriers arose to discourage foreigners from migrating there. Either there was as yet a surplus of population, as in the case of El Salvador, or the country had not developed its natural resources sufficiently to attract Europeans. Venezuela, which was quite capable of absorbing plenty of migrants, as was to become apparent in due course, had shown no evidence of this by 1891, having a migrant population amounting to only 4 percent of the total.

The tide of migration thus flowed only toward the most developed areas. The basic conditions necessary to stimulate this flow were, first, that the country concerned could produce those commodities then in demand in Europe, such as grains, meat and hides, certain fibers, and coffee; and second, that the population already there had to be sufficiently small to create a serious labor shortage. Only southern Brazil, Uruguay, and the coastal areas of Argentina met these requirements, and consequently it was toward these areas that the tide of migrants from the Mediterranean peninsulas and elsewhere flowed across the Atlantic.

Nevertheless, two countries that did not fulfill either of the above conditions, Cuba in the Caribbean and Chile on the Pacific coast, absorbed a considerable number of migrants, though of course they did not find it as easy to retain them as did those areas on the South Atlantic coastline. Cuba will be dealt with later; in Chile the government found it necessary to stimulate the somewhat sluggish flow of migrants who came of their own accord. Thus, as part of this policy, between 1883 and 1891, the Chilean government assisted the settlement of thousands of farmers from many countries in the area south of the River Bío-Bío, but a critical economic situation and the consequent revolution of 1891 interrupted the implementation of these official plans. Later, between 1908 and 1914, some ten thousand immigrants arrived each year; then, after the temporary numerical reduction during World War I, the average annual inflow came down to about half that number (Willcox, 1929). During this later stage, Chile preferred skilled workers to staff the country's incipient industries. With the opening of the Trans-Andean railway, more migrants began to arrive overland rather than by the traditional sea route. At no stage did the influx become a flood, and the country had no difficulty in absorbing them. Foreigners were never very numerous, and in 1907 they formed a mere 4.2 percent of the total population.

Within the area most favored by migrants, Argentina received the highest proportion. Table 5.1 arrives at net immigration through the numbers of second and third class passengers who arrived and departed, as recorded in the statistics compiled by the Dirección de Inmigración. The net inflow into Argentine ports between 1881 and 1935 amounted to 3,400,000. During the slightly longer period be-

TABLE 5.1 Immigration to the River Plate Area, 1881–1910 (annual net gain averaged out over five-year periods)

	Argentina	Uruguay		Argentina	Uruguay
1881–1885	55,825	4,302	1911–1915	79,774	20,213
1886–1890	115,169	10,676	1916–1920	−7,216	10,638
1891–1895	23,735	2,965	1921–1925	27,852	13,604
1896–1900	55,570	7,945	1926–1930	90,232	20,286
1901–1905	66,716	13,099	1931–1935	10,191	5,379
1906–1910	168,775	18,559			
Overall Immigration 1881–1935				3,433,110	638,330

SOURCES: For Argentina: Dirección General de Estadística, *La población y el moviemiento demográfico de la República Argentina*. Report no. 83, 1941; for Uruguay: Narancio and Capurro Calamet, 1939.

tween 1872 and 1940, Brazil received 3,300,000 (table 5.2), quite as many as Argentina. This figure is an estimate by Mortara (1947) based on the increase between censuses, not, as in the case of other countries of the area, on data recording the movement of passengers. The gross figure of migrant entries into Brazil is known, but since no exit statistics are available, it is impossible to work out accurately the net gain. The figures obtained by these two methods will never be strictly comparable. The census data may have the advantage of including even those who entered the country illegally, but omit those who entered and joined the country's work force but died before the next census.

TABLE 5.2 Influence of Immigration on the Demographic Growth of Brazil, 1872–1940

	Population increase (in thousands)			Growth rate		
Period	Overall	By excess of births over deaths	By immigration	% due to immigration	Overall	Natural	Immigration
1872–1890	4,221	3,651	570	13.5	2.01	1.63	0.38
1891–1900	2,984	2,081	930	30.2	2.42	1.82	0.60
1901–1920	13,317	12,377	939	7.0	2.12	1.86	0.22
1921–1940	10,617	9,757	859	8.1	2.05	1.87	0.18

SOURCE: Mortara, 1947.

Another risk in estimating the migration figures for the River Plate area is that of counting migrants twice, since newcomers usually tried their luck first in one of the countries flanking the estuary, and if their expectations were not fulfilled then in the other. In view of the ease of communication between the two shores, a by no means strict account was taken of such movements, and it is quite possible that many were not recorded at all. In any event, Argentina received approximately half of the total influx, Uruguay one-eighth, and Brazil the rest.

During the 1880s, the ranks of those going to "make America" swelled year by year. They did, in fact, come to stay; at least three-quarters of those who stepped ashore in Argentina remained, as can be seen in table 5.3. But the world financial and commercial crisis of 1890 disenchanted those who had, until then, dreamed of the Promised Land to the point that more people went back to Europe that year than arrived in the River Plate.

TABLE 5.3 Percentages of Immigrants Remaining in Argentina, 1857–1924, by Decades and by Country of Origin

Period	Total	Italy	Spain	Great Britain
1857–1860	55.5	54.5	53.9	38.0
1861–1870	48.4	43.7	68.8	48.5
1871–1880	32.7	24.4	55.4	31.6
1881–1890	75.8	74.2	84.7	68.2
1891–1900	49.5	47.2	55.8	46.8
1901–1910	63.5	56.7	74.8	35.0
1911–1920	22.3	–0.8	30.8	–24.6
1921–1924	68.4	76.7	58.7	–2.6
1857–1924	53.2			

SOURCE: Beyhaut et al., 1961.

The recovery from this setback was slow, except in Brazil, where all previous records were broken soon with an influx of almost a million migrants; in each subsequent decade only half this number was to arrive. (See fig. 4.) Progress in Argentina, Uruguay, and Chile was instead sustained and gradual up to the outbreak of World War I. Somewhat over 300,000 people disembarked at the busy ports of Argentina in 1913 alone, and although about half this number left, the net gain was very considerable. (See fig. 5.) Uruguay also achieved its greatest intake that year.

Thus in the period just before the Great War there was much coming and going. A small number of large landowners, in connivance with the government, maneuvered to seize most of the land, and the humid pampa only had room for tenant farmers or farmhands, neither of whom were permanent settlers. The established landholding system prevented the newcomers from acquiring property; foreigners had no incentive to remain. The result was the so-called swallow migration. Once the harvest had been gathered, the bands of reapers and their dependents took ship back to Spain or

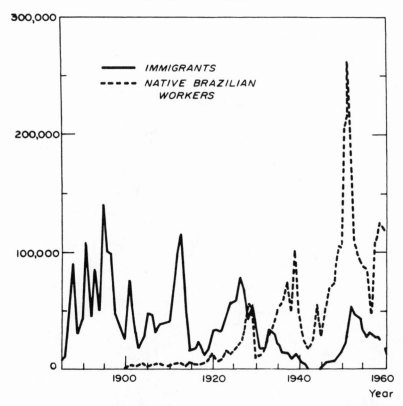

FIGURE 4. Overseas and internal migrations to the state of São Paulo (Brazil), 1885–1960. (Source: Camargo, 1968. Reproduced by permission of Editora da Universidade de São Paulo and Livro Técnico S.A. Editores.)

Italy where, owing to the seasonal differences between the two hemispheres, another harvest awaited their attention. World War I put a stop to this practice. Argentina even lost permanent residents when many citizens of the belligerent countries went back home. According to table 5.3, 25 percent more people of British descent left Argentina than came to it during the decade between 1911 and 1920.

Sea communications were reopened when hostilities ended, and those who dreamed of seeking their fortunes in South America could once again travel free of the Allied blockade and the menace of German U-boats. In addition, those who were prevented from entering the U.S.A. by new, restrictive legislation now came to South America. For some time it looked as though migration would rival prewar levels. But disillusion came soon and very suddenly. The slump of 1930, an economic crisis even worse than the one forty years earlier,

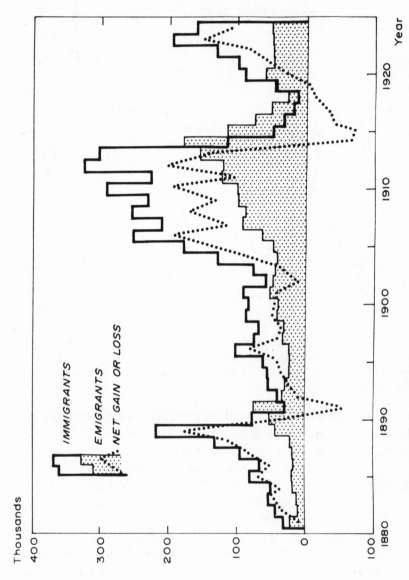

FIGURE 5. Overseas migration to Argentina, 1881–1924. (Source: Willcox, 1929.)

saw a repetition of the procession of foreign migrants packing up and making their sorry way back to the homelands they had left years before. The flood of immigrants promptly ceased, thus bringing to an end a half-century of mass migration to South America. The rate had always varied in response to differing conditions; the Great Depression, however, was not just one more event in the cycle, since for Latin America it marked the beginning of a new era.

Entry to the continent had been made along the two thousand or more kilometers of coastline between Rio de Janeiro and Buenos Aires. Where in fact did the seven million net migrants actually settle? In Brazil, three-fifths settled in São Paulo, the most prosperous state on account of the extent of its coffee plantations, its incipient industries, and its commercial vitality. The remainder went either to Rio de Janeiro, where services were increasing and light industry was beginning to appear, or to the southern agricultural and pastoral states with their temperate climate and the additional advantage of having welcomed previous migrants. Many newcomers found relatives or fellow countrymen there.

In Uruguay, the gauchos and farmers were still native-born *criollos*. According to the 1908 census, less than 4 percent of the rural population had been born abroad. On the other hand, in the capital, the only important city in the country, half the inhabitants were foreigners, including a considerable number of Argentines and Brazilians (Oddone, 1966a). Europeans had contributed to the rapid growth of Montevideo, which, from being a humble, backward town at the beginning of the nineteenth century, had become the fourth largest city in Spanish America.

The millions who went to Argentina were enough to both populate the semiempty countryside and expand the cities. Europeans spread out thinly throughout Patagonia, set foot on the inland and coastal pampa, and took firm root in the oases on the eastern side of the Andes, such as Mendoza. In 1914, nearly half the inhabitants of the four national territories of Patagonia were foreigners, while in the province of Buenos Aires they constituted 44 percent and about one in three in the provinces of La Pampa, Santa Fe, and Mendoza. The northwest was not affected for some time (Beyhaut et al., 1961). Migrants also increased the rural population, of course. In the 1880s and also during the 1890 financial crisis, when necessity drove them out of the cities, those who did not want to go back to their homelands settled in the southern countryside (Sánchez-Albornoz, 1970). In the later migratory phase, unskilled workers outnumbered farmers.

They were drawn to the urban centers, where they easily found employment in the building industry. Since the majority of those who entered the country during this period of peak immigration ended up in the cities, it should be concluded that, overall, immigration benefited the urban nuclei rather than the countryside, and thus did not fulfill the purposes envisaged by the advocates of the open-door policy.

TABLE 5.4 Proportion of Immigrants Entering Argentina, by Nationalities, 1857–1924 (in percentages)

Period	Italians	Spaniards	French	"Russians"	"Turks"	Others
1857–1860	61.77	16.85	5.52	0.60	—	15.26
1861–1870	71.04	14.28	5.25	0.26	—	9.17
1871–1880	58.28	17.07	12.54	0.16	0.26	11.69
1881–1890	58.72	18.88	11.16	0.49	0.42	10.33
1891–1900	65.66	20.31	3.95	2.69	1.79	5.60
1901–1910	45.63	36.99	1.96	4.22	3.78	7.42
1911–1920	28.83	48.89	2.09	4.71	4.87	10.61
1921–1924	45.15	30.40	0.99	0.92	2.68	19.86

SOURCE: Beyhaut et al., 1961.

The figures shown in tables 5.3 and 5.4 confirm the fact that the majority of the migrants who came to South America were from the Iberian Peninsula and Italy. The Italians were the largest group to come to Argentina, except on the eve of World War I and, of course, during it. As a result of a dispute over the conditions under which its citizens were transported, the government in Rome prohibited emigration to Argentina in 1911 and 1912. The war did not merely reinforce the effects of this temporary prohibition; it even caused a number of Italians to return home. Argentina made up for this shortage with a flow of migrants from Spain. Spaniards had, in fact been coming in rising numbers. Their highest rate of migration flow was during the first quarter of this century. Being citizens of a neutral country, Spaniards were in a favorable position vis-à-vis other nations as far as crossing the Atlantic in wartime was concerned. Yet another contingent from a Latin country came third in order of importance: the persecution of workers in France after the failure of the Paris commune, and the agrarian depression, caused many French to leave during the 1870s and 1880s. During that period, one in eight of all migrants arriving in Argentina came from France. After the flow from this source began to dry up, "Russians"—whether Slavs or not—and "Turks"—Moslems or Christians—many of whom were fleeing from political or religious persecution, took their place.

The pattern in Uruguay was similar to that in Argentina. The most numerous foreign colony in Montevideo in 1908 was the Italian one, with the Spanish following a close second. In Brazil the Portuguese, who were hardly known at all farther south, constituted a third of those entering the country, followed closely by the Italians (table 5.5). Brazil is also somewhat surprising in the number of Germans and Japanese it allowed in. The Germans came in early colonizing schemes, and these were later reinforced. Eighty-five percent of the Germans who arrived then continued to go to the southern states of Rio Grande do Sul, Santa Catarina, and Paraná, to join the descendants of the earlier settlers. The Japanese, on the other hand, did not begin to come in until very late, about 1908 (Normano and Gerbi, 1943). After that, their numbers grew slowly until at one time they were at the top of the list of migrants.

TABLE 5.5 Origin of Immigrants Entering Brazil, 1819–1959

	Number (in thousands)	Percentage
Portugal	1,718	31.0
Italy	1,614	29.1
Spain	694	12.5
Germany	257	4.6
Japan	222	4.0
Russia	125	2.3
Others	906	16.4
Total	5,536	100.0

SOURCE: Diegues, 1964.

How did each national group contribute to the new melting pot? Between 1908 and 1932 the port of Santos welcomed 198,000 Italians and 115,000 Japanese. However, after discounting those who returned home, only 26,000 Italians remained as against no less than 106,000 Japanese. Thus the net immigration of Orientals to the state of São Paulo at that time was as great as that of the Portuguese and the Spaniards, and four times as great as the Italians, although the Japanese contingent was numerically smaller (Ellis, 1934). One must therefore consider not only the entry figures but also the percentage of immigrants who took root. These can be seen in tables 5.3 and 5.6.

In Argentina only half of the immigrants stayed permanently. The proportion varied, of course, over the years. In prosperous times, three-quarters of those arriving settled. This happened, for example, between 1881 and 1890 and, to a lesser degree, between 1901 and

TABLE 5.6 Major Countries of Origin of Immigrants Remaining in the State of
São Paulo, According to Entry and Exit Records of the Port of Santos,
1908–1932 (percentages)

Portugal	42	Japan	92
Spain	52	Yugoslavia	80
Italy	13	Poland	50
Germany	18		

SOURCE: Ellis, 1934.

1910 and from 1921 on. The depression, however, reduced the numbers of migrants who remained. Of the three nationalities noted in
table 5.3, the Spaniards were most inclined to settle permanently;
the British, on the other hand, were the least likely to take root, especially after the second decade of this century. In Santos, Portuguese,
Spaniards, and Poles tended to remain in fairly large numbers, while
Italians and Germans were less inclined to stay. In view of the distance of their homeland, it is hardly surprising that the Japanese
showed fewer signs than any other group of regretting their decision
to migrate, and they consequently took firm root in their chosen
country. A very high proportion of the Yugoslav migrants also
stayed.

Permanent residence does not necessarily imply integration. A
large proportion of the Japanese women who settled in Brazil came
out specifically to marry their compatriots, or found husbands among
them after their arrival. But in view of the shortage of Japanese
women, the men more frequently married Brazilians. In any event,
the deliberate or circumstantial tendency to marry within the national groupings was very noticeable among the Japanese, as can be
seen by an examination of the marriage records of foreigners in the
municipality of São Paulo between 1934 and 1939 (table 5.7). In
general, the women of all nationalities preferred to marry within
their own national grouping. This tendency was least marked among
Spanish American women, while those from the Latin countries
of Europe and even from the U.S.A. were not over reluctant to
marry Brazilians. On the other hand, Central European and Oriental
women showed marked unwillingness to do so. The men tended to
react in the same way as did the women of each nationality, but to a
lesser degree, being slightly more inclined to marry Brazilian women.
Thus there were some ethnic groups inclined to intermarry sooner
than others, but on the whole, the situation was satisfactory. Integration through marriage—at least in urban areas, as in the specific case
quoted of São Paulo—avoided the formation of socially and culturally closed communities, on the fringe of national life.

TABLE 5.7 Marital Assimilation of Foreigners in São Paulo City, 1934–1939
(percentages)

	Foreign males married to Brazilian women	Foreign females married to Brazilian men
Portuguese	60.7	33.0
Italians	71.2	50.8
Spaniards	64.7	43.2
Germans	36.5	20.8
Austrians	30.3	22.6
Hungarians	18.9	11.1
Russians	21.6	18.4
Other Europeans	17.6	12.4
Syrians	54.1	18.8
Japanese	42.4	8.8
Americans	52.8	35.2
Spanish-Americans	81.0	65.2
Other foreigners	34.7	8.7
Average overall	50.0	28.6

SOURCE: Mortara, 1947.

The assimilation of males by marriage was partly due to the unequal sex and age distribution among the migrants. As had occurred previously with the Negro slaves, most of the European immigrants were young unmarried men. Seven out of every ten migrants arriving in Argentina between 1857 and 1924 were single males between the ages of thirteen and forty. If they decided to remain in America they would seek female companionship. But, as distinct from the case of the Negroes, their only difficulties in finding a wife were those imposed by their personal inclinations, some social prejudice, and above all, the disparity of numbers between the sexes in that motley society. In 1869, for every two women born outside Argentina there were five men who had been born overseas. This disparity not only affected foreign migrants, however, but applied to the whole population: in Argentina in 1914 there were three men to every two women.

Mass migration also greatly changed age distribution. Table 5.8 shows how the foreign migrants were mainly aged between fourteen and sixty-four. Their arrival raised the overall proportion of the population in this age group to three-fifths, while among the natives this age bracket was only 50 percent. Thus the large adult foreign population was responsible for ten additional points in this age group, above the regular proportion that would have prevailed without any migrant influx.

In Argentina, the peak of foreign influence came in 1914; 30 percent of the residents of the country in that year were not native born. At no stage in its history did the U.S.A. have such a high pro-

TABLE 5.8 Foreigners in the Population of Argentina

| | % of total | % 14–64 age group | | | Sex ratio* | | |
		Total of population	Argen-tines	Foreigners	Total of population	Argen-tines	Foreigners
1869	12.1	56.5	—	—	106	94	251
1895	25.5	57.9	48.6	85.0	112	90	173
1914	29.9	61.4	50.3	87.4	116	98	171
1947	15.8	65.2	61.9	83.7	105	100	138
1960	12.8	63.0	61.3	75.0	101	99	110

*Proportion of males to females expressed as males per 100 females.
SOURCE: Germani, 1970.

portion of foreign residents; at most it reached half this figure. At the highest point of its influx of migrants, the U.S. census of 1910 showed the foreigners living within its borders as constituting only 14.7 percent of the total population. Mortara, the distinguished Italian demographer who took refuge in Brazil during Mussolini's Fascist regime and who was responsible for many studies on the population of Latin America, endeavored to estimate how much the population growth in certain countries was due to natural growth, how much to the net immigration gain, and how much to the natural growth of the immigrant community. His study covers the period from 1841 to 1940; the numerical results can be seen in table 5.9.

TABLE 5.9 Relative Contribution of Natural Growth, Immigration, and Immigrants' Children to the Population Increases in Four Countries of the Western Hemisphere, 1841–1940 (in percentages)

	Natural growth	Immigration	Immigrants' children
Argentina	41.9	29.0	29.0
Brazil	81.0	9.4	9.6
U.S.A.	59.1	21.8	19.0
Canada	78.4	9.8	11.8

SOURCE: Mortara, 1947.

According to him, 29 percent of the increase in Argentina is directly attributable to migration, and a further 29 percent to the offspring of immigrants. Such figures outstrip by a long way those relative to the U.S.A., and even more those of Brazil and Canada. Had it not been for immigrants into Argentina, its population in 1940 would have been only six million instead of the actual figure of thirteen million. Argentina was, without doubt, the country where the influx of migrants was most significant. The U.S.A., Canada, and Brazil follow it in that order.

The proportion of foreigners in the population of Argentina began to decline after its peak in 1914. It appeared soon that the country would absorb its foreign segment in a short time. As early as 1940 Bunge could state regretfully that "cosmopolitan Argentina will soon be a country without foreigners!" But although this prophecy has taken longer to be fulfilled than Bunge imagined, it is a fact that the nonnative population is inevitably declining both in numbers and in importance. In 1970, as a result of naturalization, death, returning home, and the drying up of immigration, only 9.3 percent of the population were foreigners.

The same process took place in Brazil, but earlier than in Argentina. According to the figures in table 5.2, immigration reached its peak during the decade from 1891 to 1900. The population went up then by three million. Thirty percent of this increase was due to immigration from abroad, and 70 percent to the excess of births over deaths. Immigration alone accounted for 0.6 percent of the annual increase, almost identical to the situation in Argentina at the time. After the beginning of the present century, the contribution of immigration to population growth declined until today it is insignificant.

Cuba's independence put an end to a past of political and economic uncertainties that had affected the composition of and increase in the island's population throughout the last third of the nineteenth century. By 1898 the nation had endured two long and bloody struggles to gain its independence. Between 1861 and 1877, the intercensus period which includes the open fighting of the Ten Years' War, the annual growth rate was reduced to one-quarter of the average over the previous twenty years (0.5 percent, as against 1.9 percent between 1841 and 1860). The war and the social upheaval caused by the abolition of slavery combined to put an end to the high rates of increase noted in the previous chapter. As a result of the respite brought about by the Peace of Zanjón in 1878, the rate of growth went up by three-tenths in the following decade, to reach a figure of 0.8 percent; but this slight increase was by no means indicative of any definite improvement in the demographic situation in the colony. In the last period before independence, there was actually a decrease of 0.3 percent in the population or, in absolute terms, a drop of 59,-842. Such were the minimum results of the second and definitive war of independence. In Havana alone, the death rate in 1898 was three times that of the average over the five years prior to the war. (See fig. 6.) Le Riverend (Guerra y Sánchez, 1958) estimates that the war accounted for the lives of 200,000 military personnel and civilians,

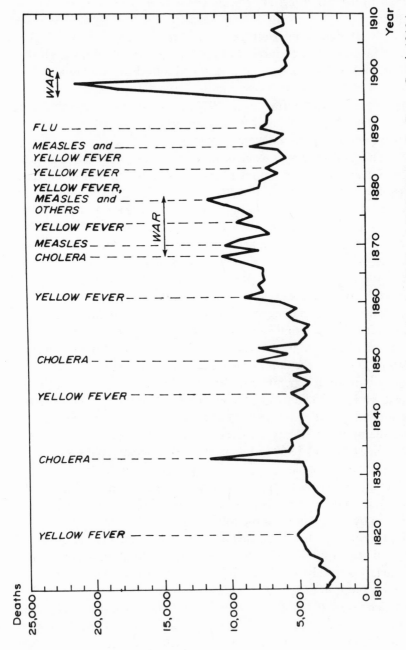

FIGURE 6. Deaths due to wars and epidemics in Havana between 1810 and 1910. (Source: Le Roy y Cassá, 1913.)

who either were killed in action or, as a result of the "concentration" policy concocted by General Weyler, the latter a precedent for similar experiments in Algeria and Vietnam.

As in every war, the birth rate went down. Between 1896 and 1899 it declined every year, from 12.1 per thousand to 8.9, and then to 5.7, only showing an increase again in the latter year to 6.1. It is hardly surprising that the number of children had dropped to only 8.3 percent of the population, according to the census taken by the American forces of occupation in 1899. This figure is about half of what one would expect to find in any age pyramid dealing with a young society. The war not only reduced the population of Cuba but also compromised its future. Furthermore, it speeded up the process of concentration in urban areas. The population problem was particularly acute in the early years of the new republic, when it was endeavoring to expand sugar production in response to the demand of its neighbor to the north and the influx of U.S. capital. Cuba consequently adopted an open-door policy. The Immigration and Colonization Law of 1906 regulated the flow. Despite the war that Cuba had just experienced with its former mother country, Spaniards arrived in large numbers, more, in fact, than those soldiers and civil servants who had been repatriated in accordance with the terms of the Treaty of Paris. Spanish influence in the island continued to be very great, but now in the productive rather than the administrative sphere. Table 5.10 shows the extent of the immigration and the overall predominance of Spaniards. The other important source of migrants was the West Indies—Haiti and Jamaica—particularly after World War I.

TABLE 5.10 Foreigners Entering Cuba, 1902–1930

Years	Spaniards	West Indians	Total
1902–1904	61,153	859	73,028
1905–1909	148,147	4,839	173,945
1910–1914	142,921	8,892	184,131
1915–1919	147,092	84,550	262,822
1920–1924	224,540	136,136	360,676
1925–1929	54,826	74,920	164,080

SOURCE: Cuba, Secretaría de Hacienda, 1902–1930.

Since no statistics are available regarding the numbers who left the island, it is impossible to establish the net gain. Presumably it was great, but there was also a very significant seasonal movement of labor between Cuba and the neighboring islands during each sugar harvest.

THE BEGINNINGS OF CHANGE

The massive migration of Europeans left an indelible mark on the host nations. Apart from the social and economic consequences, which are beyond the scope of this book, from a purely demographic point of view, it speeded up the growth of these countries, changed the geographical distribution of the population, and introduced some of the modern patterns in vital characteristics which were than beginning to become manifest in Southern Europe. The extent of the spread of these new patterns is still in dispute. Since immigration was largely restricted to those countries mentioned in the preceding pages, population increase in the other ones was mainly due to natural growth and not to the influx of foreigners.

Before examining some of the modifications that occurred in vital statistics, let us review the general trends in Latin America and its development, region by region. Table 5.11 gives the population of all the twenty-one countries of Latin America in 1850, 1900, and 1930, grouped according to the classification of Miró (1965). In the following chapters we will retain this same classification. It should be pointed out that with the passage of time the data become more and more reliable. Some figures in column 1 are mere conjectures; the census data or estimates in the third column are, however, reasonably trustworthy.

The population of Latin America doubled in half a century, between 1850 and 1900. It jumped from 30.5 million to 61 million, increasing by 1.3 percent per annum; this rate was about two-thirds higher than that of the preceding century, by no means a trifling acceleration. This rate of growth was also high in comparison with other parts of the world. Few European nations were increasing as rapidly, although they had reached at that time the culminating stage of their demographic transition. During the second period, that is, between 1900 and 1930, Latin America maintained this rate of growth and slightly increased it. It moved from 61 million to 104 million, the rate of increase being 1.7 percent per annum.

Temperate South America headed the list: overall, it trebled its population in the first half-century and doubled it in the following three decades. The growth rate moved from about 2 percent per annum in the first period to 2.3 percent during the second. Both figures are about those that would normally be recorded at a time of population explosion. Uruguay's population shot up, increasing sixfold in the brief space of fifty years. It would, of course, be difficult to main-

TABLE 5.11 Population of Latin America, 1850, 1900, and 1930 (in thousands)

	1850	1900	1930
Continental Central America			
Mexico	7,662	13,607	16,589
Guatemala	850	1,425	1,771
El Salvador	394	932	1,443
Honduras	350	443	948
Nicaragua	300	448	742
Costa Rica	125	285	499
Panama*	—	—	502
Subtotals	9,681	17,140	22,494
Caribbean			
Cuba	1,186	1,573	3,837
Puerto Rico	455	953	1,552
Dominican Republic	200	700	1,400
Haiti	938	1,270	2,422
Subtotals	2,779	4,496	9,211
Tropical South America			
Brazil	7,205	17,318	33,568
Colombia	2,243	3,825	7,350
Peru	1,888	3,791	5,651
Venezuela	1,490	2,344	2,950
Ecuador	816	1,400	2,160
Bolivia	1,374	1,696	2,153
Subtotals	15,016	30,374	53,832
Temperate South America			
Argentina	1,100	4,743	11,896
Chile	1,287	2,904	4,424
Uruguay	132	915	1,704
Paraguay	500	440	880
Subtotals	3,019	9,002	18,904
Totals for Latin America	30,495	61,012	104,441

*Until 1903 included in Colombia.

SOURCES: 1850, Spanish America: Barón Castro (1945) except for Paraguay, which is a rough estimate; Puerto Rico, which is an estimate based on Janer (1945); Haiti, an estimate based on Victor (1944); Brazil: Mortara (1947). 1900, for most countries: Miró (1965) except for Paraguay: Rivarola and Heisecke (1969); Dominican Republic and Ecuador: Barón Castro (1945); El Salvador and Guatemala, estimates based on Collver (1965); Haiti, Catholic population according to diocesan information in Victor (1944). 1930: CELADE (1970).

tain such a rate over a sustained period of time, and early signs of slowing down were becoming discernible in the first decades of the twentieth century. Argentina was not far behind its neighbor: its population quadrupled and then more than doubled. Only Paraguay showed a temporary drop. The War of the Triple Alliance plus an outbreak of cholera killed off almost two-thirds of the adult male population, and a smaller proportion of the total population. Nearly twenty years after the end of the war, the 1886 census recorded a deficit of forty thousand men. More than one woman in four was then unable to find a mate. Once Paraguay had recovered from the long-term effects of the war, its population began to increase quite rapidly during the present century.

Except for its geographical setting, Brazil ought really to be included in the group of nations listed above rather than in the tropical group. During the period under consideration, it behaved in much the same way as Chile, that is to say, it more or less doubled its population in each time lapse. It is thus in a very different position from other tropical countries, which did not have a temperate zone to absorb many immigrants, as did Brazil in its southern states.

The republics of tropical South America increased their populations at precisely one-third the rate of Brazil, and they did not experience the sudden rise at the turn of the century. Colombia was the only country to exceed the average rate for the region, and this despite its loss of Panama in 1903. Venezuela, Ecuador, Peru, and Bolivia advanced very slowly. The highlands of Peru and Bolivia experienced no population pressure whatsoever for the time being.

Continental Central America shared this sluggishness. The population of Costa Rica and El Salvador, in particular, went up especially during the first third of this century. But Mexico showed little advance and, because of its preponderant size, tended to lower the regional average. Mexico's influence in this area was thus the precise opposite to that of Brazil in the area of tropical South America: Brazil raised the regional average; Mexico depressed it. The growth rate was even further adversely affected by the Mexican Revolution during the second decade of the century. Inevitably, deaths from other than natural causes increased and the birth rate fell. At the same time there began a numerically significant movement of population out of the country. The 1920 census in the U.S.A. records the presence of nearly half a million Mexicans in the border states (Gamio, 1930). Moreover, to make matters worse, an influenza epidemic at this time dealt more severely with Mexico than with the other countries. These factors combined to bring a net loss of 825,000 inhabitants to Mexico between the centenary celebrations of 1910 and the fourth national census eleven years later. From 15.1 millions, it went down to 14.3 in 1921 (Romero et al., 1961). Once these social and political upheavals were over, the population figures again showed an upward trend. With peace came a rapid recovery, as always happens in similar situations. In the first five years after the end of the revolution, the birth rate recovered and the death rate was lower even than that prevailing during the presidency of Porfirio Díaz. (See table 5.12.)

TABLE 5.12 Birth Rate (B) and Death Rate (D) in Ten Latin-American Countries during the First Quarter of the Twentieth Century

		1900–1904	1910–1914	1920–1924
Uruguay	B	38.9	36.5	30.1
	D	13.7	13.5	12.6
Argentina	B	44.3	40.3	35.0
	D	20.0	15.6	13.8
Cuba	B	44.6	44.7	36.7
	D	23.7	21.4	19.3
Panama	B	40.3	42.0	40.0
	D	21.0	19.0	17.3
Costa Rica	B	46.9	48.9	44.9
	D	28.8	27.2	25.2
Guatemala	B	45.8	46.6	48.3
	D	35.4	33.0	33.7
Mexico	B	46.5	43.2	45.3
	D	33.4	46.6	28.4
Venezuela	B	41.8	44.5	41.2
	D	29.1	28.3	26.0
Colombia	B	43.0	44.1	44.6
	D	26.6	26.0	23.7
Chile	B	44.7	44.4	42.2
	D	31.6	31.5	31.3

SOURCES: For Uruguay and Argentina, Rothman, 1971; for the remainder, Collver, 1965.

Once Cuba recovered from its own disastrous wartime experiences, which have already been mentioned (see also the remarks regarding fig. 6), the Caribbean area—of which Cuba is the key—entered upon a period of demographic growth. The population of the area doubled in the first third of this century, thus more or less equaling the growth rate in southern South America.

To sum up, we may distinguish three main tendencies. First, there was rapid growth in the southern temperate zone and, somewhat later, in Cuba. To a great extent this is attributable to European migration. On the other hand, in the older settled areas of Mexico and South America, with few exceptions, there was a slow natural growth rate. The third tendency belongs somewhere between these two, the increase being considerable but not spectacular, and occurring particularly after the turn of the century. This is what happened in Central America and in some parts of the Caribbean area. The increase was due to natural growth rather than migration. In short, the boom experienced in the countries along the Atlantic coastline some two centuries before continued and accelerated while, conversely, the western and Andean countries, which had previously been the most important, became less significant in the Latin-American context as a whole.

In those cases where immigration played an insignificant role, what factors were responsible for the population increase? Which was more important, a gain in the number of children born, owing to a rise in the fertility rate, or a decrease in the death rate, which allowed more people to survive? In table 5.12 one can see the birth and death rate figures for some of the countries concerned. The data are for the first five-year period in each of the first three decades of this century, and these provide an idea of the trends.

The general impression given is that birth rates altered little during the period. Two countries, Colombia and Guatemala, show a gradual increase, while Uruguay, Argentina, and perhaps Cuba show a slight decrease, but in most countries the birth rate stayed fairly constant at over forty per thousand inhabitants, a situation typical of countries not yet modernized.

The same Old Regime pattern can be seen in the death rate figures. In Guatemala, Mexico, and Chile, it is over thirty per thousand per annum. Costa Rica, Venezuela, and Colombia are close to this value. On the other hand, the values for the remaining four, Uruguay, Argentina, Cuba, and Panama, vary during the first period from twenty-four to fourteen per thousand, a third below those recorded in the other countries; twenty years later they had gone down to between nineteen and thirteen per thousand. There is therefore no homogeneous pattern to be discerned in the death rates. They varied from high to low, according to the standards of the time. But whereas the birth rate was fairly stable and uniform, the death rate at the beginning of the century showed signs of altering, and the gap between the most demographically advanced countries and the most backward was widening.

Deaths in a large commercial port such as Havana (see fig. 6) reveal the hazards of life in the nineteenth century. In addition to a permanently high death rate, which fluctuated about the 40 per thousand mark, serious crises afflicted the city from time to time and took thousands of lives. The deaths recorded jumped remarkably, and these unusual upward leaps are very obvious in figure 6. The cause is indicated above each one of them. The old smallpox epidemics appear only occasionally. But yellow fever and cholera are continually reappearing. In this respect, Havana was like many other ports in Latin America. But Havana suffered, in addition, from the effects of colonial wars, which left their mark in the violent fluctuations recorded in the period of the Ten Years' War, from 1868 to 1878, and in the peak reached during the war of independence between 1895 and 1898. The last of these two wars had catastrophic consequences for the capital of the future republic. A comparison of the death rate during the period preceding the war of independence with that prevailing during the fighting, reveals the extent of the tragedy in no uncertain terms. The death rate went up two and a half times, from about thirty per thousand to seventy-two.

From this exceptional case, one should not conclude that war has played a very significant role as far as the overall death rate is concerned. No single Latin-American country has escaped such violence; revolutions as well as civil and international wars have been frequent, fostering the impression that Latin America is an unstable area. However regrettable such incidents may be, and however numerous the casualties, their effects were not very great on a national scale, except in the above-mentioned cases of Paraguay, Mexico, and Cuba. The death rate is basically linked to the problem of public health and sanitation.

Despite the hopes raised by the discovery of vaccination, the measures taken against infectious diseases during the nineteenth century were largely ineffective as was said in the previous chapter. It is very obvious that Havana in the last decades of the century had not managed to eradicate smallpox, for instance. Even more, other diseases—cholera and yellow fever—took the place of those that were brought under control.

Yellow fever was not new to the continent, but the areas affected had widened. The *Aedes Aegypti* mosquito had been established for a long time on the warm, humid coastlines of America, and the disease transmitted by it had become endemic. Havana, for example, was always under menace, experiencing seven outbreaks in the period shown in figure 6. However, the effects of these were not so catastrophic as those of cholera and smallpox. The death rate usually showed an increase of between 5 percent and 25 percent over the normal yearly figures, that is, a lower death toll than that caused by the other two diseases. Nevertheless, the repeated yellow fever epidemics did reduce the population and weaken it. In European and

American ports, that had previously been spared, its unexpected appearance had disastrous results. Increased maritime trade spread the fever to the south of Spain, Portugal, Italy, and France, as well as to ports on the eastern seaboard of the U.S.A. It reached Rio de Janeiro in its progress southward, and shortly afterward, in 1857, Montevideo. It made its unwelcome appearance in Buenos Aires soon after, where, in 1871, the most serious attack recorded cost 13,600 lives in the space of four months. Chile was smitten two years later. It should not be forgotten that yellow fever was partially responsible for the failure of the first attempt to build the Panama Canal.

Because of the way in which the virus is spread from one person to another, isolation proved an effective countermeasure. Strict international vigilance, together with drastic measures taken by local authorities, succeeded in limiting the spread of epidemics. After the end of the last century, large cities were freed of severe attacks, but its eradication from those tropical areas where it was endemic was more difficult. A Cuban doctor, Finlay, identified the transmitting agent, and this brought about control of the disease. After persistent and costly campaigns, to which the Rockefeller Foundation generously contributed, yellow fever was banished step by step from the Caribbean, restoring the health and confidence of the people of the area. Sporadic outbreaks have continued until recently, but the struggle has now shown results for more than half a century. The low death rates of Cuba and Panama, which can be seen in table 5.12, are proof of the success of the campaigns against yellow fever and malaria.

Cholera did not appear in America until the nineteenth century. Its popular name, Asiatic cholera, clearly indicates its origin. Within Asia, it is endemic in Bengal. From there, it can be traced from India to the Mediterranean and Europe, whence it made its way to America. Four or five years after the first outbreak on the banks of the Ganges, it had reached the ports of the New World.

It differs from yellow fever in that outbreaks always started as a result of the introduction of the virus from Europe. The transmitting agent never managed to establish itself in any part of America in such a way as to spread from that focus of infection to the whole continent. The seaports were the worst affected; since the infection came by sea, the coastal areas were particularly vulnerable. But distance and poor communications tended to discourage its spread throughout the continent, although outbreaks appeared inland in urban centers. Quarantine and other international health precautions controlled its spread toward the end of the last century much more effectively than was the case with yellow fever.

Since cholera is an episodic and primarily urban disease, the memory it leaves behind is worse than it might deserve, compared with the stealthy and persistent destructive action of such infections as dysentery, measles, scarlet fever, typhoid, tuberculosis, and malaria. These diseases seldom reached epidemic proportions, but were continuously present, especially in rural areas, where hygiene and medical care were inadequate. These widespread and persistent maladies, cut short the lives of vast numbers of people, especially children. Their disappearance, as a consequence of improved conditions of health and standards of living, seems to have had more far reaching effects than the eradication of yellow fever and cholera.

It is not surprising, consequently, that the capital cities were the first to introduce the changes that led to a fall in the death rate. One after another, early in this century, Latin-American cities built water mains and sewage systems. Municipal improvements made the cities look smarter and brighter and improved public hygiene. Social services became more widely available, but hospitals were provided only in the most highly populated areas. Here and there, preventive medicine began to take its place alongside the curative variety. Moreover, improvements in communications could at least guarantee regular food supplies to the markets, even if they could not ensure a better diet or make food available to those most in need. The death rate consequently went down, leading to longer life expectancy, particularly for young children.

In due course progress could advance beyond the city limits, for with a generally satisfactory standard of living, health measures could be extended to country districts. Argentina had a lower death rate than any other country in Latin America, with the exception of Uruguay. It should be remembered that Argentina's national figures cover backward areas, which Uruguay, more homogeneous though less extensive, does not have. The death rates indicated in table 5.12 compare favorably with European figures; in fact they are lower than those of the Iberian Peninsula, Italy, and central and eastern Europe. In addition, life expectancy at birth in Argentina went up from 32.96 years in the period 1869–95, to 48.65 between 1913 and 1914 (Somoza, 1971a). Mexico, Brazil, and Chile were not to achieve such a figure until forty years later.

The countries of the River Plate were also leading in another field, which other areas were to follow later. Shortly after the reduc-

tion in the death rate, the fertility rate itself declined. Recent research carried out jointly by the Instituto di Tella and CELADE
make possible an accurate account of how this came about. The phenomenon still shows up in the 1960 Argentine census. The large
number of married or widowed women of over eighty, whose reproductive period had concluded at the end of the first decade of the
century, had had 4.39 live children each. Those aged fifty to fifty-
four had had only 2.95. The latter had been at the peak of their reproductive cycle thirty years later than the first group and, when the
census was taken, had already produced all the children they were
ever going to have. Thus, in three decades, the fertility rate had gone
down by one-third (Lattes, 1967). The crude birth rates express
the same fall in a more abstract manner between the periods 1900–
1904 and 1930–34. (For the latter date see table 6.3 in the following chapter.)

The fertility rate continued to go down until approximately
1943. Since then it has remained stationary, both in Argentina and
Uruguay. In figure 7 one can see the parallel course followed by the
Uruguayan birth rate: a sustained drop for half a century, then a
leveling off, with perhaps a slight recovery at the end. The crude
reproduction rate (that is, the number of daughters born to each
woman of childbearing age at the time or, in short, the number of
future mothers) fluctuated after that date at around 1.4, with some
slight variations between Argentina and Uruguay. The replacement
of the generations was assured in both countries, since this only requires a rate around 1.0; but no great population expansion was to
be expected.

The contraction of the fertility rate was partially due to foreign
women. These either brought with them practices and ideas from
Mediterranean Europe, or managed to secure for themselves a higher
place on the social ladder than was achieved by the majority of
Argentine women, thus reaching socioeconomic levels that might
have helped to explain the difference. Whatever the reason may be—
cultural, material, or both—the fact is that the fertility rate was
originally higher among native Argentines than among women of
foreign extraction.

The 1895 census also recorded differences between the women
of Buenos Aires and those living in the provinces of the interior
(Somoza, 1968). The women of Cuyo produced one-third more
children than did those of the capital (966 children under the age of
four per thousand women in the provinces of Mendoza, San Juan,

Rate per thousand

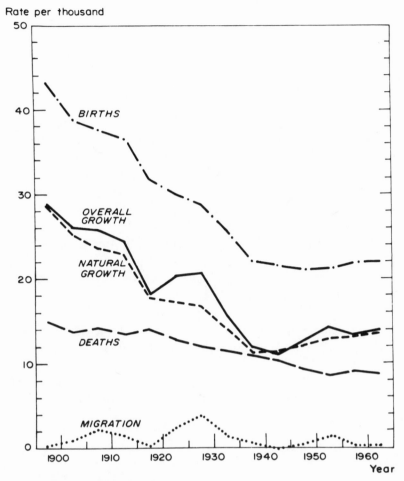

FIGURE 7. Uruguay, 1895–1964: birth, death, migration, and growth rates. (Source: Rothman, 1971.)

and San Luis, as against 711 in Buenos Aires); the women living on the Patagonian frontier had 1,110 children in that age group, or almost an additional half as many as the women in the Federal Capital.

Thus residence in town or country also brought differences. Provinces are always more fertile than big cities, as just shown, but even within the latter there were notable contrasts according to location. The analysis of the Federal Capital census of 1936 carried out by Recchini (1969) is particularly revealing. In 1936, Nueva Chicago, a working-class district, had a fertility rate 46 percent higher than that of Barrio Norte, an upper-class residential area. So far as young women were concerned, the differences between districts were higher, to as much as double. In fact, as soon as the second decade of the twentieth century the upper classes of Buenos Aires began to change their approach toward fertility and had fewer children than working-class women.

Coincidental with this stabilization of the fertility rate, the country tended to become more homogeneous. Argentina and Uruguay enjoyed the highest socioeconomic standards in the region and became quite urbanized. The great differences between provinces and different city districts tended to disappear. The place of origin or residence of the mother ceased to matter. The River Plate area prided itself on having achieved standards comparable with those in the more developed countries and on having followed a course parallel to that of Europe (Bunge, 1940).

This repeated reference to the cities of Latin America as the initiators of changes in vital standards brings us to the question of urbanization. In table 5.13, we have endeavored to summarize the extent of urbanization about the year 1900. The data are taken from the censuses nearest to that date or, when this is not available, from the most reliable official or private estimates at our disposal. None of the information is quite as accurate as that of recent years, but at

TABLE 5.13 Population Living in Cities with More Than 10,000 Inhabitants, c. 1900. Size and Rank of Capital Cities (all population figures in thousands)

Country	Date	Total Population	Cities					
			over 100,000			20,000–99,999		
			No.	Pop.	%	No.	Pop.	%
Argentina[a]	1895	3,955	1	664	16.8	7	294	7.4
Bolivia[a]	1900	1,816		—		5	132	7.3
Brazil	1890	14,334	4	825	5.8	11	394	2.8
Chile[a]	1895	2,696	2	379	14.1	4	135	5.0
Colombia	1905	4,144	1	117	2.9	6	199	4.8
Costa Rica	1892	243		—		1	30	12.3
Cuba[a]	1899	1,573	1	236	15.0	5	157	9.9
Ecuador	1889	1,272		—		3	115	9.0
Guatemala[a]	1893	1,501		—		4	140	9.3
Honduras	1901	544		—		1	24	4.3
Mexico[a]	1900	13,607	2	446	3.3	21	816	6.0
Paraguay[a]	1886	330		—		1	25	7.5
Peru[a]	1876	2,622	1	101	3.9	2	63	2.4
Puerto Rico[a]	1899	953		—		2	60	6.3
Salvador	1892	703		—		2	56	8.0
Uruguay	1900	936	1	268	28.7		—	
Venezuela[a]	1891	2,222		—		4	189	8.5

[a]Census data.
[b]Excluding rural parishes within the federal district.

least it suggests a relative size for each city and allows valid conclusions. Nicaragua, Panama, Haiti, and the Dominican Republic have been omitted from the list for lack of reliable statistics.

This table on urbanization in Latin America distinguishes between cities of three different sizes: those with over 100,000 inhabitants, those with between 20,000 and 99,999, and those with between 10,000 and 19,999. Under these three categories there are also specified the number of centers there were, and what proportion of each country's population lived in each type. The information starts, of course, with the name of the country concerned, the date of the census or estimate, and the overall population in that year. On the right is noted the proportion of citizens living in cities of over 10,000 inhabitants, that is, the true urban population. Then there follows the name of the capital city, its ranking in comparison with other capitals in Latin America, the number of its inhabitants, and the percentage of the total population which this represents. For reasons of space, the absolute figures are expressed in thousands.

To sum up, of the seventeen nations listed, eight had cities with more than 100,000 inhabitants. Of these, only Buenos Aires, and perhaps Rio de Janeiro, had more than half a million. Except for

10,000–19,999			% over 10,000	Capital	Rank	Pop.	%
No.	Pop.	%					
9	117	2.9	27.1	Buenos Aires	1	664	16.8
1	14	0.7	8.0	La Paz	11	53	2.9
19	339	2.4	10.9	Rio de Janeiro	2	430[b]	3.0
6	74	2.8	21.8	Santiago	4	256	9.5
5	72	1.7	9.4	Bogotá	8	117	2.9
3	39	16.0	28.4	San José	15	30	12.3
7	90	5.7	30.7	Havana	6	236	15.0
4	42	3.3	12.3	Quito	12	47	3.7
9	103	6.8	16.9	Guatemala	10	72	4.8
2	22	4.0	8.4	Tegucigalpa	17	23	4.3
35	467	3.4	12.7	Mexico City	3	345	2.5
2	30	9.1	16.5	Asunción	16	25	7.5
2	31	1.2	7.4	Lima	7	101	3.9
1	15	1.6	7.9	San Juan	14	32	3.4
5	52	7.4	15.4	San Salvador	13	33	4.7
1	13	1.4	30.0	Montevideo	5	268	28.7
23	316	14.2	22.8	Caracas	9	72	3.3

Brazil, Chile, and Mexico, which had developed secondary centers with more than 100,000 inhabitants (Salvador da Bahia, Recife, São Paulo, Valparaíso, and Puebla), in each country there was usually only one city that stood out well above the others: the capital. This macrocephalic tendency is evident in Uruguay and, to a lesser degree, in Argentina and Cuba. Montevideo had, in fact, no less than 28.7 percent of the total population of the country; Buenos Aires and Havana about one-sixth. However, as a general rule, it was usual for between 3 percent and 5 percent of the total population to live in the capital city. Managua, Panama, Santo Domingo, and Port-au-Prince, which are not included in the table, fall into this category.

Thus the capitals of Latin-American states were of quite modest dimensions at that time. Their size varied according to the importance of the country. Even the most populous—Buenos Aires, Rio de Janeiro, and Mexico City—were not in the same class as London, New York, or Paris; there followed a second category of capitals with a population of about a quarter of a million each, comprising Santiago de Chile, Montevideo, and Havana. Montevideo had managed to become the fifth largest, which was quite astonishing in view of the size of Uruguay itself. Of the large cities, four were flourishing commercial ports on the Atlantic seaboard: the capitals of Cuba, Brazil, Uruguay, and Argentina.

Of smaller size still were Lima, Bogotá, and, possibly, Caracas, and Guatemala City. The first two were only just over the 100,000 mark, while the other two were a little short of this figure. La Paz and Quito headed the list of the remainder, with a population in excess of 50,000. The rest had only between 20,000 and 30,000. This was typical of the size of capitals in Central America and the Caribbean, and is indicative of the obvious backwardness of these areas.

Rapid urban growth occurred only in the south. São Paulo, Montevideo, and Buenos Aires are the most outstanding examples of the spectacular advances made, all of which were effected late in the nineteenth century. Other cities also grew quickly, just fast enough to maintain their position high up on the list. Santiago de Chile and Bogotá, for example, multiplied approximately five times; Rio de Janeiro quadrupled its population, while Mexico City and Havana trebled theirs. The majority of the capital cities entered the twentieth century without any very spectacular growth. Lima, Quito,

La Paz, and Guatemala City had merely doubled their populations in the course of a century, and Caracas had not even done that.

The fact that the capital cities were small does not necessarily imply a lack of overall urbanization. Of cities in the second category indicated in table 5.13, that is, with populations between 20,000 and 99,999, there were 79 in the seventeen countries listed, including the capitals of the smaller republics; 134 cities fall into the third category, to which figure should be added a few in the countries omitted from the table. In general, a greater proportion of the population lived in cities of the second group than in the third. In Venezuela, however, centers with a population of less than 20,000 predominated.

It is not surprising that the majority of people were still living in the countryside or in rural communities. On the contrary, it is astonishing that several countries had managed to reach such an advanced stage of urbanization so early. Five countries—Argentina, Chile, Cuba, Uruguay, and Venezuela—had between 20 percent and 30 percent of their inhabitants living in towns and cities of over the 10,000 mark. But it by no means necessarily follows that a large number of cities and an extensive area of country imply a high concentration rate. Mexico had the highest number of such cities, 58, and Brazil had 34; but only 10 percent of the total population lived in them. The dimensions—size and number—and the intensity of the phenomenon do not correlate. The degree of urbanization depended rather on socioeconomic development. It is not by mere chance that the three most southerly countries and Cuba are among the most urbanized states. They have socioeconomic factors in common which are now familiar to us.

The influx of European immigrants, alterations in the death rate, incipient changes in the fertility rate, and the development of cities undermined the demographic structure that had prevailed since the upward trend started in the seventeenth century. The breakdown of the traditional order seemed to bring concrete correctives to unfavorable situations, but no one realized that this fact heralded a more widespread and more significant change.

VI

The Population Explosion

*H*ISTORY is the only one of the social sciences in which one does not have to endeavor to keep abreast of events, since by definition it deals with the past. The others rush to keep up with current events and run the risk of being aware of them too late. Irene Taeubner (1944) wrote as follows, a quarter of a century ago: "The problems of future population are less acute in the Western Hemisphere than in any other major region of the world. . . . Neither is the Malthusian pressure of a rapidly increasing population on limited resources a necessary characteristic of any portion of the New World." A few years before these words were printed, demographers changed from an attitude of confidence to one of consternation, and with good reason. Latin America's population was growing before their very eyes at an unprecedented rate. A greater proportion of food it produced was consumed locally, and economic expansion could not keep pace with the increasing demand for goods and employment opportunities.

The opinion of a person of the intellectual stature of Irene Taeubner was not an isolated one. Similar statements can be found in articles and conference papers of the time. In retrospect they are of historical value, since they were issued at a critical time, when a fundamental change was taking place in Latin America which scientists did not anticipate. The social sciences were very slow to see the change. The world became aware of what was happening in

Latin America only when the situation was already staring it in the face. Until that moment, Latin America's population appeared to be following the same path as that of the most advanced countries, though somewhat later in time. It was not easy to foresee the sudden leap forward that was to occur at a speed and on a scale never before experienced.

One phase in the growth of the population of Latin America came to an end about 1930, when the Great Depression put a stop to it. Some nations were more affected than others. The greater the degree of dependence on major world markets and the inflow of foreign investments, the greater the shock. The countries of Central America, the Caribbean, and the River Plate, together with Brazil and Chile, were the most vulnerable. Marriages and conceptions were postponed, and the birth rate went down in some cases by as much as 10 percent. Mexico, ignoring the world beyond its borders, was scarcely affected (Collver, 1968).

Once the crisis was over, the population of the area began to grow again, as can be seen in tables 6.1 and 6.2. In the first table the estimated size of the population of each country is recorded for every decade from 1940 to 1970. In most cases the figures are based on adjusted census data, with the exception of the last column, which is based on projections. When the definitive figures for the 1970s are available, they might be corrected. So far provisional information at hand shows only slight variations from the projected figures: Argentina and Chile had less than their projected number of inhabitants: 23.3 million and 9.2 million; Cuba, on the other hand, had more: 8.5 million. Meanwhile, generally speaking, the census results do confirm the accuracy of the estimates. Thanks to them, analysis can be brought up to date, instead of relinquishing it halfway through the current demographic phase. Table 6.2 records the annual growth rates computed from the preceding figures. The countries are grouped in accordance with the subregional classification already used above.

In the last three decades Latin America more than doubled its population, from 126 million to 277 million. In the last decade it increased by an average of 6,700,000 per year. This is the equivalent of adding to the region each year the combined populations of either three countries such as Uruguay, Paraguay, and Panama, or of Bolivia and Nicaragua together. The average annual growth rate in each period went up from 1.9 to 2.3 to 2.7 and finally to 2.8. No area the size of a continent has ever grown at such a rate before in the

TABLE 6.1 Total Population of the Countries of Latin America, 1940–1970
(in thousands)

	1940	1950	1960	1970
Continental Central America				
Mexico	19,815	26,640	36,046	50,718
Guatemala	2,201	3,024	3,965	5,282
El Salvador	1,633	1,922	2,512	3,441
Honduras	1,119	1,389	1,849	2,583
Nicaragua	893	1,133	1,501	2,021
Costa Rica	619	849	1,249	1,736
Panama	595	765	1,021	1,406
Subtotals	26,875	35,722	48,143	67,187
Caribbean				
Cuba	4,566	5,520	6,819	8,341
Puerto Rico	1,880	2,218	2,362	2,842
Dominican Republic	1,759	2,303	3,129	4,348
Haiti	2,825	3,380	4,138	5,229
Subtotals	11,030	13,421	16,448	20,760
Tropical South America				
Brazil	41,233	52,326	70,327	93,245
Colombia	9,077	11,629	15,877	22,160
Peru	6,681	7,968	10,024	13,586
Venezuela	3,710	5,330	7,741	10.755
Ecuador	2,586	3,225	4,323	6,028
Bolivia	2,508	3,013	3,696	4,658
Subtotals	65,795	83,491	111,988	150,432
Temperate South America				
Argentina	14,169	17,085	20,850	24,352
Chile	5,147	6,058	7,683	9,717
Uruguay	1,947	2,198	2,542	2,889
Paraguay	1,111	1,337	1,740	2,419
Subtotals	22,374	26.678	32,815	39,377
Totals for Latin America	126,074	159,312	209,394	277,756

SOURCE: CELADE, 1972.

history of the world, nor will one grow in the future if the projections made from now to the beginning of the twenty-first century are proved correct.

The subregion with the most rapid growth is no longer the temperate zone, as it was at the end of the last century and the beginning of this. The roles have been reversed, and the area that previously showed the slowest growth rate has now the fastest. Continental Central America's population has gone up roughly two and a half times, from 26 million to 67 million. Since 1940 its growth rate has been consistently above the average in Latin America. In

TABLE 6.2 Average Annual Population Growth Rate over Four Decades, 1930–1970

	1930–40	1940–50	1950–60	1960–70
Continental Central America				
Mexico	1.8	2.9	3.0	3.4
Guatemala	2.1	3.2	2.7	2.8
El Salvador	1.2	1.6	2.7	3.2
Honduras	2.6	2.1	2.8	2.3
Nicaragua	1.8	2.4	2.8	2.9
Costa Rica	2.1	3.1	3.6	3.3
Panama	1.7	2.5	2.9	2.9
Subtotals	1.8	2.8	3.0	3.3
Caribbean				
Cuba	1.7	1.9	2.1	2.0
Puerto Rico	1.9	1.6	0.5	1.8
Dominican Republic	2.3	2.8	3.0	3.3
Haiti	1.5	1.8	2.0	2.1
Subtotals	1.8	1.9	2.0	2.3
Tropical South America				
Brazil	2.3	2.6	2.9	2.8
Colombia	2.1	2.5	3.1	3.3
Peru	1.6	1.6	2.3	3.0
Venezuela	2.3	2.6	3.7	3.2
Ecuador	1.8	2.2	2.9	3.3
Bolivia	1.5	1.9	2.0	2.3
Subtotals	2.0	2.3	2.8	2.9
Temperate South America				
Argentina	1.7	1.9	2.0	1.5
Chile	1.5	1.6	2.4	2.3
Uruguay	1.3	1.2	1.4	1.4
Paraguay	2.3	1.9	2.1	1.8
Subtotals	1.7	1.8	2.1	1.8
Totals for Latin America	1.9	2.3	2.7	2.8

SOURCE: Tables 5.11 and 6.1.

the last decade it has reached the very high figure of 3.3 percent per annum, a rate that would enable it to double its population in twenty years. The area has added the population of a country like Costa Rica to its total every year.

And it is precisely Costa Rica which shows the highest growth in the whole of Latin America, without the help of immigration. Between 1955 and 1960 the annual growth rate there was no less than 3.87 percent. In 1970 Costa Rica had twice as many inhabitants as it had twenty years before. Mexico and Guatemala were growing nearly as fast. The only country in the region which started to expand its population somewhat late was El Salvador, though it is now growing so fast that its neighbors are apprehensive.

Tropical South America comes after continental Central America in upgrowth, jumping from 65 million to 150 million, more than double, in thirty years. Its general growth rate is just over the average for Latin America. Venezuela was the most dynamic country in the area, doubling its population in the last twenty years, though admittedly with the assistance of immigrants from Europe. In Brazil immigration has, on the contrary, been of little significance, in view of the semicontinental dimensions of the country. Colombia has gained proportionately even more than Brazil, and without any influx of migrants. Its growth, in fact, has been such as to cause an overflow eastward into Venezuela. Lastly, there are two countries whose expansion has started somewhat late: Peru, which is now growing rapidly, and Bolivia, which has not yet got into its stride.

In the Caribbean, the Dominican Republic's population is increasing as fast as that of Mexico, but without the economic resources of the latter. Cuba and Puerto Rico are quite restrained, by Latin-American standards. Puerto Rico's increase is comparatively slow because hundreds of thousands of its inhabitants have migrated. Haiti is somewhat off the mark, having quite a time lag to make up if it is to follow the pattern set in Spanish- and Portuguese-speaking America. The Caribbean countries as a whole have not quite doubled their population in thirty years, increasing from eleven million to twenty million.

Finally, in temperate South America the growth rate is lower, about 1.8. Population has gone up from about twenty-two million to thirty-nine, an increase of approximately 75 percent. However, this figure disguises big differences within the area: the population of Paraguay, for example, is increasing very rapidly, like the other tropical countries in the continent; that of Chile is expanding, but not overly fast, while Argentina and Uruguay are slow. The demographic curve in both countries shows a sort of ridge from the forties to the fifties, owing to the arrival of European migrants. This immigration did not last, however, and the country's population expansion has depended basically on natural growth.

The population explosion in Latin America, in short, did not affect the South American countries with a temperate climate, for their population had undergone a demographic transformation earlier; but it hit Central America, the Caribbean, and tropical South America. The explosion was most serious in Mexico, most of Central America, the Dominican Republic, the north of South America, Brazil, and Paraguay. Secondary charges went off several years later in Haiti, El Salvador, and the Andean countries—Ecuador, Peru, and

Bolivia. In El Salvador and on the Andean altiplano the peak effect has not yet been reached. In Puerto Rico the bomb was defused early by means of emigration and birth control.

The official birth and death rates in Venezuela will serve as an example to show how the explosion occurred. The results can be seen in figure 8. In the north of South America the birth and death rates followed a parallel course except for a few ups and downs, until 1935. The birth rate showed a slight tendency to move upward. The death rate fluctuated at just over twenty per thousand, the birth rate at just below thirty. For every thousand inhabitants of the republic living under the dictatorial regime of General Gómez, eight new children were gained by the group. From that time on, as if the people felt relieved by the tyrant's death, the birth rate began to increase rapidly until 1955, when it leveled out and showed no immediate tendency to fall again. The death rate appears in the graph to be descending in an almost straight line to attain its present level. The pressures that seemed to keep the two fluctuating rates within fixed bounds relaxed, and the natural growth rate speeded up. The difference between the birth and death rates, which had allowed an increase of eight new citizens per thousand per year, increased to thirty-six between 1953 and 1963, that is, four and a half times greater.

The population explosion in Latin America as a whole is, as in Venezuela, the result of a sudden fall in the death rate and a lively increase in the fertility rate, caused by the relaxation of the control mechanisms that used to prevail. Before examining in detail each of these two contributing factors in the sections that follow, let us examine tables 6.3 and 6.4. In the first of these both components of the demographic movement are given for a series of years, while the second shows the present position. Table 6.3 deals only with the ten countries we have been examining in recent pages and by way of illustration gives the relevant statistics for the first five years of each decade of the 1930s, 1940s, and 1950s. Table 6.4 shows the most recent calculations concerning the period 1965–70 for all the countries of Latin America. Comments will be found in the pages that follow.

THE LOWER THE DEATH RATE,
THE GREATER LIFE EXPECTANCY

Latin America has no reason to rest on its laurels for its achievements in lowering the death rate in the last few decades. The figure

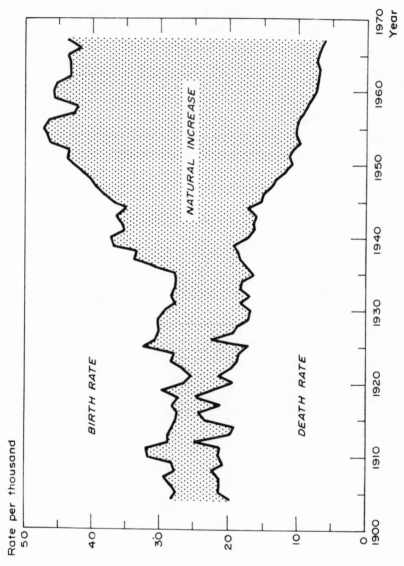

FIGURE 8. The population explosion in Venezuela: birth and death rates, 1904–1967. (Source: Carrillo Batalla, 1967; U.N., 1969.)

TABLE 6.3 Birth (B) and Death (D) Rates in Ten Countries of Latin America

		1930–1934	1940–1944	1950–1954
Uruguay	B	25.8	21.6	21.2
	D	11.5	10.3	8.5
Argentina	B	30.9	26.1	26.1
	D	12.2	10.5	8.8
Cuba	B	31.3	31.9	30.4
	D	13.3	10.9	11.3
Panama	B	37.4	39.5	38.5
	D	15.1	12.7	9.1
Costa Rica	B	44.6	42.8	45.0
	D	21.5	17.4	10.7
Guatemala	B	46.2	45.2	50.9
	D	31.7	28.5	23.4
Mexico	B	44.1	43.8	45.0
	D	26.7	21.8	15.4
Venezuela	B	39.9	41.5	44.2
	D	21.9	18.8	12.3
Colombia	B	43.3	42.2	44.0
	D	22.5	20.3	18.4
Chile	B	40.2	38.3	37.0
	D	24.5	20.1	13.7

SOURCES: For Uruguay and Argentina, Rothman, 1971; for Cuba (1950–54), adjusted by González Quiñones and Debasa, 1970; for the remainder, Collver, 1965.

TABLE 6.4 Recent Statistics Concerning Birth, Death, and Growth Rates (annual rates 1965–1970 according to CELADE estimates)

	Births	Deaths	Growth
Argentina	23.0	8.7	15.4
Bolivia	43.8	19.0	23.7
Brazil	37.7	9.5	28.2
Chile	33.2	10.0	23.2
Colombia	44.6	10.6	34.0
Costa Rica	37.3	7.4	22.9
Cuba	27.3	7.5	19.8
Dominican Republic	48.5	14.7	33.8
Ecuador	44.9	11.4	33.5
Guatemala	43.5	15.1	28.4
Haiti	43.5	19.7	24.2
Honduras	49.0	16.9	33.6
Mexico	43.2	8.9	34.3
Nicaragua	46.0	16.7	29.3
Panama	40.5	8.4	32.1
Paraguay	44.6	10.7	33.9
Peru	41.8	11.1	30.7
Puerto Rico	26.7	6.6	15.4
Salvador (El)	46.9	12.9	32.9
Uruguay	21.2	9.0	12.2
Venezuela	40.9	7.8	33.1

SOURCE: CELADE, 1971.

of ten deaths per thousand inhabitants per year still leaves room for improvement. If this rate is compared with those of the most advanced countries, such as the U.S.S.R., the Scandinavian countries, and the U.S.A., it is clear that they have achieved significantly lower levels. This average figure for so vast an area as Latin America obviously conceals widely differing situations. The eleven countries of the area least favored in this regard have an average figure among them of 14.4. In some that are particularly backward, the figure is as high as 19 and 19.7 (Bolivia and Haiti, respectively), as can be seen in table 6.4. The average for the ten most favored countries is as low as 8.3, Puerto Rico, Cuba, and Costa Rica having the lowest figures. To raise Haiti to the standards achieved by countries only a few sea miles distant from it would seem, so far, to be a slow and difficult task.

If, however, one were to compare Latin America's levels with other parts of the Third World instead of with those of the most highly developed countries, Latin Americans can feel better. Unfortunately, a large number of nations in Africa and Asia have crude death rates near those of Bolivia and Haiti. A figure twice that of the Latin American average is frequent, though even there, as in the rest of the world, the death rates are definitely falling. By comparing the present situation in Latin America with that prevailing in the other developing continents, one can appreciate how far the New World has advanced in a short space of time. When the improvement started, the death rate was approximately that experienced by the most backward Asian countries today.

If Latin America suffered from disasters of unparalleled intensity and scope during the period of discovery and conquest, it is experiencing the reverse in the twentieth century. Unprecedented progress is being made in the control of fatal diseases. Starting at the beginning of this century in urban areas, the River Plate, and parts of the Caribbean, this campaign took several decades to really get into its stride and show far-reaching results. At the end of World War I the decline in the death rate slowed down; it speeded up again in the 1930s and then, after 1940, fell everywhere at an astonishing pace. One can follow this trend up to the present day in tables 6.3 and 6.4.

In most countries the rate fell from the Haitian level to that prevailing today. In approximately a quarter of a century the pattern altered from the old traditional one to the modern one. The drop was spectacular: in Mexico, for example, it fell from 21.8 per thousand inhabitants to 8.9, in the period 1940–44; in Venezuela from

18.8 to 7.8; and in Guatemala from 28.5 to 15. The countries that had taken the lead, like Argentina, Uruguay, and Cuba, are trying to reduce their rates still further, but as their efforts are spread over a longer period, their achievements do not seem as spectacular as those in tropical America.

Without denying the practical utility of crude death rates because of the ease with which they can be calculated, recent refinements in demographic techniques have restricted their value for professional demographers. When one is endeavoring to trace the historical evolution of a country or region, or when international comparisons are being made, the systematic computation of life expectancy now competes with them in relevance. In the specifically Latin-American context, life expectancy estimates overcome the difficulties created by statistical deficiencies. It is relatively unusual to have available both a national census and vital statistics. For example, there are countries such as Uruguay which keep quite reliable records of birth and deaths, but which unfortunately have not held regular censuses. For more than half a century, from 1908 to 1963, Uruguay held no census. However, the reverse is more usual, where a country has the administrative machinery capable of holding a census from time to time, but does not keep regular, reliable registry records. Working from information on the age composition of a given population provided by a census, the demographer calculates the life tables. From them he works out the life expectancy rates for men and women. Successive censuses make apparent any alterations that have occurred in the intervening period.

A number of isolated experiments in this field, carried out originally in Brazil, Chile, and Mexico, have been followed by the work of Arriaga (1968a), who compiled a historical series of life expectancy covering seventeen countries, the ones omitted being Argentina, Uruguay, Cuba, and Puerto Rico. This study is one of the most important recent contributions to the historical demography of Latin America. An additional advantage is that the book lays the foundations for later analyses in depth, as the author himself has shown (Arriaga and Davis, 1969, and Arriaga, 1970a and 1970b).

After computing the relevant life table for each census and assessing the resulting life expectancies, Arriaga preferred to estimate the values for the years ending in zero, since the censuses were neither simultaneous nor at regular intervals. The object of this is to facilitate comparison. We will ignore the figures relative to the late nineteenth century and early twentieth, as they were based on limited examples. Unfortunately, life-expectancy figures for Costa Rica, Guatemala, Paraguay, and Brazil before 1890 are no more than rough estimates of the situation in Latin America. Let us concentrate, therefore, on the period between 1920 and 1960, since this information seems more adequate. In table 6.5, where the values are

TABLE 6.5 Life Expectancy for the Last Two Generations of Latin Americans

Year	Life expectancy	Years added in a decade	Percentage of change
1920	31.1	2.2	7.6
1930	33.6	2.5	8.0
1940	38.0	4.4	13.1
1950	46.4	8.4	22.1
1960	55.8	9.4	20.2

SOURCE: Arriaga and Davis, 1969.

summarized, one can see that in the course of two generations the number of years a Latin American could expect to live increased from 31.1 to 55.8. This would imply that where a married couple in 1920 might hope that their newborn child would enter the fourth decade of his life, another couple in 1960 would fondly imagine that their child would reach old age. But the reality was somewhat different. At the first date mentioned, large numbers of children died when only a few months old and the survivors lived well past the age of thirty-one; by the second date, fewer children were lost in infancy and nearly everyone reached sixty.

This magnificent increase in the life span coincides chronologically with the abrupt drop in the death rate. In separate columns in table 6.5 are shown the number of years added per decade and the percentage increase this represented. It is obvious that the life-expectancy rate went up rapidly after 1930. The death rates and life expectancy are not checks one on the other, but are complementary. The number of years a man may expect to live is intimately linked with the death rate for the period. They are different aspects of the same problem. Of the two types of calculation, the death rates have not been submitted to a reconstructive effort similar to that which Arriaga has applied to life tables or Collver to the crude birth rates.

Although incomplete, the series makes it possible to determine the internal rate of change and compare it with experience elsewhere. Above all, one should note the existence of two groups of countries in this regard. In table 6.6, the countries are listed in two columns in descending life-expectancy order. Thus the ten countries ranking highest in the list have, on average, a life expectancy twelve years

TABLE 6.6 Life Expectancy at Birth, 1965–1970 (both sexes)

Puerto Rico	71.2	Colombia	58.5
Uruguay	69.2	Peru	58.0
Argentina	67.4	Ecuador	57.2
Cuba	66.8	El Salvador	54.9
Costa Rica	65.1	Dominican Republic	52.1
Venezuela	63.7	Guatemala	50.9
Panama	63.4	Nicaragua	49.9
Mexico	62.4	Honduras	48.9
Chile	60.9	Bolivia	45.3
Brazil	60.6	Haiti	44.5
Paraguay	59.3		

SOURCE: CELADE, 1971.

higher than that of the remaining eleven: 65 as against 52.7. These figures differ slightly from those contained in table 6.7 (columns C and D).

The life expectancies of four groups of nations, two in Europe and two in Latin America, are noted in table 6.7. Two show the highest life-expectancy figures in each region, and two the lowest. In European group A, Arriaga (1970a) includes Great Britain, France, the Scandinavian countries, Holland, and Switzerland; in group B he includes the remainder except for Germany; among the Latin-American countries in group C, those with the highest life expectancies, are Brazil, Colombia, Costa Rica, Chile, Mexico, and Panama. Guatemala, Nicaragua, and the Dominican Republic are the only ones representing those countries with low life expectancies, in group D. Groups C and D do not provide such a wide sample as is provided in table 6.6, but they in no way contradict it.

At first glance, it is obvious that the conditions in all four groups are improving simultaneously, though not at the same pace. To make this fact clearer, the relationships shown in the last four columns have

TABLE 6.7 Life Expectancy, 1920–1960

	Life expectancy in years Europe		Latin America		Relationships between the groups expressed as a percentage			
	Most advanced countries A	Remainder B	High life exp. countries C	Lower life exp. countries D	A–B B	A–C C	A–D D	C–D D
1920	55.0	46.1	33.0	25.3	21.4	66.6	117.3	30.4
1930	59.9	50.9	36.1	27.1	17.6	65.9	121.0	33.2
1940	64.8	56.0	40.2	33.0	15.7	61.6	96.3	21.8
1950	68.8	63.4	48.9	40.7	8.5	40.6	69.0	23.4
1960	71.8	68.0	58.2	50.4	5.5	25.0	42.4	15.4

SOURCE: Columns A–D, Arriaga, 1970a.

been calculated. In 1920, seven years and eight months separated those in group C from those in group D, and this difference represented 30.4 percent of group D's life expectancy. By 1960, seven years and ten months represented a difference of only 15.4 percent The backward countries were advancing more rapidly than the more favored ones. The gap between the two Latin-American groups was narrowing.

All the less developed countries progressed at this time faster than the more' developed ones. In general, progress slows down as the logistic growth curve approaches its highest point, and this example is no exception to the rule. Groups B, C, and D in table 6.7 were advancing rapidly when group A was showing signs of slowing down. In 1960, the gap which had separated the two European groups (A and B) fifty years earlier had been narrowed from 21.4 to 5.5, that is, to one-quarter of the original figure. During the same period, both Latin-American groups had been moving closer to the level of the European nations: from 66.6 they went down to 25, from 117 to 42.4, that is, to one-third. In its own way Latin America has been involved in a broader drive. The aim is to catch up with the more favored nations.

Groups A and B achieved in about 1930 and 1940 figures which groups C and D did not attain until 1960. The most advanced countries of Latin America were then thirty years behind the countries of northwest Europe, while the most backward ones were fifty years behind. Comparing the two Latin-American groups with central and southern Europe, we find that the discrepancy was not so great: just over fifteen years in one case and thirty in the other. Somoza (1971*a*) has specifically demonstrated how the male and female life-expectancy figures of Argentina since 1880 run parallel with those of Italy. One may therefore presume that, if present trends continue, all four groups will eventually achieve the same levels. To use another analogy, one could say that the death rate today in Central America, the Andean countries of South America, and parts of the Caribbean area approximates more closely that of the *belle époque* in western Europe than that of the *ancien régime*.

A general outline of these changes having been given, one must explain what caused them. One reason hardly needs mentioning. The death rate went down as standards of living improved, incomes grew, and fatal diseases became less prevalent. Nevertheless, it has been thought worthwhile to confirm this by an examination of figure 9. In the vertical coordinate the life expectancies are recorded, and

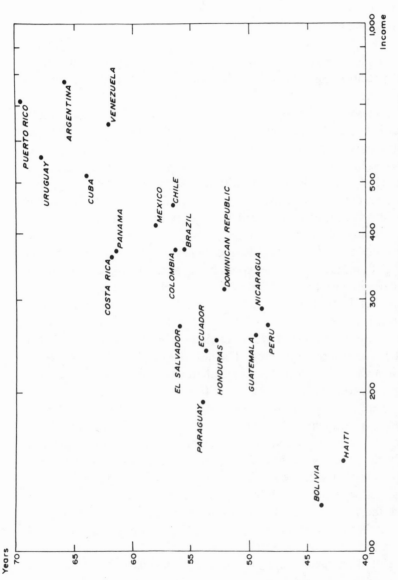

FIGURE 9. Life expectancy and per capita income in Latin America, 1960. (Sources: Arriaga, 1968; Somoza, 1971*b*; CEPAL.)

in the horizontal one, the per capita income in dollars, expressed in semilogarithmic measurements. Each country is represented by the point of intersection of two lines. The countries with higher life expectancies are among those with high annual incomes, that is, between $500 and $800. These are Cuba, Uruguay, Venezuela, Puerto Rico, and Argentina. The majority of countries have medium life expectancies, forming a second category, with incomes ranging from $250 to $500. Last of all come Bolivia and Haiti, with exceedingly low values.

The positive correlation between both variables is undeniable. Nevertheless, Paraguay and Costa Rica, with per capita incomes considerably below those of Peru and Chile, have higher life expectancies. They are smaller and consequently more homogeneous entities. However, economic conditions being equal, the results may vary according to the degree to which equality of income distribution is achieved, and the relative efficiency of public health measures.

The measurement of life expectancy is a brief, direct, and efficient, but also somewhat cold and dispassionate, way of expressing a mass of events and human experiences. A fascinating story of scientific experimentation and the persistent exercise of professional expertise lies behind each year of extended life. A vast amount of literature records the way in which the pathogenic germs of various diseases were identified and the medicines and treatments needed to combat them were discovered. The administrative framework within which medicine developed is also well known: offices, programs, staff, finance, instruction. It is easy to list the dates when the bacilli or viruses of tuberculosis, diphtheria, typhoid fever, exanthematic typhus, pneumonia, brucellosis, dysentery, not to mention cholera, yellow fever, and many other diseases, were identified in the laboratory, and the dates of the discoveries of the remedies and when they were first used. Even if it were restricted to Latin America alone, this chapter of the history of medicine would fill many pages, and however detailed the account, the reader's curiosity would be only partially satisfied. We would still not know how effective were skill and knowledge in the field.

Health statistics ought to be able to tell us precisely how the disappearance or gradual retreat of certain types of diseases affected the general death rate or extended the overall life span. No historical studies of this have yet been made, let alone on a continental scale. All the information available concerning the retreat of diseases is no more than generalizations that are probably correct, or analogies drawn from what is known to have happened in other countries or in other regions; there is very little direct observation. The main reason for this is the relative unreliability of the data on the causes of death. The United Nations' *Demographic Yearbook* for 1966 notes that, in Guatemala, only 18 percent of the deaths recorded for the previous year had death certificates signed by a doctor, in the Dominican Republic and El Salvador, 21 percent, and in Ecuador, 39 percent. The proportions in other countries were higher: Panama 55 percent, Costa Rica 58 percent, Colombia 60 percent, Mexico 69 percent, and Chile 77 percent. The *Yearbook* gives no information for other countries in Latin America, but we know from earlier volumes that Nicaragua, Paraguay, and Peru would have been no different in this respect. Add to this the number of deaths of indeterminate cause as well as underregistration, and it is not surprising that no general and reliable study has yet been made on the changing impact of the more important diseases and still less on how the death rate fell. Only in one case has this already been done.

Chile has provided the material for the first study on the changes that have occurred in the causes of death. This is not surprising, for Chile has had a National Health Service for a long time, and its statistical records have been more efficiently kept than those of any other country in Latin America. Figure 10, taken from Behm Rosas and Gutiérrez (1967), shows on two graphs, using a logarithmic scale, the changing mortality-cause pattern in that country between 1937 and 1963. The two graphs make quite clear the structural change which occurred in the relatively short span of a quarter of a century. In the left-hand graph, the death rate appears to fall from the beginning of the period covered, and particularly abruptly since 1945. It was then that antibiotics and many modern drugs became widely available. Within a few years, deaths from infectious diseases such as pneumonia, tuberculosis, infantile diarrhea, and so forth were reduced to proportions that have remained constant since then. Between 1939 and 1941, Chile seemed to be, so far as its mortality rate was concerned, close to the position of Great Britain in 1930. With the aid of antibiotics but no economic development, Chile covered in twenty years as much ground as Great Britain in fifty. The decline in infectious diseases increased also the incidence of cardiovascular diseases, of cancer, and of other maladies that affect modern societies, not to mention accidental deaths, which are constantly on the increase.

If sulfonamides and penicillins destroy viruses and bacteria, in-

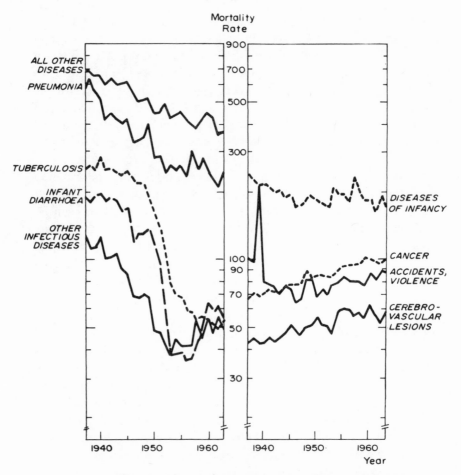

FIGURE 10. Mortality by groups of causes, Chile, 1937–1963.
(Sources: Behm Rosas and Gutiérrez, 1967.)

secticides attack the species that transmit them. The widespread use of insecticides after World War II is only second in importance to the spread of antibiotics. Within a brief space of time, DDT made inhabitable millions of square kilometers of land that had previously been of very limited use. Between 1911 and 1915, for example, 527 out of every 100,000 inhabitants of the Venezuelan llanos died of malaria each year. In 1941–45, less than half that number died, but 214 was still a sufficiently high number for travelers to avoid the area if possible (Gabaldón, 1956). Toward the end of 1945, Venezuela began an intensive national campaign, and all houses were sprayed with DDT. Nine years later, the country requested the World Health

Organization to include the greater part of the llanos in the list of those areas from which malaria had been eradicated.

Years ago, Brazil had eight million and Colombia one million square kilometers affected by malaria. Thirty million people lived in the first area and seven million in the other. The coasts of Mexico also suffered from it. As late as 1955, one in every 125,000 inhabitants in the country died of it. At the same time Peru, among the Andean nations, Guatemala, El Salvador, and Nicaragua among those in Central America, and the Dominican Republic in the Caribbean, were still subject to the scourge. By the late 1950s it looked as though eradication campaigns had been successful; the greater part of the populations concerned could be considered safe, and only a very few residual pockets of infection were left. Thus one of the commonest afflictions of the tropics became no longer a threat.

At the same time that it disposed of the *Anopheles* mosquito, the carrier of malaria, the massive spraying of DDT over forests, plains, and marshes had subsidiary effects, eliminating other harmful insects. Ordinary flies, which spread so many diseases-carrying germs, were also destroyed. This reduced sharply diarrhoea and enteritis thus saving the lives of tens of thousands of children. Besides these, many other transmissible diseases were either eradicated or controlled as a result of the combined attack of insecticides and antibiotics. Examining the tables in the *Demographic Yearbooks* in which the fifty standardized causes of deaths are listed, it will be seen that many countries record blanks where figures for infectious and contagious diseases ought to be given. For quite a number of other countries such diseases are however still the most important causes of death, though to a lesser extent than formerly.

So far as the causes of death are concerned, Latin-American countries can be divided into two groups: those for which, like Chile, the major causes are now heart disease, cancer, and accidents; and those which still have not managed to do away completely with the more traditional ways of dying. In 1959, Cubans and Uruguayans died mainly from varieties of heart disease; Dominicans and Paraguayans, from gastroenteritis (Gabaldón, 1965).

These two varieties of ways of dying also correspond to different age groups. Heart disease and cancer are mainly afflictions of maturity and old age, while infectious diseases mainly attack children. If the first type is more prevalent, those who are getting on in life are the main victims. The cause of death differs according to age. The control of infectious and contagious diseases has primarily benefited children from birth to the age of five; the death rates for infants and children have gone down.

If infant and general mortality rates were traced alongside each other, one would find that at the time the drop was faster both moved together. Deaths of children under five in many nations accounted for between one-half and one-third of the total. As this age is the most vulnerable, it was the one to show most marked improvement. When modern drugs were introduced infant mortality fell sharply bringing down the general death rate. In a comparison of the infant death rates in table 6.8 with that of the population as a whole (table

TABLE 6.8 Infant Mortality Rate in Nine Countries, 1920–1967 (per thousand live births)

	1920–24	1930–34	1940–44	1950–54	1967
Argentina	100	82	74	65	58
Cuba	135	76	61	—	44[a]
Panama	110	101	81	60	43
Costa Rica	174	160	131	88	62
Guatemala	142	125	127	110	94[b]
Mexico	178	142	105	92	63
Venezuela	153	130	120	88	41
Colombia	159	155	143	125	78
Chile	250	212	170	119	92

[a]1966. [b]1968.

SOURCE: Collver, 1965; for 1967, U.N., 1969, except for Cuba, Perez de la Riva, 1967.

6.3), one can trace the broad relationship between the two over the last fifty years. It will be appreciated that the deaths of children under the age of twelve months run more or less parallel to the overall annual death rates. At the end of the period the infant mortality rate does not fall so rapidly, or rather, the fall in the death rate for other age groups proceeds faster.

Health care yielded remarkable results when it adopted foreign innovations. But to reduce infant mortality further, improvements in living conditions were needed. Chile again can serve as an example The infant death rate in figure 11 is shown to be in inverse relationship to the number of births occurring in hospitals and to the increase in the per capita gross national product. In other words, the greater the national income and the better the obstetrical attention in hospitals, the lower the infant mortality rate. The time span covered is 1940–68 (Behm Rosas et al., 1970). It is obvious that the static deathrate figures after 1953 coincide with a stagnant period so far as economic growth is concerned. The decline in the death rate that

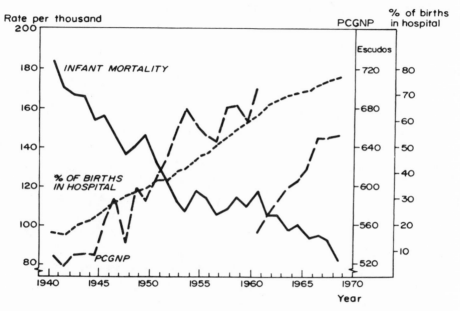

FIGURE 11. Infant mortality rates, per capita gross national product (PCGNP), and percentage of births in hospitals, Chile, 1940–1968. (PCGNP in 1961 escudos. Official figures of CORFO and ODEPLAN. The PCGNP line is discontinuous because of a change in the method of calculation. Source: Behm Rosas et al., 1970, and *Actas de la Conferencia Regional Latinoamericana de Poblacción*, Vol. I. Reproduced by permission of El Colegio de México.)

began about 1960 can be linked with the resumption of economic progress. It should be noted in passing that the lack of continuity in the line indicating the gross national product, expressed in constant price terms (Chilean escudos in 1961), is due to a change in the way this was calculated.

Despite improvement, the infant death rate in Chile is still high today owing to the persistence of certain adverse social and economic factors. One should bear in mind how the death rate varies according to differing social strata. It has been demonstrated that the infant death rate in 1957 was greater among working-class people than among persons in other social strata. Among the former, the infant death rate was 126 for every thousand live births, as against 67. That is to say that working-class children were disadvantaged by 88 percent compared with the children of higher social classes (Behm Rosas, 1962). The same study proves that the difference between the two groups is even greater in the postnatal period, when medical attention is more sporadic than in the neonatal period, and consequently the child is more exposed to those socioeconomic factors which affect him through the family. The relative stabilization of infant death rates in Argentina, Uruguay, Chile, and Cuba, which are the most advanced countries, leads one to suppose that a further drastic reduction in infant mortality requires the resumption of the former pace of socioeconomic change, or to carry out the radical social transformation which some seem to be aiming at.

At the present time infant mortality rates are spread over a wide range, some being twice as high as others. Table 6.8 gives a specimen set for 1967, where the worst figures shown are double those for the most developed countries. There is room for enormous improvement, more, in fact, than the figures suggest; one must bear in mind that these are national averages, and that there is uneven distribution not only among classes, but also between the urban and rural population. The day when all countries will share the best values is, regrettably, in the fairly distant future. The city enjoys some advantage over the country in this respect, and it is the city child who has a better chance of survival than his country cousin.

This rule is of such general application that it is the exception rather than the rule that is worth noting. Infant mortality in Colombia, for example, was of the order of 141, 147.1, and 109.5 in the 1930s, 1940s, and 1950s, respectively; the rate in the capital, Bogotá, was worse than the national average during the first two decades (192.9 and 162.9) and was only just better in the last decade (104). The same thing happened in Mexico during the same periods: as against a national average of 131.4, 112, and 85.7 infant deaths per thousand live births, the Federal District recorded 151.5, 142.3, and 84.8. The same situation can be seen in a smaller country, El Salvador: 132.3, 108.3, and 79.8 as the national average, against 196.9, 135.9, and 90 in the capital during the same decades (Robinson, 1963). These facts militate against the assumption that urbanization and socioeconomic development always march hand in hand. Owing to intense immigration and a proletarianization of the lower social strata, the urban explosion frequently depresses living conditions. Mexico City and Bogotá passed through this stage in the 1930s and 1940s; San Salvador was still in it in 1960. Buenos Aires, a metropolis of long standing, went through it some time earlier; in 1950–59 infant mortality in the capital was almost half the national average.

The exceptionally rapid lowering of the death rate from 1930 onward has inevitably brought about changes in the demography of Latin America, some directly, such as the steep increment of its inhabitants, the high proportion of youth in the population, and the rise in fertility. Others are secondary effects, such as the geographical distribution of the people—migration, urbanization—the numbers joining the work force, as well as population pressure on income distribution and on the costs of improvements in the fields of education and public health. Having dealt with the natural growth of population in the introductory portion of this chapter, we will now consider two immediate changes brought about by the fall in the death rate and the related increase in life expectancy: the presence everywhere of enormous numbers of young people, and the fertility expansion. Further consequences will be dealt with separately.

REJUVENATION

With the survival of large numbers of children who would previously have died, the youthful portion of the population expanded enormously. The increase in the fertility rate unleashed in its turn successive throngs of children, while transoceanic immigration had hardly any significant effect on the age structure of the population except in a few cities, such as Caracas. Of three parameters, two dynamic and one inert, it was the lowering of the death rate which was the prime cause of this overflowing of the fountain of youth. If the rate had remained at its 1930 level, thirty years later there would have been twenty-seven million fewer people in the eleven countries studied by Arriaga (1970a). The reduction in the death rate, however, meant that they survived, and three-fifths of these were under the age of fifteen in 1960. This internal flux thus brought about a large gain in the numbers of young people in proportion to the size of the adult population.

The accumulated effects of this tendency during four decades are shown in table 6.9, where one can see the percentage of the total population represented by the 0–14 and 15–19 age groups in all the republics of Latin America. These two categories are added together in column 3. More than half the population of Latin America is now under the age of twenty, and two-fifths are under fifteen. In Central America, including Panama, the averages are 56.8 percent and 46.1 percent in the above age groups, absolutely astonishing proportions. Only in the four most socially developed countries, Argentina, Uru-

TABLE 6.9 Proportion of the Population Under the Age of Twenty in 1970
(in percentage)

	Age groups			1960–70 variation		
	0–14	15–19	0–19	0–14	15–19	0–19
	1	2	3	4	5	6
Argentina	29.3	8.9	38.2	–1.4	0.5	–0.9
Bolivia	42.6	10.1	52.8	0.7	–0.2	0.6
Brazil	42.0	10.5	52.5	–0.7	–0.3	–0.5
Chile	39.3	10.2	49.6	–0.6	0.7	0.2
Colombia	47.0	10.5	57.5	1.1	0.4	1.6
Costa Rica	45.6	11.1	56.7	–2.0	1.4	–0.6
Cuba	34.5	9.7	44.2	–1.6	–0.1	–1.7
Dominican Republic	47.6	10.8	58.4	0.3	0.6	0.9
Ecuador	46.9	10.3	57.1	1.5	0.3	1.7
Guatemala	44.9	10.7	56.5	–0.5	1.0	0.4
Haiti	42.5	10.2	52.6	0.5	0.0	0.4
Honduras	46.7	11.3	58.1	–0.7	1.7	1.0
Mexico	46.4	10.4	56.7	0.8	0.5	1.3
Nicaragua	47.1	10.6	57.7	0.5	1.0	1.5
Panama	44.7	10.0	54.7	1.2	0.0	1.2
Paraguay	46.5	10.8	57.3	–0.4	0.8	0.4
Peru	45.0	10.2	55.3	0.4	0.2	0.7
Puerto Rico	36.8	10.9	47.7	–5.9	0.4	–5.6
Salvador (El)	47.1	10.2	57.3	1.7	0.6	2.3
Uruguay	28.2	8.2	36.3	0.1	0.2	0.2
Venezuela	45.2	10.6	55.8	0.2	0.9	1.1

SOURCE: CELADE, 1971.

guay, Cuba, and Chile, does the proportion of young people under twenty fall below 40 percent, and those under fifteen, below 30 percent.

Percentages in table 6.9 may disclose similar or dissimilar stages in the same evolutionary process. Nations with predominantly adult population, such as Argentina, are proceeding in the same direction according to changes in age composition as countries with a predominantly youthful population, such as Costa Rica. In both cases youth is on the decrease. However, low rates of change may indicate also the opposite. Bolivia and Haiti, for instance, record such low rates; but their demographic change process has hardly begun, and they have a long way to go.

The distinction of stages within the same line of evolution— beginning, culmination, and recession, and its intermediary positions —can be inferred from the comparison of age structures in 1970 and 1960. Columns 4, 5, and 6 in table 6.9 reveal the changes that have occurred, either in a positive or in a negative direction. In this comparison, El Salvador, Ecuador, Panama, and Colombia show the highest increase of all in the 0–14 age group, an indication that the influx of children continues and that the population is becoming younger there. Also, in Bolivia, Peru, Haiti, and Mexico the youngest bracket is expanding, while in Venezuela, the Dominican Republic and Nicaragua, although it still increases, it does not show the highest growth. Boys and girls 15 to 19 years old make up the faster growing group, as if the crest of the wave has passed from the younger group and reached the adolescents. Last of all come the countries with a minus sign prefacing the 0–14 age group figures. This feature suggests the arrival of maturity. Puerto Rico, Costa Rica, and Honduras belong to this group, followed closely by Chile, Guatemala, and Paraguay. From the remaining four nations, the proportion of youth below 20 years is shrinking; among the aging countries, Uruguay seems to be rejuvenating slightly, while Argentina carries on.

The graphic representation of a preponderantly youthful population is an elegant pyramid, stretching from an enormously wide base to the advanced-age peak. The sex distribution to left and right is almost identical. It is true that the fall in the death rate was, on the whole, kinder to women than to men. The greatest improvement came during the reproductive years, an indication of improved pre-natal and maternity services (Arriaga, 1970*a*). The overall distinction, however, is very slight.

Two age pyramids are reproduced in figure 12 by way of example. The one on the left is for Guatemala in 1950 and it conforms to what has just been said above; the one on the right is for Uruguay in 1957. This profile is thick, with a narrow base and a gradual narrowing toward the peak; the upper strata are much broader. Uruguay has an aging population in which children and adolescents together form only one-third of the total. Uruguay is the most extreme case of this in Latin America, but Argentina is approaching it. Naturally it is the adjacent plains that are similar, not the remote areas of the interior. Cuba and Chile are on the same road, but some way behind.

The physical, social, and educational needs of this increased youthful population constitute a heavy burden for the countries concerned. In the eight countries studied by Arriaga (1970*a*), 31.3 percent of the population had to support 68.7 percent. Thus every person in employment had to provide for 2.2 people. This average is a 12 percent increase on what would have been his responsibility if the population explosion had not occurred. The burden would have been even greater had it not been for the influx of women into the work force. In Mexico, for example, 4.3 percent of the female popu-

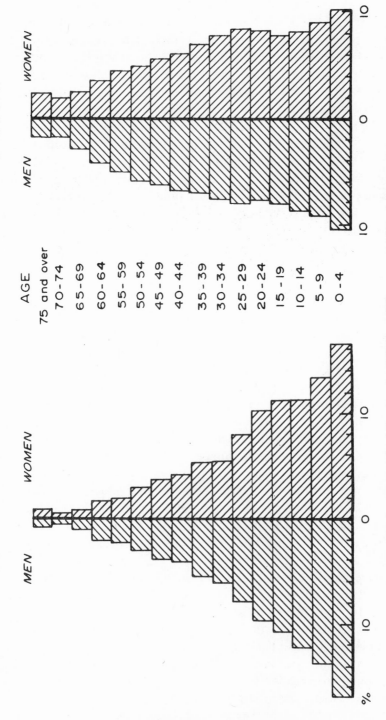

FIGURE 12. Age pyramids of Guatemala (1950) and Uruguay (1957), in percentages.
(Sources: for Guatemala, IASI, 1959–60) : for Uruguay, Cataldi, 1964.)

lation was working in 1940; this figure went up to 8.6 percent in 1950 and to 11.6 percent in 1960. Compared with more advanced societies in which nearly half the female population works beyond the confines of the home, these figures are low.

This greater degree of dependence aggravated social and economic conditions, which were already far from good. One of the fields, for example, in which the sudden increase in the youthful element of the population slowed down progress is education. If adequate budgetary provision was to be made for the extra pupils, it meant that the cost of education went up, so far as every wage earner was concerned, or if money was not made available, the standard of education provided inevitably went down. Whichever way one looks at it, the fall in the death rate did not have a favorable effect either on the economy or on educational standards.

This fact and many other arguments have been adduced to maintain that this exceptional population increase is preventing Latin America from emerging from a state of underdevelopment and that there is no hope of improvement until this is brought under control. The benefits of economic growth—it is said—cannot be distributed until this continuous growth of consumers has been checked and countries can create capital more rapidly. The present state of Uruguay ought to shake one's faith in such beliefs. As Solari (1967) has pointed out, Uruguay has stabilized its population growth and has achieved sociocultural levels that make it more like Europe than the rest of its sister republics, and yet it has not succeeded in throwing off the yoke of underdevelopment. Thus the validity of the above proposition is still open to question. A static population is compatible with economic stagnation, as it has been for hundreds of years. What is more, an aging population brings new problems of its own. Sauvy would find in Uruguay a good illustration for his thesis that an expansion of the inactive, elderly population distorts an advanced national social security system and renders it unworkable, for lack of adequate numbers of people to share the social costs.

FERTILITY OUT OF CONTROL

The theory of demographic transition, so often referred to, which was formulated to give coherence to a mass of empirical observations about the development of the population of Europe from the end of the eighteenth century onward, came in time to be accepted as of general application. As with every attempt at conceptualization, it presents of necessity a simplified view of the historical process. It is hardly to be expected that every country or region would follow the same pattern.

It seemed beyond possible doubt that Latin America would follow the general trends. Bunge (1940) had titled one part of his study on the population of Argentina "The demographic drama of a young country." In it he reflected the population preoccupations that demographers and politicians of the 1930s had voiced as a result of the reduction in the European fertility rate, including the racist tone of the argument. Argentina, superficially populated, shared the low reproduction rates of the economic and cultural metropolises on the other side of the Atlantic. The fears of Bunge and his colleagues overseas did not materialize, as is well known, and fertility rates improved after World War II.

With some variation as a result of massive immigration, Argentina and Uruguay, the first countries to undergo a demographic change, followed the European example. It is hardly surprising, therefore, that it became generally accepted that Latin America as a whole would behave in the same way when its turn came, that is, that when the death rate fell, the fertility rate would slowly adjust to the situation. But these predictions did not come true: reproduction, on the contrary, broke through all barriers.

Official birthrate figures do not give a very accurate impression of the increase that occurred. The figures shown in table 6.3 (p. 189) give an imperfect idea of the rise that occurred from 1930–34 onward. This initial period is not a good starting point for comparison, moreover, since the fertility rate had gone down considerably as a result of adverse economic circumstances. Later fertility rates seem at most to show a recovery to previous levels, but do not suggest a vast increase.

Demographers now prefer to fill out the basic picture provided by the crude rates with more detailed measurements. In addition to making up for omissions, they differentiate among the diverse factors that affect reproduction, such as the sex and age of both the parents and the children. For example, the lowering of the infant mortality rate, that is, of children under the age of five, immediately enlarges the whole population. By thus increasing the denominator by which births are divided, the rate diminishes in a mathematical form that does not correspond to alteration in the fertility rate. Migration, too, alters the balanced distribution of the sexes and consequently lowers or raises the fertility rate, depending on the migrating group and on whether they are emigrants or immigrants. Whatever the distortion, adjustments must be made in order to arrive at the effective birth rates. Those given in figure 13 eloquently portray the enormous fertility expansion that has occurred in most Latin-American countries since 1935.

Collver (1965), the man responsible for the calculations, thus confirms what had previously been maintained in unilateral studies.

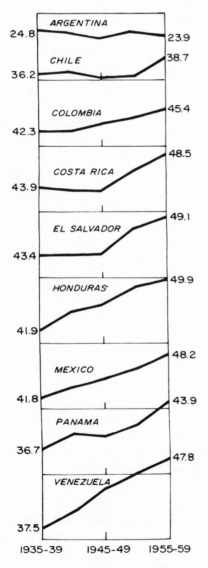

FIGURE 13. Trends of standarized birth rates since 1935.
(Source: Collver, 1965.)

Saunders (1958) had indicated, for example, how the fertility rate of Brazilian women increased phenomenally between the 1920 and 1950 censuses, especially in the north, the northeast, and the center, the most depressed areas. The method employed in this study was to work out the ratio between the number of children in the 0–4 age group and the number of women of child-bearing age, that is the 15–49 age group. Mortara had frequently used this method before him. Carleton (1965), however, quite correctly observes that the numerator consists of the number of surviving children born during the preceding five-year period, and that consequently any alteration in the infant mortality rate affects the ratio. This objection, among others, lessens the significance of this index, and the method is not now used very frequently.

Collver's thesis, as well as confirming some previous observations, produced additional evidence which led to open questioning of the validity of the demographic transition theory in the form in which it has so far been expressed concerning Latin America. Robinson (1963) had begun such questioning. Two years after the publication of Collver's book, three articles almost simultaneously suggested that the theory needed reconsideration. These were those of Gendell (1967), Arriaga (1967b), and Zárate (1967b). Gendell maintained that the socioeconomic development of Brazil had not been accompanied by any correlative reduction in the fertility rate and that, consequently, it was essential to reexamine the preconceived ideas concerning the relationship between economic growth and a lowering of fertility. Arriaga, basing his argument on the case of Venezuela, pointed out that the lowering of the mortality rate had actually raised the crude reproduction rate. Zárate finally attacked the belief that industrialization necessarily causes a lowering of the fertility rate, by demonstrating how in Mexico it has gone up from 1940 onward, and how the urban fertility rate and its changes are inversely proportional to the population employed in the secondary sector of the economy, that is, in industrial activity.

In a recent book, Arriaga (1970a) has again returned to the fray, not this time with just one more suggestion, but with a proposition of general application. If factors such as the length of the reproductive period and the age at which sexual relations start have a bearing on the fertility rate, then the longer a couple live the longer will be their reproductive life. In fact, as large numbers of women were surviving who would previously have died, the fertility rate could not help going up. The husband's survival was also a significant factor, since this gave each couple a longer reproductive life together. Arriaga is categorical on the matter: the fertility increase is the result of the drop in the mortality rate. None of the other factors involved occurred as rapidly as did the fall in the death rate, and consequently the rise in the fertility rate was inevitably rapid too.

In the middle of the twentieth century, women were more prolific and produced exceptionally large numbers of children, thus ensuring very large generations in the future. The crude reproduction rate for Latin America about 1965 was approximately 2.6 (U.N. *Demographic Yearbook*, 1969). This means that every mother who completed her child-bearing years in the conditions prevailing in the region produced 2.6 daughters, or approximately one and a half times more than the number required for the replacement of the present generation. Thus the three girls produced by every two mothers in excess of requirements would, in due course, add their quota to the birth rate. Sustained growth is guaranteed in these circumstances. But nine countries—Costa Rica, the Dominican Republic, Ecuador, Mexico, Paraguay, Guatemala, El Salvador, Honduras, and Peru—have a rate in excess of three girls per mother; most of the remaining countries have a figure that fluctuates about the average. Three countries, on the other hand, have a figure of less than two: Uruguay (1.4), Argentina (1.5) and Puerto Rico (1.9).

The addition to the world population of so many mouths is a source of worry to those responsible for their reception. The social, economic, and administrative problems presented by their unexpected arrival are worse than were foreseen and, with good reason, are considered very serious indeed. One can thus not be surprised that any sign of an early drop in the fertility rate is anxiously awaited. As the situations in city and country are very notably different, and in view of the fact that Latin America is tending to urbanize, one might predict the future of the birthrate and hopefully wait for an end to the present phase of frenzied expansion. For that very reason the difference between urban and rural behavior is of particular interest, not merely because it is a distinctive feature of demographic structure, but also because a better understanding of it may provide an indication of future trends.

This thought underlies the inquiries into urban fertility that have been carried out in eight capital cities of a variety of types. The cities concerned are Buenos Aires, Rio de Janeiro, Mexico City, Santiago de Chile, Caracas, Bogotá, Panama, and San José. Later research has added three other cities to the list, Guatemala City, Guayaquil, and Quito. For comparative purposes, parallel studies have also been carried out in rural areas in Chile, Colombia, and Mexico. The results available, summarized in Miró and Martens (1968), show that country areas in Mexico have a fertility rate one-quarter above that prevailing in the capital, whereas in Chile the parallel proportion is almost one-third. There are very marked differences between capital cities. Buenos Aires records an average of 1.49 live births to women between the ages of twenty and forty-nine, as against more than double that in Mexico City and Bogotá (3.26 and 3.16, respectively). The cities that most closely approximate to the situation in Buenos Aires are Rio de Janeiro and Santiago de Chile.

Every prediction depends on an interpretation of history. Brito (1969) applies this criterion and explains these discrepancies as due to the time factor and not to geographical position. Buenos Aires has completed its demographic change, while Mexico City has not. According to him, the great cities have different fertility rates because they are at differing stages within the same evolutionary cycle. Thus at best one obtains an a priori view of the sequence. The chronological or linear study, on the other hand, highlights each phase in a way that naturally cannot be done by the mere juxtaposition of cross sections.

Is it not possible, for example, for the urban fertility rate to expand contrary to any linear conception of change, even to the extent of temporarily closing the gap between it and the rural rate? Arriaga (1968b) maintains that it is; Chile provides the case in point. According to Weeks (1970), the crude birth rates there went up between 1952 and 1960 in the metropolitan areas. Meanwhile the rural rates appeared to decline. However and bear in mind that there was an alteration in the age structure of the population—fertility did not, in fact, decrease. On the contrary, it experienced a slight increase. For the same reason, urban fertility increased at an astonishing rate. With adjustments made, the birth rate actually went up by 21 percent. Weeks asserts that the concentration of health and social services in the cities caused this reaction there rather than in the countryside, as is obvious. He thus concludes that the process of urbanization in Chile depends on the natural growth of the population in the cities as much as on the influence of social and economic development. Lastly, it should be noted that the fertility rate which went up most was that of women between the ages of twenty and forty living in the large cities, precisely those who had reached child-bearing age about 1940 or shortly thereafter. The youngest, on the other hand, showed a tendency to have smaller families.

The present debate on fertility extends to cover all the factors that affect it. Economic development per se is no longer accepted quite so uncritically as bringing about a reduction in the birth rate. The suggestion that a decrease in the birth rate is almost automatically caused by a greater number of women going out to work is doubted (Heer and Turner, 1965). Even contraception and sterilization are quite compatible with a high birth rate. The discussion on fertility now consists of very general assertions and of concrete statements contradicting them. So far there appears to be no common ground between the two, for lack of a theoretical alternative and a historical perspective to support them.

While facets and explanations are being questioned, the population explosion is reaching its peak. It is doubtless risky to maintain this, for secondary explosions such as those now occurring in Haiti, Bolivia, and El Salvador cannot be excluded, and conception may remain high for awhile in many places, higher, of course, than planners would like. Several indications suggest that some nations have already turned the corner. Costa Rica's birth rate is on the downgrade, despite high fertility levels (Gómez, 1970). Venezuela and even Brazil are possibly at a similar juncture. Argentina, Uruguay, Puerto Rico, Cuba, and Chile preceded them. Mexico, Panama, and Honduras seem to have reached their respective peaks prior to the descent.

So far no mention has been made of marriages. Is this because marriage has no bearing on fertility? Here one must differentiate between the legal bond and conjugal life. In 1965 Puerto Rico, with the highest crude marriage rate (10.3), although a moderate figure for other areas, boasted one of the lowest birth rates. Just across the sea, the Dominican Republic, with a very high fertility rate, had the lowest marriage rate in Latin America: 3.5 newlyweds per thousand inhabitants (U.N., *Demographic Yearbook*, 1969). The biological facts do not require the institutional framework. The necessity of legal sanction or religious sacrament for the effective union of man and woman has long been questioned in Latin America. It was because of this that *mestizaje* first started, despite the barriers set up by colonial legislation and the social prejudices which the republics inherited. The lack of legal bond or religious sacrament has similarly been no restraining influence on the twentieth century population explosion.

TABLE 6.10 Free Unions and Illegitimacy in Fifteen Countries in Latin America, 1950

	Proportion of women living in consensual unions to each 100 married women	Percentage of illegitimate births
Guatemala	213.1	73.2
Panama	116.6	73.0
Dominican Republic	107.4	59.8
El Salvador	104.3	61.3
Honduras	98.0	64.4
Nicaragua	76.1	56.3
Venezuela	71.9	56.6
Peru	56.3	43.3
Paraguay	44.7	47.4
Ecuador	30.9	32.7
Mexico	25.7	24.1
Colombia	24.4	27.0
Bolivia	22.4	22.2
Costa Rica	17.3	23.7
Chile	7.3	17.1

SOURCE: Mortara, 1965.

In table 6.10 (column 1) can be seen the number of women living in consensual unions for every hundred married women, in about 1950. The proportions in several countries are extremely high, varying from a 2:1 proportion to a mere 7.3 percent figure for Chile. The natural result is noted in the second column. The proportion of illegitimate births is enormous: nearly three-quarters in Guatemala and at least one-sixth in Chile. The family and matrimonial standards of the ordinary people of Latin America cannot be compared with concepts which, according to the thesis of Hajnal (1965), belong only to a European context and a historical cycle of limited extent and duration.

A civil or a church ceremony is not, of course, any guarantee of the stability of a marriage, nor does concubinage presuppose sexual promiscuity. The concentration of free unions and illegitimacy during the early child-bearing years of the mothers' lives indicates that many of the associations are eventually legalized, not after the first pregnancy but after a long and fertile period of cohabitation. Consequently, there is a change also in the status of the children born before this decision is made.

The relative decline of free unions with the passage of time suggests that forces are now at work favoring the spread of the marriage bond. Mortara (1965) has observed that, when the 1950s are compared with the previous decade, legal marriages have increased by

90 percent in Honduras, 71 percent in Panama, 69 percent in Venezuela, 36 percent in El Salvador, and 15 percent in Puerto Rico. The phenomenon is more marked in the older age groups than among the young, and he attributes this to efficient missionary activity, without denying that the alteration might be due in part to an improvement in the functioning of registry offices. In many countries, social security plans deny benefits to a wife and children whose legal status has not been officially proved, thus compelling many rural and industrial workers to marry in order that their families may receive medical attention, allowances, and pensions. These advantages are, of course, more tempting to those who are living together permanently than to the young who have only just started out on a relationship of this kind. It is possible to witness nowadays open-air ceremonies in a sports' stadium, in which hundreds or thousands of couples come together and are married en masse under the aegis of the president. The attempts that modern states are making to achieve social integration are spreading more widely standards that, for historical and cultural reasons, were not previously accepted by the masses.

There are numerous different types of unions, and it is an extremely complex and difficult matter to classify them. Consequently, there is little one can say reliably about the influence that each type has had on fertility. In general, the forms of relationship that replace official marriage do not produce larger families, as has been pointed out by Mortara (1961). Conversely, the rapid population growth rate in countries where consensual unions are common, such as Guatemala, the Dominican Republic, and Venezuela, does not appear to indicate that such unions have been any obstacle to procreation.

A few final observations must be made with regard to present-day attitudes and policies regarding fertility. Such an unusual population growth as that experienced by Latin America creates economic, social, and human problems in the short term and tends to frustrate all the efforts made to improve living conditions. It is obvious that the population increase almost completely absorbs any rise in the gross national product. Between 1960 and 1967 Latin America's GNP increased at the rate of 1.7 percent per year per inhabitant, while that of the developed countries went up by 3.7 percent (CELADE, 1968). The relative position of Latin America is deteriorating. Its share of the total world product is decreasing. Although it has seen some vague possibility of improving its economy, it has had to use its scarce resources to provide for an overflowing population. Occasionally the standard of living has even gone down seriously.

Undoubtedly the achievements in lowering the mortality rate, which have in part been the cause of the present situation, cannot but attract general sympathy, nor would anyone wish controls of a Malthusian type over population growth; hence the only possible discussion necessarily centers around the fertility problem. Everyone ardently wishes all possible lives to be saved, but at the same time no one wishes to encourage an unreasonable increase in the number of new lives.

The position opening up in the present debate is opposed to that of the populationist policies of the nineteenth century, but for the same reasons. In the last century the nations welcomed European immigrants with open arms, and today they are trying to control the numbers of their own new citizens being born. In both aspects, economics is at the root of the problem. Previously there was a need for labor, and now there is an excess of mouths to feed.

The echo that the modern thesis finds outside the ambit of the economists is nevertheless the opposite of that which it aroused in the past. A policy in favor of immigration and of encouraging natural population growth was consistent with the atavic desires of the family and of the state and with traditional religious beliefs. In our day, those who favor birth control are propounding a theory that is contrary to those feelings and beliefs.

Several Latin-American dictators have, in recent years, declared themselves against any form of birth control. Their opinions express a belief entrenched of old in the minds of bureaucrats and especially of the military that men, by their sheer weight of numbers, uphold the power of a state. Pope Paul VI, in his encyclical "Humanae vitae," has reiterated the Roman Catholic church's position against birth control. The declaration has added more fuel to the fire of debate rather than altered people's behavior. In short, many people have proclaimed their individual right to resist external pressures whose motivations they neither understand nor share.

To those arguments have been added those of the Marxists, whose influence is growing in Latin America. In their view of historical reality, the lack of balance between population and the economy is a false problem. Underscoring their humanistic beliefs, they maintain that production methods must be adapted to suit the population, and not vice versa. For Marxists, the present imbalance between resources and population growth is an example of the failure of capitalism to face up to the problems of the contemporary world. They quote in support of their doctrine the example of China, where, in our day, despite an enormous increase in population, the people's basic aspirations, which had been frustrated for centuries, were satisfied, and conditions were created for further development. The points of contact between this thought and the doctrines of the church or the policies of certain conservative governments are superficial. There is no reason to equate opposition to contraception for supernatural or other reasons with attitudes that do not exclude it on principle.

There are many who, for reasons of individual freedom, maintain that anyone who so wishes should have access to information that will enable him to control the size of his family. They do not, for that very reason, feel that they have the right to dictate in such matters to any other couple. Gynaecologists and obstetricians, who are in daily contact with human worries and are therefore more aware than most of the situations involved, wish to avoid, among other risks, the physiological damage to women's health resulting from unwanted pregnancies or from abortions. Any of the above arguments, including the Marxist one, are based on less prosaic reasoning than those which propose a reduction in the birth rate as a supplement to development planning or as an alternative to the lack of any plan.

Latin America does not, at the moment, have any global population policy. The attitudes of the governments vary from those that are in favor of birth control, as in Peru and Ecuador, to those, such as Brazil and Argentina, that steadfastly oppose any regulation of the size of families. In other countries there is a gradual shifting of attitude from one of tolerating the activities of private organizations that favor birth control, to one of more and more active collaboration of the health authorities with family-planning programs. In Puerto Rico the government assumes responsibility for the overall control of population, although it leaves the actual execution of its policy to semiofficial agencies. Thus, in contrast to the last century, there is no general agreement on an acceptable population policy. In view of the diversity of conditions, there is probably no reason either why any such unified policy should exist.

While the problems created by a high fertility rate are getting worse, the birth control programs are at present making hardly any noticeable headway, which confirms the skeptical attitude with which they are regarded by Davis (1967). A recent estimate (García, 1970) points out that a total of 793,000 new patients are seen each year in all the private and government family-planning clinics in the whole of Latin America, excluding Puerto Rico, or, in other words, little more than 1 percent of all the women of child-bearing age. The insignificance of this number is emphasized when one realizes that in Latin America three million more women annually enter the fertile stage of their lives. Present plans do not even begin to deal with the minimal requirements of the population.

VII

The Drift to the Cities

T*HIS* chapter examines further the effects of the contemporary population explosion. The aspects under consideration
deal not with the growth itself but with population distribution within
Latin America. As a rule, the greater the population, the greater its
concentration. However, since the increase was neither uniform nor
always in accordance with the needs of each place, people were
tempted to move. The degree of attraction or rejection exerted by a
given area impelled them in several directions. The exodus from the
countryside provided an outlet for surplus population sending it
toward more dynamic areas. Sometimes it went still further, not
merely mobilizing the excess but even lowering the original size
of the rural population. The cities received a proportion of these
migrants.

Before dealing with internal movements—migration from one
country to another within Latin America, movement from one agricultural area to another, or the drift to the cities—a different movement will be considered: migration to and from Latin America. Such
movement is very minor compared with the situation examined two
chapters earlier, but it is nevertheless very significant, not because of
the numbers involved, but because of the mere fact of its occurrence.
An astonishing event is happening before our very eyes—a reversal
in the old pattern of migration.

"CHILDREN ARE THE BEST MIGRANTS"

In the 1940s Barreto (1947) launched this nationalistic motto, which is the very reverse of Alberdi's. The difference between Alberdi and Barreto is, however, that the contemporary sociologist was never systematic nor did he have a deep influence on Brazil's restrictive policy, whereas the nineteenth-century thinker's staunch convictions are imprinted on the constitution and the human composition of his country. In his way, Barreto expresses how much Latin America has changed in three-quarters of a century. He argued quite logically that instead of thinking of bringing in immigrants the government should first of all seek to deal with the infant mortality rate. Once this problem had been solved, he had no objection to immigrants—he was no xenophobe—but he set conditions for their admittance. He proposed a selection based on the physical and intellectual quality of the individual and his ability to assimilate. Cultural affinity was for him an important requisite, as it favored the integration of the foreigner and would prevent Brazil from having to make any alterations in its way of life. Barreto thus clearly manifested an anti-Japanese prejudice.

To encourage immigration when infant mortality rates remained high was, of course, a flagrant contradiction, especially at that time. It was a different matter a century earlier, but in the twentieth century there were many ways to reduce the death rate, and many countries had done so. The internal growth rate that would occur when the death rate was lowered would render immigration unnecessary. And so it proved.

At the time of the Great Depression, Brazil, like other countries which had traditionally received immigrants, found that its population was in excess of the resources and opportunities available during a crisis. Many foreigners then returned to their home countries and those who were on the point of migrating did not do so. But this time the Latin American nations did not just rely on a spontaneous ending of the migrant flow, as they had before in lesser crises. Legislation closed the open doors. Uruguay suspended the entry of foreigners for a year in July 1932, and when a new law was introduced, it made the Instituto Nacional de Trabajo the agency responsible for granting admissions (law of 23 November 1937). Argentina shut off immigration between 1931 and 1935 and, after 1940, ceased to allow indiscriminate admission to foreigners. The purpose of the new law was to channel all applicants to the countryside. Chile adopted a similar colonization policy, but not an immigration one. Mexico prohibited the entry of foreign workers in 1936 and would only admit those people who could show adequate means of support, with one exception, which will be mentioned later. Panama, in 1938, in turn restricted entry, and the Dominican Republic in the same year reserved 70 percent of all jobs for its own nationals (Costanzo, 1944).

The general desire was to prevent employment conditions from getting worse and thus aggravating social problems, which were quite bad enough as it was. But no country went as far as Brazil, where the reaction moulded the new Vargas constitution of 1934. This set an immigration limit, which was fairly high as well as a system of quotas according to country of origin. Brazil agreed to admit, per year, 2 percent of the total number of persons of each nationality who had entered the country during the preceding fifty years, that is, from 1883 onward. Thus there were allowed in each year 27,000 Italians, 23,000 Portuguese, 12,000 Spaniards, 3,500 Japanese, 3,100 Germans, and so forth. The Decree-Law of 18 September 1945 reiterated the intention of "preserving and developing, in the ethnic composition of the population, the most suitable characteristics of the European ancestry, and of defending the Brazilian worker." In 1958 a bill was presented to the parliament suspending immigration and using the funds of the agencies that dealt with it to finance internal migration. Barreto justified a posteriori what was written into these laws.

The emotions awakened by war in Europe tempered the strictest of these positions, and economic recovery at a later date fostered the belief that these Latin American countries were promised lands for immigrants. The restrictions could be a necessary, but temporary, evil. The first country to admit large numbers of Europeans was precisely one which never before received any significant number of them. Combining humanitarian sentiments with the populationist policy then in favor within the party in power, Mexico, during the progressive presidency of General Cárdenas, welcomed tens of thousands of excombatants from the Spanish Republican army who were forced into exile when the Civil War ended in 1939. These refugees were highly trained workers and professional people, and their presence was of great benefit to the economic and cultural development of Mexico. Chile, Cuba, and Santo Domingo, particularly, welcomed smaller numbers of Spanish exiles. By its very nature this immigration was restricted, both in numbers and in duration, once the emergency was over.

A broader and more lasting stream of migrants eight years later arrived in another country which had hardly been touched by the flood that came to Latin America early in the century. In 1939 Venezuela created an Instituto Técnico de Inmigración y Colonización. The purpose was to establish foreign colonists in the country's interior to replace the Venezuelan peasants who left their jobs there in search of better opportunities. The oil industry, then booming, paid much higher wages than those available in the farmland. Venezuelan agriculture was in the doldrums. In the first two years, thousands of Portuguese crossed the Atlantic, but World War II curtailed communication and cut down the number of immigrants. Once the war was over, massive immigration began again. This time, the first to arrive were Spaniards.

The main object of the authorities was still to provide agricultural workers. The selection of immigrants was the responsibility of the Instituto Agrario Nacional after 1948, but the experiment was a failure. The outcome was that, in 1961, 270,409 foreigners were living in the capital, as much as 20 percent of the population of the metropolitan area of Caracas, which includes parts of the neighboring state of Miranda. Table 7.1 shows the net annual gain due to

TABLE 7.1 Net Immigration to Argentina, Brazil, and Venezuela from 1946 to 1957
(in thousands)

	Argentina	Brazil	Venezuela
1946–47	30.7	17.0	11.9
1948–49	237.4	23.5	58.8
1950–51	190.8	82.5	49.6
1952–53	64.1	153.1	67.4
1954–55	58.1	100.5	97.6
1956–57	27.6	65.6	84.7
Totals	608.7	442.2	370.0

SOURCES: For Argentina, the transoceanic migration according to information provided by local authorities, International Labour Office, 1959. For Brazil, the number of migrants entering, as recorded at the port of arrival, less those who left. (For lack of Brazilian exit statistics, these numbers have been calculated from data provided by Italy, Spain, and Portugal of the number of returning migrants. The number of migrants of other nationalities returning home are unknown, but were relatively few.) The same source as for Argentina. For Venezuela, the total immigration, including that from other Latin-American countries, especially Colombia, Carrillo Batalla, 1967.

immigration to Venezuela during the period 1946 to 1957. Apart from the Spaniards, who made up 30 percent of the number of those born overseas, the most numerous foreign colonies in 1961 were the Italian, forming 22 percent and the Portuguese, 8 percent (Carrillo

Batalla, 1967). Since 1958 more people have left the country than have entered it (Morales-Vergara, 1971). As a result of this, and because of the gradual naturalization of residents, Venezuela has absorbed a high proportion of those foreigners who entered the country in the 1950s. On a smaller scale than that experienced by other South American countries at the time, the immigration to Venezuela is nevertheless the only recent example of a country open to mass migration, and consequently, also, the only one where the influx made as much impact on the society of the welcoming country as it did in the River Plate area and in southern Brazil years earlier.

In 1946, Argentina and its vast neighbor to the north were already well-established countries. The new migrants found there long-established residents of their own nationalities and an atmosphere long accustomed to the presence of foreigners. The foreign communities formed excellent reception centers, and the prevailing attitude was one of tolerance. The difficulties which their predecessors had had to face seventy years earlier did not arise. Their social status, too, was different from that of their predecessors. Usually they were not peasants or manual workers; on the contrary, many came with some technical training or specialization, or with some financial resources with which to set up lucrative businesses. Their settling in was easy, apart from the prevalence of a nationalist feeling, which had not existed in the cosmopolitan atmosphere at the end of the nineteenth century.

The fact that the new wave of migrants was different from the old is also evident in their versatile attitude and deliberate choice of where to go. They were not men driven by necessity, but they were well aware of the opportunities offered by different countries. During the opulent years of the Perón regime they came to Argentina, but when the economy weakened, they lost interest in the country and went off in search of new horizons. Brazil attracted them after the return to power of Vargas. Then they were drawn to Venezuela in the lavish days of the Pérez Jiménez régime.

Italians, Spaniards, and Portuguese were once again the most numerous contingents to cross the Atlantic. In the days immediately after World War II, Italians made up nearly half the total numbers, Spaniards one-quarter, and Portuguese just over one-sixth. From 1958 onward the Spaniards were the most numerous, closely followed by the Portuguese and then the Italians (Morales-Vergara, 1971). According to Diegues (1964), about 60 percent of the migrants going to Brazil between 1953 and 1957 disembarked at

Santos, the port of São Paulo, and only just over a third at Rio de Janeiro. In Argentina they all entered through the port of Buenos Aires, and the majority remained there. Caracas contained about two-thirds of the foreign residents of Venezuela.

The new arrivals were in a different position from that of their predecessors, for they encountered stiff competition for jobs from local rural migrant laborers. In the countryside there was an excess of manpower for the agricultural industries, which were either stagnating or in the process of mechanizing, and the country people flocked in the thousands to the big cities to take on any jobs they could get. Being less demanding over the question of wages, they almost monopolized the menial occupations there. Quick to learn and assimilate, they then forced their way upward into the jobs which, because of the qualifications demanded, had fallen into the hands of foreigners. Within an expanding economy the latter would have been able to remain, but the postwar boom did not continue and the economy began to falter. About 1960, the migrant tide was reversed, and more foreigners left Latin America than came to it.

The economic recovery of the Old World also attracted European migrants to return and prevented the departure of those who had intended to migrate. Thousands of jobs became available in the industrial centers in the north of Italy, and in France and Germany, which local labor could not fill. When Latin America ceased to offer migrants rosy prospects, Europe offered them alternative ones, not quite as attractive, apparently, but closer to home.

When the influx of workers from neighboring countries proved insufficient—Sicilians and Neapolitans to the north of Italy, Spaniards, Yugoslavs and Greeks to Germany, Portuguese and Spaniards to France, for example—Europe then recruited workers from overseas. Algerians, Moroccans, and Turks came in to work in the fields and in the factories. Sauvy (1962) calls this new phenomenon the inversion of the centuries-old current of immigration.

In the nineteenth century, the industrial centers of Europe attracted the excess labor available in the nearest backward agricultural areas. Their ability to absorb such people never rose to such an extent as to prevent several million Europeans from migrating overseas. In the third quarter of the twentieth century, the western portion of the politically fragmented continent of Europe is repeating the experience. This time it is attracting labor from farther afield, from as far as Greece, the Mezzogiorno of Italy, the Algarve in southern Portugal, and even from across the Mediterranean.

Latin America is also sharing in this worldwide change. Its own rapid natural population increase has made immigrants unnecessary. There are too many workers. It sends them not to Europe, but nearer home, to another highly productive area. With the exception of the three thousand Puerto Ricans sent to distant Hawaii before 1898 to work on the sugar plantations (Senior, 1947), and a handful of Negroes whose return to Africa has given a Brazilian atmosphere to some places on the Gulf of Guinea (Verger, 1968), Latin Americans have never emigrated to countries outside the American continent. Since the end of the last century, migrants have crossed the northern frontier of the region into the U.S.A. It was the turn of peons born south of the Rio Grande to go north, rather than of American colonists to come south to Mexico, as had been the case at the time of the secession of Texas. This shift of population within the same type of country is international only in an administrative sense.

Later the situation was to change. In 1910 there were some 200,000 people in the U.S.A. who had been born in Mexico. Two-thirds of them lived just across the river in the border state of Texas; the rest were spread out over New Mexico, Arizona, Colorado, and California. Twenty years later there were one and a half million Mexicans or their descendants living there, mainly in California and Colorado. There was a pause during the Great Depression; then, when migration began again, Mexicans were to go as far north as the Chicago-Gary and Detroit industrial complex (Hernández Álvarez, 1966). This migration was no longer only of "wetbacks." Today it is urban and industrial. Like his Algerian counterpart, the Mexican experiences the same disillusionment. Every year between 1960 and 1964, the U.S.A. granted temporary entry permits to an average of 233,000 Mexican workers, and a further 43,000 a year were given permission to reside in the country permanently (Grebler et al., 1970). These figures do not include those who continued to enter the country illegally. At the present moment there are some five million *chicanos*, as this ethnic group is called, living in the U.S.A., 90 percent of them in the southwestern states and California.

A similar movement is that of Puerto Ricans to New York. However, the situation is different, for two reasons. Owing to the fact that Puerto Rico is an island, leaving it is always a more deliberate act than that of the Mexican departing from Tamaulipas, Chihuahua, or Baja California, especially since the destination is a metropolis nearly three thousand kilometers away in a latitude and climate that are so different that the migrant can be in no doubt that he is quitting Latin America. On the other hand, since Puerto Rico is a Commonwealth associated with the U.S.A., and its inhabitants pass as American citizens, their departure for the mainland will not be registered as an international movement. Apart from the statistical sampling taken at San Juan airport, the only way of gauging the extent of this flow is by an examination of census returns. According to the 1940 census, there were 100,000 Puerto Ricans living in the metropolitan area of New York City. In 1950 there were 226,000 and another 75,000 actually born there. Ten years later the number had trebled: 600,000, with another 300,000 born in New York. In 1970 both categories together totaled one and a half million. They are concentrated in New York, though separate colonies exist in Chicago and Philadelphia.

These figures give an imperfect idea of the size of this shift of population, since there is a permanent movement to and fro. In recent years the number of those returning to the island has increased. After a while many Puerto Ricans go home to start a new life in San Juan or some other city with the savings or training they have acquired. Thus the migration of Puerto Ricans to New York has the characteristics of a typical migration from countryside to city.

The long-established Cuban colony in Florida and Louisiana has been expanded since the setting up of the socialist state in Cuba, with the arrival of political exiles. The Havana-Miami air corridor, the usual means of exit, has already transported 200,000 Cubans, mainly from the middle and upper classes. There are now more than 600,000 Cubans resident in the U.S.A.

Some hundreds of thousands of Dominicans and Haitians also live in the U.S.A. This fact is easily explained, both by geographical proximity and by the vast difference between the American economy and that of the two Caribbean countries concerned. Migration from Central and South America is more difficult, but people have, nevertheless, come from these two areas. There are now quite large colonies of Colombians, Ecuadorans, Argentines, and others living in the cities of the eastern seaboard and on the coast of California. Altogether they number about half a million people.

Much more important than the numbers involved is the quality of these migrants. A substantial proportion of these Latin-American migrants entering the U.S.A. are engineers, scientists, doctors, and other professional people, and also skilled workers (González, 1968, and Oteiza, 1969). This is a select migration, which enriches the recipient country and impoverishes countries that are not, themselves, highly developed. The "brain drain" widens the technological gap between the developed and underdeveloped Americas.

The U.S.A. has attracted trained personnel through good employment opportunities and the higher salaries offered, but it must be admitted that many were driven from their country of origin because of the poor use certain countries made of their human resources or because of political restrictions imposed at certain historical junctures. This migration perhaps also indicates that trained personnel are available in some countries in greater numbers than can be profitably employed in the present economic situation. This does not mean an excess in absolute terms; it means rather an imbalance within specific economic contexts. Although to a lesser degree than the U.S.A., Europe has also attracted some professional people and scientists from Latin America.

Not all of this movement results in a net loss to the region. Some professional people return home after years of training and use in their own country the experience they have gained. This aspect of the question has not been studied and is not at all easy to measure, but it should not be disregarded on that account. Finally, it should be noted that the "brain drain" will not last forever; since 1968, North America has ceased to be able to absorb so many professionals, and the number of those going has declined as a result (Oteiza, 1971).

Lastly, one should bear in mind that the inversion of the traditional migration pattern does not rule out the possibility of further migration to Latin America, even though objective conditions may not be favorable. It it does occur, it will necessarily be much more selective than in the past.

THE FLIGHT FROM THE LAND

Besides rendering inappropriate the indiscriminate immigration of foreigners, the lowering of the infant mortality rate and the consequent increase in the population had an unexpected outcome. Either driven by necessity or attracted by better opportunities, the country dwellers had always been prepared, as a last resort, to abandon their lands. In fact, there have always been some who left in search of more fertile land or for the cities. This time, as agriculture did not keep in step with the accelerated growth of the rural population, many people had no option but to leave.

During the last forty years, agriculture has developed in Latin America more slowly than any other economic sector. In general, one may even say that it has stagnated. The changes or innovations introduced have not altered the traditional character of primary production. Land tenure still combines extensive estates and intensive but uneconomic small holdings. Technology did not make up for years of neglect; consequently, low yields continued to be produced from the available resources. Productivity increased slowly, as though unaware of the enormous incentives offered by a continually expanding market (CEPAL, 1963).

In these circumstances, living conditions in the country areas did not alter either. The stratification of society did not reduce the extreme polarization from which it suffers. All participation of the lower orders in the ownership and the benefits of land continued to be resisted, and they were even denied the advantages of civilization that were taken for granted by others. The income, food, education, housing, and even health of rural communities continued to be the lowest in the whole social scale, and in many places conditions were appalling.

By this time, however, the country dweller was no longer entirely isolated. Roads now reached places previously accessible only by rough bridle tracks, and versatile motor transport was providing prompt and regular services along them. If the new route did not bring with it the normal advantages of civilization, it did, of course, make the rural population aware of them. On foot or by truck, alone or in a group, out of work or full of ambition, the peasant began to leave his land rather than continue to drag out a fruitless existence.

This picture broadly applies even in certain special cases. Sometimes mass migrations were caused by climatic conditions which suddenly made large regions uninhabitable; such was the case with the droughts in Northeastern Brazil. Sometimes mechanization was responsible for a labor surplus in one area or another. Not even agrarian reforms in Mexico, Bolivia, and Venezuela have succeeded in retaining people on the land. It is too early to tell what will be the results of the very recent measures introduced in Cuba, Peru, and Chile, but it is unlikely that they will be very different from those experienced in earlier attempts.

When one places such migratory movements against the background of rural population density, it is not very easy to understand the need for such a general exodus. If one disregards the people living in towns of over twenty thousand inhabitants, then only in certain areas—Haiti and the Dominican Republic, the central valley of Mexico, the Pacific coast of Guatemala and El Salvador, the highlands of Costa Rica and Colombia, and in the vicinity of the Paraguayan capital—are there to be found rural population densities of over fifty persons per square kilometer (map 2). The figure is between twenty and fifty in eastern and western Cuba, central Mexico, the greater part of the Pacific slopes of Central America, the sierras of Colombia which carry over into the Venezuelan Andes, the coasts of Venezuela, Ecuador, and northern Peru, the central valley of Chile, the province of Tucumán in Argentina, the central coastal regions in the state of São Paulo, and the northeast of Brazil. The remaining areas do not reach a figure of twenty inhabitants per square kilometer, and there are, besides, great areas in Lower California, the Petén, Amazonia, the Atacama Desert, and Patagonia that do not have even one. Some of these sparsely populated areas are inhospitable and arid, such as northern and southern Chile, where it is doubtful whether any flourishing agricultural or cattle-raising community could ever exist. Other areas, however, are a very different matter; the Amazon basin is a case in point. In short, there are some places where saturation has been reached but which, with a change in the system of landholding and better management, could support a greater number of people. Compared with Europe and Asia, Latin America does not appear overpopulated. The rural population of the area is excessive only in relation to the amount of land suitable for cultivation, the technology available, and the pattern of land ownership and land utilization.

This should not be taken as suggesting that the drift from the land would immediately be reversed if the system were changed and if the extensive capital investment needed by agriculture were provided. It is more probable that, if the means were available, the exodus would, on the contrary, be speeded up. Mechanization, the prime necessity for the modernization of agriculture, would free millions of people who are now bent over their fields, using primitive farming methods. If an out-of-date agricultural system is today driving peasants from the land, a more efficient one would not retain them but merely ensure better conditions for those remaining behind.

By and large, the country areas of Latin America are becoming depopulated. In some places the numbers remain stationary, despite a high natural population increase, thus showing only a relative drop. Such is the case in northeast Brazil. In vast areas in the coastal provinces and in the northwest of Argentina, as well as in Uruguay, the loss is, however, absolute. With every census the numbers recorded in the rural areas grow fewer.

Between 1960 and 1970, the rural population of Latin America as a whole increased from 109 million to only 125 million. "Rural population" was used here in the strictest sense to mean inhabitants of villages with less than 2,000 people. This increase was only about 1.3 percent per year when the overall population increase was more than double, or about 2.8 percent. During the same period, the non-rural population increased from 97 to 148 million. There was obviously an enormous migration from the countryside to the cities.

Argentina provides a concrete example. Map 3 shows recent trends in a historical perspective. The three diagrams indicate the number of interprovincial and international migrants at the end of each census period, 1895–1914, 1914–1947, and 1947–1960. This is the only possible way of estimating the long-term migration between the large administrative units of the country, for lack of any statistics concerning internal migration. Symbols within each of the three maps record the positive or negative figures produced by a comparison between two censuses. Each symbol represents ten thousand migrants and distinguishes between Argentine nationals and foreigners. The symbols are recorded within the territory to which they refer; an enlargement of the map of the Federal Capital is shown in an inset, and in the third map the area in the inset has been expanded to include Greater Buenos Aires. Though minute in an area compared with that of the whole country, the capital is extremely important, demographically, as can be seen.

The general tendency at the turn of the century is quite clear. The influx of foreign migrants to the capital, to the riverine provinces, and to Mendoza, Patagonia, and the Chaco is obvious, while the rest of the country provides only a very small contribution to the population of this area. Nevertheless, the very small exodus of people from the northwest and from the Mesopotamia (the provinces of Corrientes and Entre Ríos) is the beginning of a typical movement, which was to increase with the passage of time.

During the second period, the flow of European migrants slackens, although it is still significant within the most favored area. The south and west continue to receive foreign migrants. Elsewhere, native Argentines have replaced them as migrants. The northwest and the Mesopotamia thus show a net population loss, but so do some of the central provinces, such as La Pampa, San Luis, and even Córdoba. The men and women of the interior move principally to the Federal Capital and neighboring areas, but rural people are still attracted to the riverine provinces or the Chaco frontier.

In the third period, the foreign element has become a trickle, except in the suburbs of Buenos Aires. All the provinces have population losses except for those in the extreme north, west, and south,

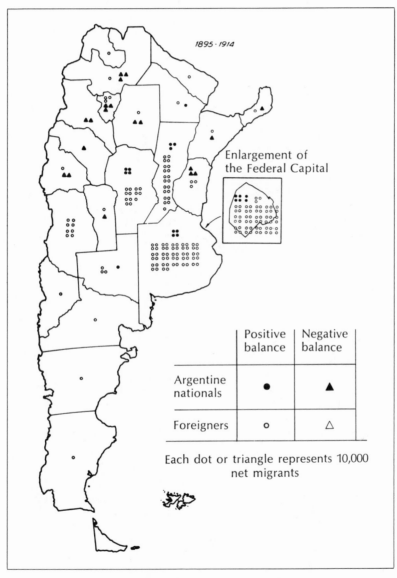

MAP 3. Argentina: Migration to and from each province at the end of the intercensal periods 1895–1914, 1914–1947, and 1947–1960, differentiating between Argentine nationals and foreigners. (Source: Recchini de Lattes and Lattes, 1969.)

where migration from neighboring countries is responsible for an increase. The Mesopotamia loses its population at an unprecedented rate; the riverine provinces, the paradise of immigrants a half-century earlier, also loses considerable numbers. The northern areas also continue to lose a number of their native inhabitants, but not as many as previously. The Federal Capital itself, somewhat confined within

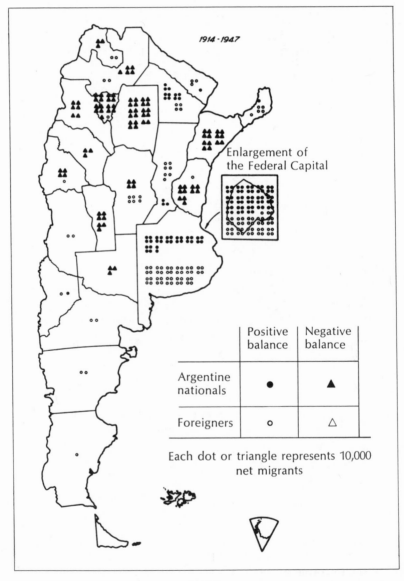

1914-1947

Enlargement of the Federal Capital

	Positive balance	Negative balance
Argentine nationals	●	▲
Foreigners	○	△

Each dot or triangle represents 10,000 net migrants

MAP 3.

the limited area assigned to it eighty years earlier, loses residents to the surrounding suburbs, a feature typical of modern sprawling connurbations. Where do the native Argentines of the interior and the Federal Capital itself go? With the exception of Mendoza, which is still growing, they are all crowded into the vicinity of Buenos Aires. Thus at the moment, migration from the countryside is contributing

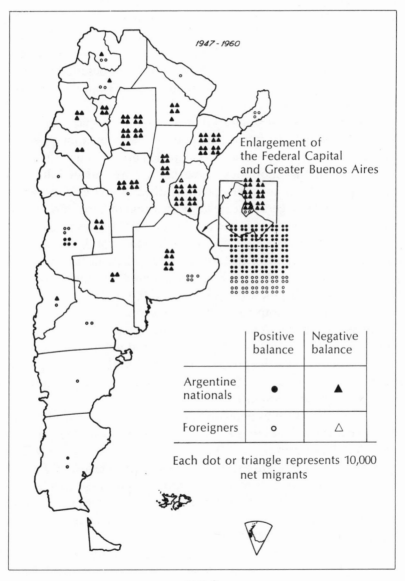

1947 - 1960

Enlargement of
the Federal Capital
and Greater Buenos Aires

	Positive balance	Negative balance
Argentine nationals	●	▲
Foreigners	○	△

Each dot or triangle represents 10,000 net migrants

MAP 3.

primarily to the growth of the metropolis. So far this century, Argentina has consequently reversed its earlier migration trends: from clamoring for agricultural workers from Europe, it has gone on to depopulate the countryside so recently settled, in order to expand its one large city.

Before examining this exodus at its point of arrival—urbanization—we will first consider those few recent examples in which people have moved from one rural area to another. In some cases this was exclusively an internal movement, but in others a crossing of frontiers was involved. The term *international migration*, though it is the appropriate technical term from a civil servant's point of view, nevertheless seems too weighty a phrase to describe the mere crossing from one bank of a river to another or from one side of a mountain to another.

When millions of square kilometers of the tropics were freed from endemic diseases, it was only natural that population pressures should cause these virgin lands to be opened up. Although the initial effort involved was enormous, these lands were full of future potential. Yellow fever, malaria, and other diseases no longer presented a problem, and pioneers have never been afraid of hard work. Under these new conditions, life in the equatorial belt became no more difficult than in many other parts of the inhabited world. The opening up of the vast reserves of the Amazon basin has, in fact, begun in several places. Demographers have been unaware of this; only geographers are watching these developments with interest.

So far there is nothing about this adventure that amounts to a frontal assault on nature; clearings to date amount to no more than scratches on the vast expanse of the equatorial jungle. Vegetation is difficult to tame, and the progress made is not always the result of spontaneous colonization. Most frequently it is achieved by means of costly government assistance.

In Peru, the surplus population of the sierra has been advancing down the eastern slopes toward the forests below, entailing a descent from altitudes of between 2,500 and 4,500 meters above sea level to an area ranging from 800 to 2,000 meters, or even below 800 meters in the case of the lower forest zones. Spontaneous migration has followed down the narrow eastern valleys gouged out by the Tambopata, Inambari, Urubamba, Apurímac-Ene, and Huallaga rivers, but does not proceed very far. Farther on, in the jungle area proper, official activity is centered on the Madre de Dios River, in the neighborhood of Puerto Maldonado, along the length of the Ucayali River,

especially toward Pucallpa, and is also encouraging the development
of Iquitos, far away on the Amazon itself. The army has set up bases
along the Brazilian and Colombian frontiers, and elsewhere has tried
out joint civilian and military settlements. The armed forces provide
the necessary infrastructure for the economic success of the new settlements; the air force provides transport for passengers, supplies,
and produce. The Universidad Nacional de Huamanga and private
institutions, such as the Banco de Fomento Agropecuario, have been
granted land to experiment with, using their own colonization methods (Eidt, 1962). During the presidency of Belaúnde Terry, the
government concentrated its attention on the construction of the
carretera marginal de la selva (the Eastern Highway along the edge
of the jungle) in the hope that it would open up a frontier to attract
development and transport the products of the region. The selva area
has increased its population three times as fast as that of the sierra,
thus showing evidence of the dynamic growth of the region. Nevertheless, its growth rate is lower, even in relative terms, than that of
the urban population on the coast. So far, the eastern area has not
made any significant contribution to the alleviation of the problem
of the great concentration of population on the coast, nor has it fully
satisfied the hopes placed in its resources.

To the south, in Bolivia, the migration of the *coyas*, the inhabitants of the altiplano, has gone on along the banks of the Beni River,
on the Mojos plains, where cattle ranching is flourishing, and in
Santa Cruz. This latter area has emerged from its isolation to become
of growing importance in the political and economic life of the country. For the colonists, removed from the heights of the altiplano, ac-
climatization has sometimes proved difficult, and as is to be expected,
friction has arisen between the *coyas* and the local *cambas*.

In Colombia, also, there has been some migration eastward by
people living in the sierra. The mountains themselves have dictated
the areas from which these migrants have come, and the river valleys
have determined the direction in which they have gone. Those coming from Pasto have followed the Mocoa River downstream; those
from Huila have gone into Caquetá, beyond the town of Florencia;
those from Bogotá have progressed beyond Villavicencio and followed the banks of the Meta River downstream; those from Sogamoso, farther north, have moved on to the plains of the department
of Boyacá (Crist and Guhl, 1956). In thirteen years, between 1951
and 1964, the population of the eastern llanos doubled.

In Venezuela, at the foot of the Sierra de Portuguesa, intensive agriculture is gradually taking the place of herds of cattle, which previously wandered over this grassland area, and between 1950 and 1961 the geo-economic area of Acarigua-Araure more than doubled its population (Vila and Pericchi, 1968). Nevertheless, the most spectacular change has occurred in the Guayana region. A large mining and industrial city has sprung up overnight at the junction of the Caroní and Orinoco rivers. The agricultural and cattle-raising areas in its vicinity have shared in its prosperity.

Finally, one must examine the remaining country in South America that is expanding its internal colonization. Settlement is proceeding in northwestern Paraná and São Paulo, spreading into Mato Grosso, and also extending from another spectacularly booming city, the new capital, Brasília. (See map 4.) Movement north-

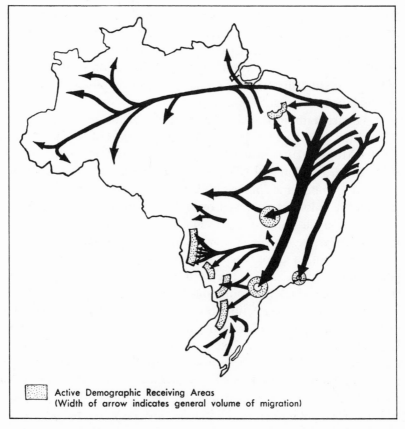

Active Demographic Receiving Areas
(Width of arrow indicates general volume of migration)

MAP 4. Brazil: Internal migration, ca. 1960. Source: After A. H. Neiva, in Stycos and Arias, 1966.

ward through the state of Goiás follows the route of the highway linking the capital with Belém do Pará. Another current southward through the forested area of the state of Maranhão will join up with this. But the great undertaking that is still in the future, which Brazil is initiating with the construction of the Transamazonian Highway, will be the settlement of the torrid plains through which the Amazon itself flows. The Brazilian government hopes that it will be able to channel to this area the surplus rural population of the northeast, a region that suffers from chronic economic depression. So far the only settlements in the area are the same ones that huddled along the banks of the Amazon between Belém and Manaus during the last century, in the days of the rubber boom.

Apart from Amazonia, the only rural areas to receive currents of internal migration are the coastal areas of South America, Central America, and northern Mexico. Along the Pacific coast and in some low-lying areas along the Atlantic, there has occurred what one might term a "march to the sea." Tacna, in southern Peru, and several northern valleys have been receiving migrants from the altiplano and the sierra. A similar drift is occurring in Ecuador. The mountain people from Chimborazo, Azuay, and Pichincha come down to the coast of Guayas, first as seasonal workers on the banana plantations and in the rice and cane fields, and then to settle permanently. In Venezuela, the eradication of malaria and the building of roads have opened up to economic activity the area between the Cordillera del Norte and the southern shore of Lake Maracaibo. Cattle raising and banana plantations have attracted a rural population to this previously unhealthy area. Owing mainly to the influx of Colombians, its population has trebled.

In Central America, areas abandoned centuries ago have been resettled, on both the Pacific and the Caribbean coastlines. In Costa Rica, for example, the plantations of Puntarenas on the south coast and Limón on the north are attracting the excess work force from the plateau (Jiménez Castro, 1956, and Sandner, 1961). The same thing is happening in Guatemala, particularly in the department of Izabal (Zárate, 1967a), but there has also been a symbolic migration of Kekchí Indians into the department of El Petén, a former center of the classical civilization of the Mayas (Adams, 1965). Leaving the altiplano, the Kekchíes are moving down to resettle lands that have been abandoned since pre-Columbian times. In the far north of Mexico, both in the west in Baja California del Norte, and in the east in Tamaulipas, there has been a similar movement toward the coastal areas. Irrigation has brought into cultivation arid country on the Pacific coast, and other types of intensive agricultural methods have provided new jobs for the farmers in adjacent areas. Contrary to what has happened elsewhere in Mexico, the rural population has increased.

International migration within Latin America, or rather, rural population movements as distinct from the usually reciprocal seasonal migrations between neighboring countries, have had an effect in three main reception areas: Honduras, the west of Venezuela, and the north and south of Argentina.

The migration of Salvadorans to Honduras went unnoticed, except by interested parties and some specialists, until the world in general suddenly became aware of it as the root cause of the war between the two countries in July 1969. It is difficult to think of any war caused so explicitly by population pressure. So far as El Salvador was concerned, the attempt was not to acquire more territory to ensure more living room for its population, but merely to safeguard the rights of Salvadoran migrants in Honduras, many of whom had lived there for many years. For decades Salvadoran peasants, unable to acquire land, and with no industries to employ them—suffering, in other words, from unemployment or underemployment, which affected one-third of the work force in 1964—had no alternative but to cross the frontier into Honduras. There was little physical difference between the two countries, but in the latter there were considerably more opportunities. Thirty percent of the migrants acquired property there after a while, and nearly half succeeded in becoming tenant farmers on private or state land, thus securing considerably improved living standards (Vieytez, 1969).

According to the most conservative estimates, there were 60,-000 Salvadorans living in Honduras when the war began, but others suggest that they made up about 10 percent of the total population of the host country. In any case, Honduras has 20 inhabitants per square kilometer, while El Salvador has 150. Prompted by their desire to face up to the problems of agrarian reform, the authorities in Honduras ordered all foreigners off the land they were occupying, without even the opportunity to acquire Honduran citizenship. Tens of thousands of Salvadorians would thus have had to return to their own country. The result of the ensuing war has seriously affected attempts to bring about economic integration by means of the Central American Common Market.

The presence of about 100,000 Colombians in the western states of Venezuela has given rise to friction between the two governments, but never to such an extent as that generated in Central America. Two-fifths of these migrants were settled in Táchira in 1961, replacing the Venezuelans who moved to Caracas or the Maracaibo oil fields.

The situation in Argentina is complicated. Three neighboring countries are involved. After the disastrous Chaco War, which shook Bolivian society to its very roots, the peasants of the southern altiplano used to take part in seasonal migrations to the neighboring provinces of Argentina to help with the harvests, and especially with the sugar harvest in Tucumán. The agrarian reforms resulting from the 1952 Bolivian revolution kept the peasants for some years on the lands thus acquired, but social and political changes could not keep up with the population explosion. In 1957, migration started again, but this time many remained permanently instead of returning home, and these former migratory laborers slowly gravitated toward the industrial belt and the shantytowns of Buenos Aires.

Migration from Paraguay was similarly motivated by the Chaco War, the population explosion and, in addition, by a serious internal political crisis, the 1947 civil war. When it ended, many tens of thousands of people from all parts of the country and from all social strata —politicians and professional people in particular—had to seek sanctuary in exile. The persistent persecution of the opposition by the Colorado party in power caused the departure of a constant stream of select migrants, whose very militancy indicated the intended temporary nature of their stay in Argentina. After 1957 political pressure relaxed, but a deteriorating economic situation, at least in relation to the rapidly increasing population, together with the attraction exerted by the colonies of earlier emigrés, maintained a flow of migrants. The temporary nature of this political and economic exodus gradually became more deliberate and permanent, and instead of being restricted to the neighborhood of the Paraguayan frontier, the new current also spread out as far as Buenos Aires (Rivarola, 1967).

A third group of migrants entered Argentina through the mountain passes in the southern Andes which lead from Chile to the *meseta* of Patagonia. The peons on the cattle ranches, the oil workers, and the coal miners are Chileans. In some of the southern provinces of Argentina as many as half of the inhabitants have arrived from the other side of the cordillera.

URBANIZATION

During the last thirty years, the population explosion has transformed Latin America from a rural and agricultural area into a markedly urban, if not industrial, one. Two-fifths of its population are now concentrated into cities with more than twenty thousand inhabitants.

Urban tradition has roots in the prehistoric period, when the continent could boast cities comparable in size with those of the Old World. During the colonial period, cities developed into an almost continental network, and their political, social, and economic importance was continually increasing. In the postindependence period, their growth did not at first continue, but later became widespread. Even before the present period of phenomenal expansion, Latin America had achieved a fairly advanced degree of urbanization, considering its limited industrial capacity and its generally low population density, as was pointed out some years ago by Davis and Casis (1946). The current expansion of the cities is thus no novel feature in the cultural and material life of the area.

The cities of Latin America have rapidly increased in size in the last few decades, but a considerable proportion of the functions they fulfill already existed, and those just acquired, to the astonishment of sociologists and economists, do not fundamentally alter the role they play. The cities have, of course, changed in shape and obviously their problems are different from those of the nineteenth century. Nevertheless, the lack of a well-established industrial base and the preponderance of tertiary activities do not make the physical differences between the past and the present so sharp as would be expected. Except for minor features of building which tend to make all modern cities look alike, many Latin-American cities seem large-scale versions of the old, rather than the local rendering of a modern city.

In the historical description that follows, we have left out of consideration the effects of urbanization on the economic, social, psychosocial, and even political life of the countries concerned, however currently interesting and attractive the subject may be. Anthropologists, planners, economists, sociologists, as well as ordinary people interested in contemporary problems are quite legitimately concerned about the ways in which the urbanization of Latin America is redistributing the population of the area, and about its implications for the future. The scope of this book, however, only allows for a consideration of the demographic and ecological extent of the change. In accordance with the distinction made by CEPAL (1968), this examination will be, not of the urbanization *of* society, but of urbanization *in* society, a simple aspect of a doubtless wider problem, which is outlined in the works of Urquidi (1969) and Ouijano (1967), among others.

The systematic growth of cities is now a worldwide phenomenon, but, as can be appreciated from table 7.2, it is especially

TABLE 7.2 Urban Growth Rates between 1940 and 1970 in Specific Regions of the World (percentage of annual increase in cities with more than 20,000 inhabitants)

	1940–50	1950–60	1960–70*
Africa	4.5	5.4	4.4
Latin America	4.8	5.5	4.2
Southern Asia	4.3	4.3	4.0
Eastern Asia	2.5	4.6	3.7
U.S.S.R.	0.6	4.5	2.8
North America	2.4	3.2	2.1
Europe	0.6	1.7	0.8

*Provisional estimates of urban population for 1970.
SOURCE: U.N., 1969.

typical of the developing countries of southern Asia, of Africa, and above all, of Latin America. For two decades the fastest annual growth rate has been in the latter area, and it is only in the last decade that Africa has taken the lead.

Why this sudden desire to crowd together in the houses and streets of cities? Primarily, the accelerated growth of urban areas of Latin America is due to the population explosion, as has already been pointed out. With the population of the country areas growing faster than the resources to support it, the people living there have been compelled to sever their links with the land. By a variety of routes many found their way to the outskirts of the local metropolis. Migration provided an outlet for the surplus rural population produced by a high natural growth rate.

The country people of northwest Argentina, the Mesopotamia, La Pampa, and even neighboring countries drifted to Buenos Aires and to a few inland cities (Recchini de Lattes and Lattes, 1969). In Brazil, migrants from the countryside had a wider choice open to them: they could go to places other than the time-honored centers of Rio de Janeiro and São Paulo—particularly the latter (see fig. 4, p. 157). They could go, for example, to the new, expanding cities of

Minas Gerais, Paraná, Rio Grande do Sul, and Goiás, not to mention the new federal capital, Brasília, erected in the middle of an empty central plateau.

Caracas emerges during this period as the undisputed great metropolis of Venezuela, a privileged position it had not previously attained. People flocked to it from all the states of the federation, but especially from the Andean states in the west. Only the oil fields of Maracaibo could compete significantly with the capital as a magnet for migrants from the country (Friedmann, 1966). Lima's position of predominance, as distinct from Caracas, was of long standing. Its status is even higher now. The highland Indians swarm down to it from the rugged mountains of the Andes; but the inhabitants of the coastal valleys to the north and south also come, and in almost equal numbers (Matos Mar, 1968). Colombia, like Brazil, can offer a variety of promising centers: there is, of course, the capital, Bogotá; there are also leading centers of economic activity in the valleys, such as Medellín and Cali, and Barranquilla on the Caribbean coast.

From all parts of Mexico, the north, the south, and the center, men and women converge on the Federal District. The former Aztec capital has grown enormously. Yet despite this continual drift toward the age-old capital, the traditional tendency for people to move to and concentrate on the central plateau is now no longer quite so overwhelming, for there has also been a drift northward especially toward the cities close to the border with the U.S.A. (Whetten and Burnight, 1956; and Tabah and Cosio, 1970).

Although to a lesser degree than the six examples above, the other Latin-American countries have also experienced movements of the same kind. To mention two of the smaller ones, Guatemala and the Dominican Republic, the urban population has also grown there strikingly, due to the permanent influx of people from the countryside.

Is it possible to give a more accurate idea of the extent of the exodus from rural areas to the cities? If this migration had not occurred, according to an argument put forward by Ducoff (1965), one could conceive that the population of the countryside and the city would have increased side by side, each at its own natural rate of increase. The difference between the two growth rates would, therefore to some extent, reflect the amount of migration that has actually occurred. According to recent estimates, the population of Latin America increased by 33 percent between 1960 and 1970 (U.N., 1969); in cities with over 20,000 inhabitants, the increase was 54 percent, while elsewhere it was only 23 percent. Thus the urban population grew faster than the rural one. If the latter had increased at the rate of the area as a whole, it would now have a population of some 190 million, about 14 million more than it actually has. These missing millions would presumably represent the excess population that migrated to the cities during the decade in question.

Let us now repeat this calculation over a longer period, from 1940 to 1970, approximately the duration of the current demographic explosion to date. The rural population appears to have lost some 51 million as compared with what would have been if it had increased at the rate prevailing in the area as a whole. That number of people probably migrated to the cities. They represent 63 percent of the total population increase of the urban areas after thirty years.

Looked at in this light, the vast extent of the rural exodus can be appreciated. The figures advanced should not, however, be taken too literally. Based on hypotheses of questionable validity, they are of merely speculative value. The initial hypothesis, for example, held that both urban and rural populations grew in a symmetrical manner, when this is hardly ever so. Rural growth rates are usually higher. Consequently, the population of the country areas should have increased by more than the amount estimated in the previous paragraph. Conversely, the hypothetical figure of 51 million migrants during the period 1940 to 1970 includes children born to them after their arrival in the cities, who otherwise would have been born in the country. These children constitute a rural bonus to the growth of the urban centers although how could it be denied that they were actually city born? It seems, then, that perhaps the real drift from countryside to city is less than is suggested by the first rough calculations. Finally, the original hypothesis fails to take into account any possible international migration, or administrative changes such as the clustering of small outlying villages within city limits or the reclassification as urban of places whose size previously denied them such status.

At this stage, to arrive at any overall figure with any semblance of reliability seems difficult; nevertheless, the whole question of migration from country to city is now being examined from an entirely different point of view. Instead of an oblique approach to urbanization, there is now an attempt to ascertain the extent of the cities' own natural population increase. Arriaga (1968b), for example, by a complete reversal of perspective, has calculated the natural urban growth rate of some countries. The difference between this figure and that revealed by the actual population figures would indicate the extent of the influx to the cities. In this way, Arriaga found that more than half of the population expansion in the cities of Mexico, Venezuela, and Chile seems due to internal, natural growth. If, as was pointed out in the previous chapter, the natural growth rate in metropolitan areas is sometimes higher than in the rest of the country, then it is not surprising that natural reproduction should have been responsible for a greater proportion of urban population increase than has so far been supposed.

To sum up, careful research country by country is essential before generalizations can be made on the causes of urban growth. In Mexico, studied by Unikel (1968), it seems that the flow was not regular. The peak period appears to be from 1940 to 1950; during the following decade migration tended to decline. By comparing urban migration in various countries similar phases in this process will appear which did not all occur at the same time but at differing intervals.

To pass from the source of these migratory movements to the changes themselves, table 7.3 shows the estimated urban population of all the countries of Latin America in 1940, 1950, and 1960. A distinction is made between urban centers of over 20,000, 100,000, and 500,000 inhabitants. To save space, the figures are given in millions. It should be noted that not all countries figure in every category, and that some achieve only a fraction of one million.

The figures given in table 7.3 differ from those in other texts dealing with the urban population of Latin America. The standards adopted by different national census bodies are responsible for the existence of varying interpretations of the term *urban*. Depending on the country concerned and the date of the census, townships with as few as 2,500, 2,000, 1,500 or even 1,000 inhabitants are classified as urban. Elsewhere such administrative and quantitative criteria are disregarded, and classification as urban is bestowed in accordance with the number or kinds of public services that a locality does or does not have. On other occasions the basis for the classification is simply not given. To avoid a comparison of data of such a heterogeneous nature, and bearing in mind that nowadays townships with less than 20,000 inhabitants still tend to be closely linked with agriculture, we have adopted a system of classification increasingly used by international organizations, which ignores the differing census classifications and restricts the use of the term urban to cover townships or cities with a population in excess of 20,000. In larger

TABLE 7.3 Urban Population of Latin America, 1940–1960 (estimates in millions of inhabitants)

	20,000+			100,000+			500,000+		
	1940	1950	1960	1940	1950	1960	1940	1950	1960
Continental Central America									
Mexico	3.5	6.1	12.2	2.2	3.8	8.3	1.7	3.0	6.2
Guatemala	0.2	0.3	0.6	0.2	0.3	0.4	—	—	—
El Salvador	0.2	0.2	0.4	—	0.1	0.2	—	—	—
Honduras	0.1	0.1	0.2	—	—	0.1	—	—	—
Nicaragua	0.1	0.2	0.3	—	0.1	0.2	—	—	—
Costa Rica	0.1	0.2	0.3	0.1	0.2	0.2	—	—	—
Panama	0.2	0.2	0.4	0.1	0.2	0.3	—	—	—
Caribbean									
Cuba	1.4	1.9	2.7	0.9	1.2	1.8	0.8	1.0	1.4
Puerto Rico	0.4	0.6	0.7	0.2	0.4	0.5	—	—	—
Dominican Republic	0.1	0.2	0.6	—	0.2	0.4	—	—	—
Haiti	0.1	0.2	0.3	0.1	0.1	0.2	—	—	—
Tropical South America									
Brazil	6.6	10.8	20.3	4.8	7.6	13.6	3.6	6.0	11.8
Colombia	1.3	2.5	4.8	0.8	1.6	3.4	—	0.7	1.8
Peru	0.9	1.4	2.6	0.6	1.0	1.7	0.6	1.0	1.6
Venezuela	0.7	1.7	3.3	0.4	1.0	2.2	—	0.7	1.3
Ecuador	0.4	0.6	1.1	0.3	0.5	0.8	—	—	—
Bolivia	0.4	0.6	0.8	0.2	0.3	0.6	—	—	—
Temperate South America									
Argentina	5.8	8.8	11.4	4.2	6.5	8.9	3.5	5.2	8.0
Chile	1.8	2.5	4.0	1.2	1.6	2.4	1.0	1.2	2.0
Uruguay	0.8	1.0	1.4	0.6	0.8	1.0	0.6	0.8	1.0
Paraguay	0.1	0.2	0.4	0.1	0.2	0.4	—	—	—

SOURCE: U.N., 1969.

conglomerations, distinctions based on function, legal status, size or density of population, type of township, or the provision of public services are less significant, and it is fairly certain that the towns concerned will possess all the appropriate characteristics.

But the difficulties involved in discriminating between urban and country populations do not end here. Large modern cities spread beyond their administrative boundaries and invade surrounding districts, which become associated with the city proper in every sense except the legal one. Legal acknowledgment of an accomplished fact always lags behind the social realities. Since administrative criteria necessarily continue to be accepted for the gathering of official statistics, published data are always inevitably behind the times. Planners and demographers have not been able, nor have they wanted, to disregard the real size of cities; thus such terms as Greater Buenos Aires and Greater Santiago have arisen, lacking legal sanction, but nevertheless providing a *modus operandi*. However, for lack of agreement on the boundaries and size of such areas, which are nowadays constantly expanding, the figures that different research workers are referring to do not cover identical territories. Their conclusions are therefore not always comparable. The addition or exclusion of particular areas whose classification is doubtful makes for considerable variation. The problem is particularly difficult in the case of certain federal capitals. The metropolitan area of the capital does not coincide with that assigned to it in law. After occupying the whole federal district, Buenos Aires spread out continuously into the surrounding province. Mexico City and Caracas, on the other hand, have expanded into neighboring states without having first occupied all the rural areas existing within the federal district and even without having absorbed all the other urban centers within it.

As has been pointed out above, every comparative analysis demands that the basic data be elaborated with the same criteria. When listing the cities in Latin America which at the moment have more than half a million inhabitants (table 7.4), an overall, single source has therefore been preferred to the figures provided by different national agencies, for these are difficult to correlate. The conversions and projections of the International Population and Urban Research Office of the University of California, Berkeley, although made according to norms which some may not share, at least are consistent. Davis (1969) has published estimates of the size of metropolitan areas in 1950, 1960, and 1970. On this basis he has computed the growth rates for the two decades mentioned, as shown in table 7.4. In the last column on the right, the cities have been numbered in order of rank.

Having introduced the two tables, let us examine the state and evolution of the cities of Latin America in recent years. In 1960, the countries with the largest overall populations also had the highest absolute number of inhabitants in urban centers over the 20,000 mark. Brazil, the country with the highest population (see table 6.7, p. 193), had some 20 million people living in such centers; Mexico had about 12 million, and Argentina over 11 million. Then came Colombia with nearly 5 million, Chile with 4 million, and Venezuela with 3.3 million. These urban masses represented 29 percent of the total population of Brazil, a third or almost a third in Mexico and Colombia, 43 percent in Venezuela, and over 50 percent in Argentina and Chile. On average, 35 percent of the population of Latin America lived in urban centers with 20,000 inhabitants or more, a proportion similar to that in the U.S.S.R. and lower than

TABLE 7.4 Cities of Latin America with over Half a Million Inhabitants in 1970

	Population (in thousands)			Annual growth rate		Size ranking
	1950	1960	1970	1950–60	1960–70	
Continental						
Central America						
Mexico City	2,234	2,832	3,541	2.4	2.3	4
Guadalajara	378	737	1,364	6.9	6.3	14
Monterrey	332	597	1,009	6.0	5.4	17
Ciudad Juárez	122	262	532	7.9	7.3	32
Guatemala	294	474	770	4.9	5.0	24
Caribbean						
Havana	1,081	1,549	1,700	3.7	0.9	12
Santo Domingo	182	367	650	7.3	5.9	29
San Juan	429	542	819	2.4	4.2	20
Tropical South America						
Rio de Janeiro	3,052	4,692	7,213	4.4	4.4	3
São Paulo	2,449	4,537	8,405	6.4	6.4	2
Recife	693	1,115	1,794	4.9	4.9	10
Pôrto Alegre	434	894	1,842	7.5	7.5	9
Belo Horizonte	353	781	1,728	8.3	8.3	11
Salvador da Bahia	417	656	1,032	4.6	4.6	16
Fortaleza	270	515	982	6.7	6.7	18
Santos	248	409	675	5.1	5.1	28
Belém do Pará	255	402	634	4.7	4.7	31
Curitiba	181	362	724	7.2	7.2	25
Brasília	—	142	503	—	13.5	34
Bogotá	607	1,241	2,500	7.4	7.3	6
Medellín	341	579	1,090	5.4	6.5	15
Cali	269	486	915	6.1	6.5	19
Barranquilla	287	414	645	3.7	4.5	30
Lima-Callao	947	1,519	2,500	4.8	5.1	6
Caracas	694	1,280	2,147	6.3	5.3	8
Maracaibo	236	405	682	5.5	5.3	27
Guayaquil	259	450	800	5.7	5.9	23
Quito	210	314	500	4.1	4.8	35
La Paz	300	400	500	2.9	2.3	35
Temperate South America						
Buenos Aires	5,213	7,000	9,400	3.0	3 0	1
Rosario	560	672	806	1.8	1.8	22
Córdoba	426	589	814	3.3	3.3	21
Mendoza	256	427	712	5.2	5.2	26
La Plata	325	414	527	2.4	2.4	33
Santiago de Chile	1,275	1,907	2,600	4.1	3.1	5
Montevideo	609	962	1,530	4.7	4.7	13

SOURCE: Estimates in Davis, 1969.

those in North America (58 percent) and Europe (45 percent). On the other hand, the proportion is much higher than that prevailing in the rest of the Third World (U.N., 1969). According to these figures, Latin America is already one of the most urbanized regions in the world.

The largest countries are not necessarily the most urbanized. Argentina and Chile, for example, had a higher urbanization rate than other, larger countries, as can be appreciated. Argentina even surpassed Mexico, in numbers of people living in cities of over 100,-000 and of over 500,000 inhabitants (table 7.3). Comparing the subregional figures, we find the following proportions: Temperate South America had 53 percent of its population living in urban areas, a figure not much lower than that of North America and northern Europe; continental Central America (31 percent) and tropical South America (30 percent) approximated the figure for eastern Europe; and the Caribbean had the lowest proportion in the region, 24 percent.

By having recourse to a more rigorous system of measurement, one can emphasize even more the high urbanization rate in some Latin-American countries and the disparity existing between the advanced and the backward ones. The standard of measurement in question is the number of people living in cities of over 100,000 inhabitants as recently as 1970. Figure 14 indicates the proportion of each country's population living in cities of this size. Argentina and Uruguay stand out: more than half of their inhabitants live there. Among the most populous countries, Brazil, Colombia, Chile, Cuba, and Venezuela show a proportion of approximately one-third. Of the leading countries, only in Mexico is the dispersal of the population in the country and the small towns still so great that only one-fifth live in towns and cities of the size indicated. Haiti and Honduras, at the bottom of the list, are the least urbanized. Other countries in Central America and the Andes do have a higher urbanization rate than these two, but even when all of their small populations are added together, it does not invalidate the statement that Latin Americans as a whole are tending more and more to live in large cities.

In 1960, only nine countries had cities with populations of more than half a million. The Central American republics, those in the Caribbean, with the exception of Cuba, and the smaller countries of South America did not figure in this select group. By 1970, however, the group has been joined by five more countries: Guatemala, the Dominican Republic, Puerto Rico, Ecuador, and Bolivia. So now two-thirds of the countries of the region have cities that fall into this category. In 1960 there were only twenty cities in Latin America of this size; in 1970 there were thirty-six. Similarly, in the same period, the number of cities with over a million inhabitants has increased from ten to sixteen. Concentration is speeding up. In Latin America

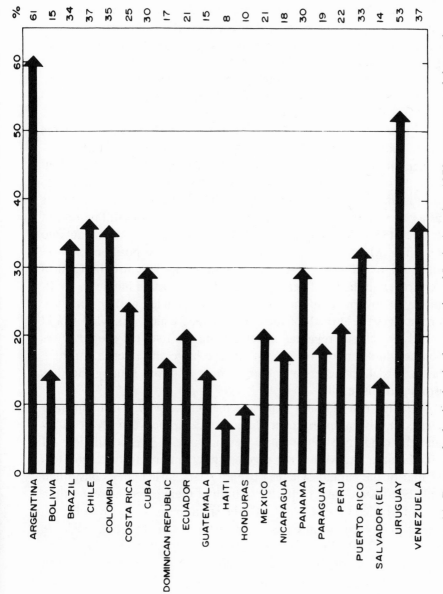

FIGURE 14. Degree of urbanization in the countries of Latin America, 1970: percentage of the total population living in cities with over 100,000 inhabitants. (Source: Davis, 1969.)

there are also seven cities with over two and a half million inhabitants (table 7.4). Of the eleven largest cities in the world, three are in Latin America: Buenos Aires, São Paulo, and Rio de Janeiro (Davis, 1969).

The large cities attract people from the smaller ones. This fact can be verified by examining the way the urban population itself is distributed. In 1960, seven out of every ten Argentines and Uruguayans living in urban centers were to be found in the cities with over half a million inhabitants; for Peruvians and Brazilians the figure was six; for Cubans, Mexicans, and Chileans it was five; and for Colombians and Venezuelans, four.

It was this tendency for the population to concentrate in large cities that gave rise to the idea that it was typical of all Latin-American countries for one city in each to become disproportionately large in relation to the country as a whole and to predominate over all the others (Browning, 1958). The Latin-American republics as a rule suffered from macrocephalia. This distortion still persists in temperate South America and in Peru, where Buenos Aires, Santiago de Chile, Montevideo, and Lima are in unrivaled positions both in size and in all other respects. The same applies also in Central America and the Caribbean. Political Balkanization implies a multiplicity of governments and administrative agencies, and this, in turn, encourages the growth of the capital cities, which otherwise would merely have been regional centers, while the national economic resources do not allow for more than one large city in each. In these cases it is sheer necessity rather than any special leaning that has produced this result.

In the rest of Latin America, the tendency which might have existed has been reversed. In Mexico, the gap between Mexico City and the other two major cities has narrowed. The populations of Guadalajara and Monterrey together now amount to three-quarters of that of the capital, whereas twenty years earlier they constituted only one-third. The growth rate of both of them is much greater than that of Mexico City (table 7.4). The situation is the same in Brazil, where many provincial cities are growing faster than either Rio de Janeiro or São Paulo. In fact, Brazil has never really suffered from the existence of a primate city. São Paulo came to compete early with Rio de Janeiro both in size and in importance. Moreover, in the last few years Rio de Janeiro has been deprived of its former status as the nation's capital with the transfer of the government to inland Brasília. In Ecuador, too, the most densely populated city, Guayaquil, does not house the seat of government; Quito, the capital, has a far smaller population. Neither in Colombia nor in Venezuela is the capital as disproportionately large in comparison with other major cities as is the case in temperate South America. Although the capitals have some advantage over the others in regard to population growth, the pull exerted by the regional centers is strong. Both Medellín and Cali in Colombia, for example, attract significantly large numbers of people.

In view of the above, one city dominance should be regarded not as a permanent feature of Latin America as a whole, but rather as typical of a few particular countries with specific characteristics. It also occurs in some other countries as the temporary result of intense polarization in the early developmental stages, but this may well weaken in due course. What does stand out, however, is that South America seems destined to develop megalopolises. Argentina is well on the way to having the first, stretched out along the right banks of the River Paraná and the River Plate estuary. From north of Rosario to south of Buenos Aires, there is a whole string of cities. Another similar development seems likely to form a continuous linear city linking São Paulo to Rio de Janeiro. It is not beyond the scope of the imagination to see the same thing happening in Venezuela between Valencia and Caracas. In Chile, the gradual merging of Santiago with Valparaíso and Viña del Mar is already taking place.

It seems almost certain that the process of urban expansion is by no means over in Latin America or elsewhere in the world, despite the warnings given that industrial and urban development will lead to the pollution of the biosphere. The speed at which urbanization is proceeding in the countries of Latin America is not uniform; in some the process seems to be slowing down, while in others it continues unabated.

In this respect, the countries of the region can be divided into three groups, according to Wingo (1967). Uruguay is typical of the first, where urbanization started early and is now nearly over, so that its cities are expanding very slowly. Further expansion seems likely to be due to natural population growth only, which is very slow. Argentina, Chile, Cuba, and Puerto Rico, whose population expansion is also relatively slow, fit into the same category in varying degrees. At the other end is Haiti, where urban development is equally slow, but for opposite reasons; there, the demographic changes that will lead to accelerated urban growth have not even begun. Bolivia and El Salvador are the two other countries where similar developments seem likely in the near future. Venezuela is typical of the remaining group, the one in which rapid urban development is now occurring. All the other countries in Latin America, with Brazil in the lead, fall into this category, though the speed of expansion varies. Mexico and Costa Rica are beginning to slow down; the Dominican Republic, however, a late entrant in the field, is proceeding very fast. Although the peak rate has not yet been reached in some countries, on the whole the majority seem to have passed it, as is apparent in table 7.2. The concentration of population is continuing, but more circumspectly and less one-sidedly than before, since the capital cities no longer have a monopoly of what development there is.

Fast expansion in so short a time has altered the configuration of Latin-American cities. The old city, which went through various phases of growth, became downtown. Occasionally the commercial heart itself has moved to the periphery, as in the case of Caracas. The area around the main square looks depressed and is saved only by the fact that governments, for symbolic reasons, insist on remaining in their traditional locales, and consequently banks and other institutions also stay. Residential districts, on the other hand, tend to move out along radial arteries, either in search of expansion, or of a specific natural feature, such as the seashore or the hills, but also in imitation of the living habits prevalent in other parts of the world. The old mansion in the city is demolished to make room for blocks of offices and apartments, while in the suburbs the reasonably well-to-do middle classes insist on building single-family houses.

The changing city has a disorderly, almost chaotic look about it. An old family mansion stands beside a towering block, while the modern suburbs are surrounded by barren lands. In the pockets left by urban expansion, a nameless huddle of makeshift homes springs up overnight, sometimes managing to turn itself into a permanent, immovable slum. The new arrivals in the cities can find nowhere to live—neither in the working-class areas of the old, half-demolished city, nor anywhere else—so they turn to squatting in order to provide a roof over their heads. They usually have to be content with waste land on the banks of a river, along a railway line, on a refuse tip, or else they climb precariously up the steep slopes of the surrounding hills. Thus, in every growing city there have sprung up shantytowns, which the fertile popular imagination has baptized with a variety of names, depending on the country in question—*favelas* (Brazil), *villas miserias* (Argentina), *callampas* (Chile), *cantegriles*

(Uruguay), *barriadas* (Mexico), or *cerros* (Peru)—but all implying poverty and squalor.

Life is hard in these improvised communities, lacking all public services, from the most elementary ones, such as water supplies, sewerage, and electricity, to transport. The distinction between these slums and the other parts of the cities is therefore not merely one of topography. The contrast between them and the ultra-modern city only a few minutes away is striking. Shantytowns are the inevitable outcome of the unexpected influx of people from the countryside, as well as of the iniquitous way in which investment and income is distributed. It is also a symptom of the imbalance between economic and demographic growth.

It is precisely this imbalance which had led Urquidi (1969) to describe Latin-American cities of today as "premature" and to forecast that matters will go from bad to worse if the serious problems besetting them are not resolved in time. Fortunately the slum is disappearing in some places as large blocks of modern housing are erected through a huge expenditure of public funds. However, since the backlog extends to some millions of homes, it is doubtful whether Latin America can solve the problem in the immediate future. Even if it could, it will still be a complex matter to piece together adjacent and conflicting elements in such a way as to fashion an integrated and viable city harmoniously related to the rest of the country.

VIII

The Year 2000

*W*E have rapidly covered an extensive time span—
from prehistory to the present day, from the palaeolithic nomad to
the sedentary city worker; it is impossible to conclude without wondering what the future holds in store for humanity. Such curiosity is
quite natural; yet prediction is no easy matter, for there are so many
imponderables and we have already seen what spectacular changes
are possible.

A long-term forecast is, of course, out of the question. But the
year 2000 is not so far ahead—only just over a quarter of a century
away. The factors that will have a bearing on the fertility rate during
the intervening period are already at work. The generation of women
now just entering upon the fertile period of their lives will then only
be beginning to reach the end of it. Without the intervention of wars,
technological catastrophes, or other unforeseen circumstances, it is
extremely likely that the demographic variables will continue to operate in accordance with their present behavior. It is therefore not
impossible to make some quantitative projections. The attempt is
worthwhile even at the risk of being proved wrong, as may very well
be the case.

In making this calculation it is essential to make quite clear
from the beginning the hypotheses upon which it is to be based. An
examination will now be made of the basic variables affecting demographic growth—fertility, mortality rates, and migration—in an en-

deavor to establish what is likely to happen to them during the remainder of this century.

The first hypothesis is that there will be no repetition of transoceanic migrations on anything like the scale of those which have occurred so far. The industrial countries have no need to export their populations, and Latin America, the area with the highest natural growth rate in the world, is even less likely to invite or attract the surplus population from the underdeveloped countries of Africa and Asia. On the contrary, in accordance with current trends—the inversion of the traditional migration pattern—it is by no means improbable to suppose that Latin Americans will themselves migrate to the more developed areas in both the Old World and the New. This process is already under way. And it is likely that the migrants will be confronted with increasingly rigid restrictive legislation, especially if there are economic recessions. Thus the migratory flow will probably not be very large. Internal migrations within the region will be able to resolve the tensions inherent in purely local population shortages or surpluses.

The mortality rate has now reached a moderate level, but it will presumably drop even further before the end of this century. However, the endeavor to control the death rate has now reached a stage of diminishing return, and spectacular changes such as those brought about by the introduction of antibiotics and pesticides in the 1940s are unlikely to materialize. The epidemiological transition discussed by Omran (1971), which admittedly has not yet been completed in some parts of Latin America, has replaced deaths due to infectious diseases by others caused by cancer or heart disease. One does not have to be a fervent believer in medical science to be certain that within the next quarter of a century cancer will have been brought under control and that great strides will have been made in the treatment of heart disease. Mature adults who now die from these complaints will grow old more placidly, but this medical achievement will have little affect on the death rates of children or young people, who are less susceptible to such afflictions. Life expectancy will, of course, rise. However, other degenerative diseases will carry off people at a more advanced age. Even if the death rate could be reduced to one-half its present figure, the resultant increase, though doubtless considerable, would not compare with that experienced at the beginning of the population explosion era. Thus projections in this respect do not show signs of excessive change.

Fertility, on the other hand, is quite a different matter. Because the internal factors controlling it are so little understood, it is that much more difficult to predict the future. Death is an involuntary act, since, with rare exceptions, the individual has no say in the matter; it is dependent on conditions controlled by science and technology. Conception, however, is the result of a conscious act of volition. Society has some influence on the matter by advancing expectations or inculcating beliefs that encourage or discourage procreation, but, in the last resort, the decision whether to have a child rests with the couple concerned. Thus the behavior of the fertility rate depends on one's evaluation of the efficacy of birth control policies and on how social and economic conditions evolve between now and the year 2000.

Bourgeois-Pichat and Taleb (1970) have demonstrated that the zero population growth slogan expounded in the press and by official circles in the U.S.A. is an unrealistic objective for Latin America in purely theoretical terms and without going into the moral questions involved. The conclusion is based on a projection of the population of Mexico. In view of the present demographic characteristics of the country, the object could not be achieved by using either of the two possible alternatives. Each of them would require drastic government intervention in the matter of birth control, and there is not the slightest indication that Mexico would be prepared to adopt such a policy. Even in the unlikely event of its doing so, such violent fluctuations in the birth rate would occur that, in the year 2000, the country would still be in the position of having a population surplus. Apparently the most one can hope for is that the reproduction rate will by then have been reduced to one, a more modest achievement than that of a zero growth rate. In this event the nation would continue to expand for awhile, owing to the present age composition of the population.

The idea of family planning has been better received than was expected. Religious and other taboos are of less importance than was thought. Latin Americans are prepared to adopt contraceptive practices if they can see the advantage of doing so. On the other hand, the family-planning campaign in the area has been in operation for only ten years, and in some parts for a much shorter time, so that it does not seem unreasonable to suppose that its influence will spread in due course. Ad hoc clinics can distribute all the necessary pills or other contraceptive devices, but what guarantee is there that people will abandon their preference for having large families? It has been pointed out that many women who submitted to sterilization already had four children. They fully accepted the idea of contraception, but their ideas about the size of their ideal family had altered little. The doubts expressed by Davis (1967) about the prospects for family planning have some substance.

To date, only improved living conditions and better education have been shown to have caused some real reduction in the fertility rate. The better the degree of economic security and the higher the standard of education, the lower the number of children deemed necessary. But the road leading to that goal is a long one and it is being proceeded along very slowly. In view of the nature of current social and power structures, and the fact that they are presently being called into question, it is impossible to predict what educational, social, and economic regime will predominate in Latin America at the end of the century, and what degree of improvement will have been achieved in these three fields by then.

One possible prognostication is that the factors influencing demographic growth will continue to follow today's lines. Extrapolations based on this hypothesis appear in table 8.1. In it are condensed a wide range of estimates made by CELADE (1971). Successive columns show the size of the population in each country, the birth, death, and growth rates, together with such complementary information as life expectancy and general fertility rates. Finally, to give an idea of the relative youthfulness of the population of Latin America, the number of children under the age of fifteen is shown as a percentage of the total population. The total population figures given refer to the situation in the middle of the year 2000. All the other figures, except those in the last column, are based on the average over the last five years of the century. The countries are listed in subregional groupings, and for each of these latter, subtotals or arithmetical averages are given.

In the year 2000, Latin America will have a population of some 642 million inhabitants. With this figure it will outrank Europe (527)—U.S.S.R. not included (353)—and the U.S.A. and Canada combined (354). Only Africa (768) and, of course, eastern and southern Asia (3,458) will have larger populations (U.N., 1966). If these estimates prove correct, the population of Latin America will, for the first time, be more numerous than that of the Old World, and twice as large as the populations of North America and of the U.S.S.R. (See fig. 1, p. 7.) These relative proportions will undoubtedly affect the region's relationship with the rest of the world.

TABLE 8.1 Latin America in the Year 2000: Demographic Projections.

	Popula-tion (in millions)	Birth rate	Death rate	Growth rate	Life expectancy	General fertility rate	% under age 15
Continental							
Central America							
Mexico	135.1	33.3	4.1	29.2	72.8	4.5	41.7
Guatemala	12.4	33.7	6.4	27.3	67.2	4.5	41.7
El Salvador	10.4	43.1	5.2	37.5[b]	69.9	6.0	47.7
Honduras	7.2	39.2	7.3	32.4[b]	64.6	5.3	44.0
Nicaragua	5.5	39.3	7.1	32.2	65.9	5.5	44.2
Costa Rica	3.7	26.4	4.5	21.9	70.8	3.2	34.8
Panama	3.6	34.5	4.2	30.3	73.2	4.4	42.0
Subtotals	177.9	35.6[a]	5.5[a]	30.1[a]	69.2[a]	4.8[a]	42.1
Caribbean							
Cuba	14.3	23.7	6.6	17.1	73.6	3.2	31.1
Puerto Rico	3.9	18.3	7.4	8.9[b]	73.9	2.5	26.1
Dominican Republic	12.5	39.6	5.5	30.2	67.8	5.5	45.5
Haiti	12.3	40.3	10.1	34.1	60.0	5.6	43.5
Subtotals	43.0	30.5[a]	7.4[a]	22.6[a]	68.8[a]	4.2[a]	36.6
Tropical South America							
Brazil	215.5	31.8	5.1	26.7	72.0	4.3	39.2
Colombia	56.7	30.5	4.2	26.7	72.8	4.3	39.2
Peru	33.5	32.9	4.9	28.0	70.9	4.4	40.3
Venezuela	26.1	31.0	4.7	26.3	71.7	3.8	38.3
Ecuador	16.1	36.2	5.2	31.0	69.4	5.0	43.5
Bolivia	10.1	36.7	10.4	25.8[b]	57.6	5.2	41.1
Subtotals	358.0	33.2[a]	5.7[a]	27.3[a]	68.7[a]	4.4[a]	40.3
Temperate South America							
Argentina	35.3	18.2	9.4	9.5[b]	70.7	2.4	25.7
Chile	16.3	24.8	5.7	19.1	72.9	3.1	32.5
Uruguay	4.0	17.6	8.8	8.8	74.4	2.4	25.6
Paraguay	6.6	34.9	4.3	30.6	71.5	4.6	42.0
Subtotals	62.2	23.9[a]	7.0[a]	17.0[a]	72.4[a]	3.1[a]	31.5
Totals for Latin America	645.1	31.7	6.2	25.4	69.6	4.2	38.2

[a]Average not weighted.
[b]Includes slight interregional migratory movements.
SOURCE: CELADE, 1971 (except Chile, CELADE, 1972)

Changes in the geographical distribution of the population within the area will also bring about changes in the present relationships between nations or their groupings. Brazil will then have as many inhabitants as the whole of Latin America had in 1960, and Mexico slightly more than the subcontinent in 1940. Portuguese-speaking America will then have a population two-thirds the size of that of the U.S.A., and Mexico, two-fifths. Brazil and Mexico will stand out well in front of the other countries of Latin America.

Colombia will lead the next largest group, a short way ahead of Central America, if centripetal forces prevail in the area at last and it succeeds in becoming a unified whole, with 42.8 million inhabitants —a population larger than that of Spain. Peru and Argentina will by then be a match for each other. At the head of the last group will be Venezuela and Chile, with Uruguay and Puerto Rico bringing up the rear.

In a comparison of this distribution with that preceding the population explosion (1930, table 5.11, p. 169), the main differences that can be noticed are as follows: While Brazil in the year 2000 will still have, as in 1930, exactly one-third of the total population of Latin America, Mexico will have increased its share proportionately from one-sixth to one-fifth. Argentina's share, on the other hand, will have been reduced by one-half—it will have only 5.5 percent at the turn of the century, compared with 11 percent in 1930. In general, the pendulum that favored temperate South America will have swung away to benefit Central America and tropical South America.

The gap separating the two groups of countries indicated by Miró (1966*b*) will have narrowed; as far as demography is concerned, Latin America will be more homogeneous. The fertility rate will continue to be low in the more developed countries. The replacement of the generations will be safely assured, but there will be no large surplus. The population will not have a disproportionately large number of young people, since only a quarter of the total will be under the age of fifteen. On the other hand, the remaining countries will still show signs of having but recently emerged from a situation in which three-quarters of the republics of Latin America had birth rates of about 40 per thousand (table 6.4, p. 189). El Salvador and Haiti with a figure in excess of this will then be exceptions to the rule. The average birth rate for Latin America as a whole will have dropped considerably: it will have fallen from 38 per thousand to 31.7, significantly lower than Africa's rate at that time. Nevertheless, Latin America's birth rate will still be double that of Europe and considerably higher than that prevailing in the U.S.S.R. and North America (U.N., 1966). Nevertheless, fertility will have begun to decline.

As for the death rate, countries where the figure is now low will have lost their lead, and will show an even poorer record than that of some countries that are now behind them. Argentina and Uruguay, for example, will have the highest death-rate figures in the area, with the exception of Bolivia. Since these countries will suffer from no higher disease rate than that of the remaining countries of the area, the difference is explained by the different age composition of the population. In any case, the gap between the extremes will have been reduced. If these forecasts prove correct, Argentina will have the same life-expectancy rate as Peru, whereas today there is a ten-year differential between them. To generalize, one may say that Latin America will have achieved life-expectancy rates comparable with those of the industrialized countries in 1960 (see table 6.7, p. 193). The crude death rate will be the lowest in the world, having gone down from 10.1 to 6.2. It will be lower than that of Europe, the U.S.S.R., and North America (11.2, 8.7, and 7.9, respectively) (U.N., 1966).

In the year 2000, Latin America will still be experiencing the results of the population explosion that began some sixty years earlier. The violence of the eruption will have ended, but the dust resulting from it will not have settled. The growth rate will be about 25.4 per thousand inhabitants, three points lower than today's figure. By reason of its growth rate and age composition, Latin America will continue to belong to the developing world, together with Africa and Asia, showing a fertility rate still only poorly controlled.

One legacy bequeathed by the population explosion will give us the key to the future environmental conditions of life in Latin America. The United Nations has already made a projection of the urban and rural population of the world at the end of this century (U.N., 1969). According to this, the majority of the 638 million inhabitants of Latin America (the estimate is slightly less than the preceding one) will be living in towns or cities of over 20,000 inhabitants: 342 million, as against 296 million remaining in rural areas or in small towns. In other words, 54 percent will be urban and 46 percent rural. Latin America will be unlike other developing areas of the world in this regard, for in Africa and Asia 71 percent of the inhabitants will be living in the countryside as against 29 percent in urban areas. From this it follows that the distribution of the work force among the various economic activities will be different in Latin America from that in Asia and Africa. In Latin America only a small proportion of the population will be employed in the primary sector. The majority will be working in the secondary and tertiary sectors.

The rural Latin Americans of the beginning of this century will have disappeared, and their grandchildren will be crowded into the concrete jungle of the cities. It is interesting to speculate on what their problems will be and what they will make of their lives, but since such matters are of a subjective nature, they cannot be quantitatively expressed and remain beyond the scope of this work.

Finally, it should be pointed out that this future mathematically extrapolated is by no means certain. It is determined not by any mysterious outside forces, but by human beings. Whether the population falls short of or exceeds the estimates is up to them. Either they will wait for the future submissively or they will take the necessary steps to ensure that it is both prosperous and pleasant. It will be up to them to determine what their aims are and how they can be achieved.

Bibliography

ASTERISKS are used to indicate the most useful titles. The names of some institutions or reviews have been abbreviated as follows:

AIIH	Anuario del Instituto de Investigaciones Históricas (Rosario)
AL	América Latina (Rio de Janeiro)
Annals	The Annals of the American Academy of Political and Social Sciences
CELADE	Centro Latinoamericano de Demografía (Santiago de Chile)
CRLP	Conferencia Regional Latinoamericano de Población (Mexico)
D y E	Demografía y Economía (Mexico)
HAHR	The Hispanic American Historical Review
IASI	Inter-American Statistical Institute (Washington, D.C.)
IPC	International Population Conference. New York 1961; London 1969
MMFQ	Milbank Memorial Fund Quarterly (New York)
RBE	Revista Brasileira de Estatística (Rio de Janeiro)
U.N.	United Nations. Population Division (New York)

Adams, R. N. 1965. *Migraciones internas en Guatemala. Expansión agraria de los indígenas kekchíes hacia El Petén.* Guatemala.

Aguirre Beltrán, G. 1946. *La población negra de México, 1519–1810.* Mexico.

Alcedo, A. de, 1786–1789. *Diccionario geográfico-histórico de las Indias occidentales o América.* 5 vols. Madrid.

Alden, D. 1963. "The Population of Brazil in the Late Eighteenth Century: A Preliminary Study." *HAHR*, 43 (2): 173–205.

Álvarez Amézquita, J., et al. 1960. *Historia de la salubridad y de la asistencia en México.* 4 vols. Mexico.

Aparicio, F. de, and H. A. Difrieri (ed.). 1961. *La Argentina. Suma de geografía* (especially Vol. 7), Buenos Aires.

Arango Cano, J. 1951. *Inmigrantes para Colombia.* Bogotá.

Aranguiz Donoso, H. 1969. "Notas para el estudio de una parroquia rural del siglo XVIII: Pelarco, 1786–1796." *Anales de la Facultad de Filosofía y Ciencia de la Educación*: 37–42.

Arcila Farías, E. 1957. *El régimen de la encomienda en Venezuela.* Seville.

Arcondo, A. 1972. *Población y mano de obra agrícola. Córdoba 1880–1914.* Córdoba.

Arriaga, E. A. 1967*a.* "Rural-Urban Mortality in Developing Countries: An Index for Detecting Rural Underregistration." *Demography,* 4 (1): 98–107.

————. 1967*b.* "The Effect of a Decline in Mortality on the Gross Reproduction Rate," *MMFQ,* 45 (3): 333–52.

*————. 1968*a. New Life Tables for Latin American Populations in the Nineteenth and Twentieth Centuries.* Berkeley.

————. 1968*b.* "Components of City Growth in Selected Latin American Countries." *MMFQ,* 46 (2): 237–52.

*————. 1970*a. Mortality Decline and Its Effects in Latin America.* Berkeley.

————. 1970*b.* "The Nature and Effects of Latin America's Non-Western Trend in Fertility." *Demography,* 7 (4): 483–501.

————. 1972. "Impact of Population Changes on Education Cost." *Demography,* 9 (2): 275–93.

Arriaga E. A. and K. Davis, 1969. "The Pattern of Mortality Change in Latin America." *Demography,* 6 (3): 223–42.

*Aschmann, H. 1959. *The Central Desert of Baja California: Demography and Ecology.* Berkeley.

Ávila, F. B. de. 1956. *L'immigration au Brésil.* Rio de Janeiro.

————. 1964. *Immigration in Latin America.* Washington, D.C.

Ayarragaray, L. 1910. *La constitución étnica argentina y sus problemas.* Buenos Aires.

Azara, F. [1790] 1943. *Descripción e historia del Paraguay y del Río de la Plata.* Buenos Aires.

Azevedo, T. de. 1955. *Povoamento da cidade do Salvador.* 2d ed. São Paulo.

Balán, J. 1969. "Migrant-native Socioeconomic Differences in Latin American Cities: A Structural Analysis," *Latin American Research Review,* 4 (1): 3–51.

*Barón Castro, R. 1942. *La población de El Salvador. Estudio acerca de su desenvolvimiento desde la época prehispánica hasta nuestros días.* Madrid.

————. 1945. "La población hispanoamericana a partir de la Independencia," *Estudios demográficos*: 185–245.

————. 1959. "El desarrollo de la población hispanoamericana (1492–1950)," *Journal of World History,* 5 (2): 325–43.

Barrera Lavalle, F. 1911. *Apuntes para la historia de la estadística en México, 1821 a 1910.* Mexico.

Barreto, C. 1947. *Estudos brasileiros de população* (2d. ed.). Rio de Janeiro.

————. 1951. *Povoamento e população. Política populacional brasileira.* Rio de Janeiro.

Barriga, V. M. 1951. *Los terremotos de Arequipa, 1582–1868. Documentos de los archivos de Sevilla y Arequipa.* Arequipa.

Bates, M. 1957. *The Migration of Peoples to Latin America.* Washington, D.C.

Bazzanella, W. 1960. *Problemas de urbanização na América latina. Fontes bibliográficas.* Rio de Janeiro.

―――. 1963. "Industrialização e urbanização no Brasil." *AL*, 6 (1): 3–26.

*Behm Rosas, H. 1962. *Mortalidad infantil y nivel de vida.* Santiago de Chile.

Behm Rosas, H., and H. Gutiérrez, 1967. "Structure and Causes of Death and Level of Mortality: An Experience in Latin America," *U.N. Proceedings of the World Population Conference, 1965.* Vol. 3, pp. 391–94.

Behm Rosas, H., et al. 1970. "Mortalidad infantil en Chile: tendencias recientes." *CRLP*, Mexico, Session 1/7.

Benítez Zenteno, R. 1961. *Análisis demográfico de México.* Mexico.

Berberena, S. I., and P. S. Fonseca. 1909–1914. *Monografías departamentales.* 14 fasc. San Salvador.

Besio Moreno, N. 1939. *Buenos Aires. Puerto del Río de la Plata. Capital de la Argentina. Estudio crítico de su población, 1536–1936.* Buenos Aires.

―――. 1943. "Rosario de Santa Fe. Cartografía y población, 1744–1942." *Revista del Museo de La Plata* (new series), 1 (Geología no. 7): 259–98.

Bethell, L. 1970. *The Abolition of the Brazilian Slave Trade: Britain, Brazil and the Slave Trade Question, 1808–1869.* Cambridge, England.

Beyhaut, G., et al. 1961. *Inmigración y desarrollo económico.* Buenos Aires.

Beyer, G. H. (ed.). 1967. *The Urban Explosion in Latin America: A Continent in Process of Modernization.* Ithaca.

Boeri, L. I. 1963. *Catálogo de estadísticas publicadas en la República Argentina.* Buenos Aires.

*Borah, W. 1951. *New Spain's Century of Depression.* Berkeley.

―――. 1962. "Population Decline and the Social and Institutional Changes of New Spain in the Middle Decades of the Sixteenth Century." *Akten des 38 Internationalen Amerikanistenkongresses, Wien, 1960.* Vienna. Pp. 172–78.

―――. 1964. "America as Model: The Demographic Impact of European Expansion upon the Non-European World." *XXXV Congreso Internacional de Americanistas, México, 1962.* Vol. 3, pp. 379–87.

*―――. 1970. "The Historical Demography of Latin America: Sources, Techniques, Controversies, Yields." In Deprez, 1970, pp. 173–205.

*Borah, W., and S. F. Cook. 1960. *The Population of Central Mexico in 1548: A Critical Analysis of the Suma de Visitas de Pueblos.* Berkeley.

―――. 1962. "La despoblación del México Central en el siglo XVI." *Historia mexicana*, 12 (1): 1–12.

*―――. 1963. *The Aboriginal Population of Central Mexico on the Eve of the Spanish Conquest.* Berkeley.

―――. 1966. "Marriage and Legitimacy in Mexican Culture: Mexico and California." *California Law Review*, 54 (2): 946–1008.

―――. 1969. "Conquest and Population: A Demographic Approach to Mexican History." *Proceedings of the American Philosophical Society*, 113 (2): 177–83.

Bourgeois-Pichat, J., and S. A. Taleb. 1970. "Una tasa de crecimiento demográfico nulo en los países en vías de desarrollo al año 2000: ¿sueño o realidad?" *D y E*, 5 (1): 77–92.

Boxer, C. R. 1969. *The Golden Age of Brazil: 1695–1750: Growing Pains of a Colonial Society* (3d ed.). Berkeley.

*Boyd-Bowman, P. 1964 and 1968. *Índice geobiográfico de cuarenta mil pobladores españoles de América en el siglo XVI.* 1 (1493–1519), Bogotá; and 2 (1520–1539), Mexico.

Brady, T. M., and J. V. Lombardi. 1970. "The Application of Computers to the Analysis of Census Data: The Bishopric of Caracas, 1780–1820." In Deprez, 1970, pp. 271–78.

Brannon, M. P. 1943. "Desarrollo histórico de la estadística en El Salvador." *Proceedings of the American Scientific Congress.* Washington, D.C. Vol. 8 (*Statistics*), pp. 263–78.

Brito Figueroa, F. 1966. *Historia económica y social de Venezuela.* 2 vols. Caracas.

Brito V., E. M. 1969. "La fecundidad según status socioeconómico. Análisis comparativo de las ciudades de México y Buenos Aires." *D y E*, 3 (2): 156–87.

Bromley, J., and J. Barbagelata. 1945. *Evolución urbana de la ciudad de Lima.* Lima.

*Browning, H. L. 1958. "Recent Trends in Latin American Urbanization." *Annals*, 316: 111–20.

Browning, H. L., and W. Feindt. 1969. "Selectivity of Migrants to a Metropolis in a Developing Country: A Mexican Case Study," *Demography*, 6 (4): 347–57.

————. 1971. "Patterns of Migration to Monterrey, Mexico," *International Migration Review*, 5 (3): 309–24.

Bueno, C. [1763–1779] 1951. *Geografía del Perú virreinal (siglo XVIII).* Publicado por D. Valcárcel. Lima.

Bunge, A. E. 1940. *Una nueva Argentina.* Buenos Aires.

Burnight, R. G. 1963. "Estimates of Net Migration, Mexico, 1930–1950." *IPC New York 1961.* London. Vol. 1, pp. 412–18.

Cacopardo, M. C. 1969. *Argentina: aspectos demográficos de la población económicamente activa en el período 1869–1895.* Santiago de Chile.

*Camargo, J. F. de. 1960. *Êxodo rural no Brasil. Formas, causas e conseqüências econômicas principais.* Rio de Janeiro.

————. 1968. *A cidade e o campo. O êxodo rural no Brasil.* São Paulo.

Camisa, Z. C. 1968. "Assessment of Registration and Census Data on Fertility." *MMFQ*, 46 (3, part 2): 17–37.

Carleton, R. O. 1965. "Fertility Trends and Differentials in Latin America." *MMFQ*, 43 (4, part 2): 15–31.

*————. 1969. *Aspectos demográficos de la infancia y de la juventud en América latina.* Santiago de Chile.

Carmagnani, M. 1963. *El salariado minero en Chile colonial. Su desarrollo en una sociedad provincial: el Norte Chico, 1690–1800.* Santiago de Chile.

*————. 1967. "Colonial Latin American Demography: Growth of Chilean Population, 1700–1830." *Journal of Social History*, 1 (2): 179–91.

*————. 1970. "Demografia e società. La struttura sociale di due centri mineri del Messico settentrionale (1600–1720)." *Rivista Storica Italiana*, 82 (3): 560–91.

Carmagnani, M., and H. S. Klein. 1965. "Demografía histórica: la población del obispado de Santiago, 1777–1778," *Boletín de la Academia Chilena de la Historia*, 72:54–74.

Carneiro, Felipe, J. 1948. "Historia da imigração no Brazil. Una interpretação." *Boletim geográfico*, 6 (69): 1009–44.

———. 1960. *Imigração e colonização no Brasil*. Rio de Janeiro.

Carvalho, A. V. W. de. 1960. *A população brasileira (Estudo e interpretação)*. Rio de Janeiro.

Carr-Saunders, A. M. 1936. *World Population*. Oxford.

Carrasco, P. 1964. "Tres libros de tributos del Museo Nacional y su importancia para los estudios demográficos." *Congreso Internacional de Americanistas, México 1962, Actas y Memorias*. Mexico. Vol. 3, pp. 373–78.

Carreira, A. 1968. "As companhias pombalinas de navegação, comércio e tráfico de escravos entre a costa africana e o nordeste brasileiro." *Boletim cultural da Guiné portuguesa*, 23: 5–88, 301–454.

Carrillo Batalla, T. E. 1967. *Análisis cuantitativo y cualitativo de la economía de la población venezolana*. Caracas.

Casañas, O. 1965. "La población de Santa María (Catamarca) entre los censos nacionales de 1869 y 1895." *AIIH*, 8: 181–220.

Casas, B. de las. 1953. *The Tears of the Indians*. Stanford.

Cataldi, A. 1964. *La situación demográfica del Uruguay en 1957 y proyecciones a 1982*. Santiago de Chile.

CDI. 1864–1884. *Colección de documentos inéditos relativos al descubrimiento, conquista y organización de las antiguas posesiones españolas*. 24 vols. Madrid.

CELADE, 1963. "Differential Migration in Some Regiones and Cities of Latin America in the Period 1940–1950. Methodological Aspects and Results." *IPC, New York 1961*, London, Vol. 1, pp. 468–80.

———. 1968. "Crecimiento de la población de la región de América latina, 1920–1980." *Boletín demográfico*, 1.

———. 1969. *Chile. Población económicamente activa. Migración. Seguridad social. Fecundidad. Mortalidad, Fuentes de datos demográficos*. Santiago de Chile.

*———. 1970. "América latina: población total por países, año 1970." *Boletín demográfico*, 6.

*———. 1971. *Boletín demográfico*, 8.

———. 1972. *Boletín demográfico*. 10.

Centre National de la Recherche Scientifique. 1965. *Problèmes des capitales en Amérique Latine*. Paris.

Centro de Estudios de Población y Desarrollo. 1966. *I Seminario nacional de población y desarrollo, Paracas, 1965*. Lima.

———. 1972. *Informe demográfico del Perú*. Lima.

Centro de Estudios Económicos y Demográficos. 1970. *Dinámica de la población de México*. Mexico.

Centro de Investigación y Acción Social. 1966. *La revolución demográfica. Estudio interdisciplinar del caso colombiano*. Bogotá.

Centro Latino Americano de Pesquisas em Ciências Sociais. 1965. *Situação social da América Latina*. Rio de Janeiro.

*CEPAL. 1963. *El desarrollo social de América latina en la postguerra*, Buenos Aires.

————. 1968. "La urbanización de la sociedad en América latina." *Boletín económico de América latina*, 13 (2): 211–29.

————. 1969. *Estudio económico de América latina 1968*. New York.

Cervera, F. J., and M. Gallardo, 1966–1967. "Santa Fe 1765–1830: historia y demografía." *AIIH*, 9: 39–66.

Cervera M. 1907. *Historia de la ciudad y provincia de Santa Fe, 1573–1853*. Vol. 1, Santa Fe.

*Chang-Rodríguez, E. 1958. "Chinese Labor Migration into Latin-America in the Nineteenth Century," *Revista de Historia de América*, 45/46: 375–97.

Chao, M. del P. 1965. "La población de Potosí en 1779." *AIIH*, 8: 171–80.

Charry Lara, A. 1954. *Desarrollo de la estadística nacional en Colombia*. Bogotá.

*Chaunu, H. and P. 1955–1960. *Séville et l'Atlantique (1504–1650)*. 8 vols. Paris.

Chaunu, P. 1964. "Pour une 'géopolitique' de l'espace américain." *Jahrbuch für Geschichte von Staat, Wirtschaft und Gesellschaft Lateinamerikas*, 1: 3–26.

*Chevalier, F. 1963. *Land and Society in Colonial Mexico: The Great Hacienda*. Berkeley.

Cho, L. J. 1964. "Estimated Refined Measures of Fertility for all Major Countries of the World." *Demography*, 1 (1): 359–74.

Cieza de León, P. [1553] 1945. *La Crónica del Perú*. Buenos Aires.

Cline, H. F. 1949. "Civil Congregations of the Indians in New Spain, 1598–1606." *HAHR*, 29 (3): 349–69.

Cofresí, F. 1951. *Realidad poblacional de Puerto Rico*. San Juan.

Colin, M. 1966. *Le Cuzco à la fin du XVII et au début du XVIIIe siècle*. Paris.

*Collver, O. A. 1965. *Birth Rates in Latin America: New Estimates of Historical Trends and Fluctuations*. Berkeley.

————. 1968. "Current Trends and Differentials in Fertility as Revealed by Official Data." *MMFQ*, 46 (3): 39–48.

Colmenares, G. 1969. *Encomienda y población en la provincia de Pamplona (1549–1650)*. Bogotá.

*————. 1970. *La provincia de Tunja en el Nuevo Reino de Granada. Ensayo de historia social (1539–1800)*. Bogotá.

Comadrán Ruiz, J. 1969. *Evolución demográfica argentina durante el período hispano (1535–1810)*. Buenos Aires.

Consuegra, J. 1969. *El control de la natalidad como arma del imperialismo*. Buenos Aires.

Contreras, J., et al. [1971]. *Fuentes para un estudio de demografía histórica de Chile en el siglo XVIII*. Concepción.

Cook, N. D. 1965. "La población indígena en el Perú colonial." *AIIH*, 8: 73–110.

———— (ed.). 1968. *Padrón de los indios de Lima en 1613*. Lima.

*————. 1970. "The Indian Population of Peru, 1570–1620." Ms.

Cook, S. F. 1937. *The Extent and Significance of Disease Among the Indians of Baja California, 1697–1773*. Berkeley.

———. 1940. *Population Trends Among the California Missions Indians*. Berkeley.

———. 1941–1942. "Francisco Xavier Balmis and the Introduction of Vaccine to Latin America." *Bulletin of the History of Medicine*, 11: 543–57; 12: 70–89.

———. 1946a. "Human Sacrifice and Warfare as Factors in the Demography of Pre-Colonial Mexico." *Human Biology*, 18 (2): 81–102.

———. 1946b. "The Incidence and Significance of Disease Among the Aztecs and Related Tribes." *HAHR*, 26 (3): 320–25.

———. 1947. "The Interrelation of Population, Food Supply and Building in Pre-Conquest Central Mexico," *American Antiquity*, 13 (1): 45–52.

———. 1949a. *The Historical Demography and Ecology of Teotlalpan*. Berkeley.

*———. 1949b. *Soil Erosion and Population in Central Mexico*. Berkeley.

———. 1955. "The Epidemic of 1830–1833 in California and Oregon." *Publication on American Archeology and Ethnology*, 43 (3): 303–26.

———. 1970. "Migration as a Factor in the History of Mexican Population: Sample Data from West Central Mexico, 1793–1950." In Deprez, 1970, pp. 279–302.

*Cook, S. F., and W. Borah. 1957. "The Rate of Population Change in Central Mexico, 1550–1570." *HAHR*, 37 (4): 463–70.

*———. 1960. *The Indian Population of Central Mexico, 1531–1610*. Berkeley.

———. 1963. "Quelle fut la stratification sociale du centre du Méxique durant la première moitié du XVIe siècle?" *Annales. Economies. Sociétés. Civilisations*, 18: 226–58.

———. 1966. "On the Credibility of Contemporary Testimony on the Population of Mexico in the Sixteenth Century." *Summa Anthropologica en homenaje a Roberto J. Weitlaner*. Mexico. Pp. 229–39.

———. 1968. *The Population of the Mixteca Alta, 1520–1960*. Berkeley.

*———. 1971. *Essays in Population History: Mexico and the Caribbean*. Vol. 1. Berkeley.

———. 1972. "Aging in Latin America During the Past Century." Ms.

Cook, S. F., and L. B. Simpson. 1948. *The Population of Central Mexico in the Sixteenth Century*. Berkeley.

Cooper, D. B. 1965. *Epidemic Disease in Mexico City, 1761–1813. An Administrative, Social and Medical Study*. Austin.

Corcoran, T. F. 1945. "Crecimiento de la población de la República de Panamá." *Estadística*, 10: 21–17.

Cordero, E. 1968. "La subestimación de la mortalidad infantil en México." *D y E*, 2 (1): 44–62.

Corredor, B. 1962. *La familia en América latina*. Madrid.

Cortés Alonso, V. 1965. "Tunja y sus vecinos." *Revista de Indias*, 25 (99–100): 155–207.

Cortés y Larraz, P. [1768–1770]. 1958. *Descripción geográfico-moral de la diócesis de Goathemala*. Guatemala.

Corwin, A. F. 1967. *Spain and the Abolition of Slavery in Cuba, 1817–1886.* Austin.

Costa, A. de J. da. 1965. *População da cidade da Baía em 1775.* Bahia.

*Costanzo, G. 1944. "The Policy of Immigration and Settlement in the South American Countries." *International Review of Agriculture,* 35: 81E–118E.

Crist, R. E., and E. Guhl. 1956. "Pioneer Settlement in Eastern Colombia." *Annual Report of the Board of Regents of the Smithsonian Institution.* Publication 4272, pp. 391–414.

CRLP, 1972. *Actas.* 2 vols. Mexico.

Crosby, A. W. 1967. "Conquistador y pestilencia: The First New World Pandemic and the Fall of the Great Indian Empires." *HAHR,* 47 (3): . 321–37.

Cuba. Secretaría de Hacienda. 1902–1930. *Inmigración y movimiento de pasajeros.* Havana.

Curtin, P. 1968. "Epidemiology and the Slave Trade." *Political Science Quarterly,* 83 (2): 190–216.

*———. 1969. *The Atlantic Slave Trade: A Census.* Madison.

Dahl, V. C. 1960. "Alien Labor in the Gulf Coast of Mexico, 1880–1900." *The Americas,* 17 (1): 21–35.

Daly, H. E. 1969. "El problema de la población en el Nordeste de Brasil: sus dimensiones económicas e ideológicas," *D y E,* 3 (3): 279–307.

Dávila Padilla, A. 1625. *Historia de la fundación y discurso de la provincia, de Santiago de México, de la orden de predicadores* (2d ed.). Brussels.

Davis, K. (ed.). 1950. *Corrientes demográficas mundiales.* Mexico.

*———. 1964. "The Place of Latin America in World Demographic History." *MMFQ,* 42 (2): 19–47.

*———. 1967. "Population Growth Policy: Will Current Programs Succeed? *Science,* 158 (3802): 730–39.

*———. 1969. *World Urbanization, 1950–1970.* Vol. 1: *Basic Data for Cities, Countries and Regions.* Berkeley.

Davis, D., and A. Casis. 1946. "Urbanization in Latin America." *MMFQ,* 24 (2): 186–207; and (3): 292–314.

Debuyst, F. 1961. *La población en América latina. Demografía y evolución del empleo.* Bogotá.

Denevan, W. M. 1966. *The Aboriginal Cultural Geography of the Llanos de Mojos of Bolivia.* Berkeley.

———. 1970. "The Aboriginal Population of Tropical America: Problems and Methods of Estimation." In Deprez, 1970, pp. 251–69.

Deprez, P. (ed.). 1970. *Population and Economics.* Winnipeg.

Díaz de Yraola, G. 1947. "La vuelta al mundo de la expedición de la vacuna." *Anuario de estudios americanos,* 4: 105–62.

Diégues Júnior, M. 1964. *Imigração, urbanização e industrialização.* Rio de Janeiro.

*Dobyns, H. F. 1963. "An Outline of Andean Epidemic History to 1720." *Bulletin of the History of Medicine,* 37 (6): 493–515.

*———. 1966. "Estimating Aboriginal American Population. 1. An Ap-

praisal of Techniques with New Hemispheric Estimate." *Current Anthropology*, 7 (4): 395–416.

Dobyns, H. F., and M. C. Vásquez (ed.). 1963. *Migración e integración en el Perú*. Lima.

Dorselaer, J., and A. Gregory. 1962. *La urbanización en América latina*. 2 vols. Bogotá.

Ducoff, L. J. 1965. "The Role of Migration in the Development of Latin America." *MMFQ*, 43 (4, part 2): 197–216.

Durand, J. D. 1967a. "World Population Estimates, 1750–2000." U.N. *Proceedings of the World Population Conference, 1965*, 2: 17–22.

*———. 1967b. "The Modern Expansion of World Population." *Proceedings of the American Philosophical Society*, 111 (3): 136–59.

*Durand, J. D., and C. A. Peláez. 1965. "Patterns of Urbanization in Latin America." *MMFQ*, 43 (4, part 2): 166–91.

Eguilaz de Prado, I. 1965. *Los indios del Nordeste de Méjico en el siglo XVIII*. Seville.

Eidt. R. C. 1962. "Pioneer Settlement in Eastern Peru." *Annals of the Association of American Geographers*, 52 (3): 255–78.

———. 1971. *Pioneer Settlement in Northeast Argentina*. Madison.

Elizaga, J. C. 1963. *Formas de asentamiento de la población en América latina*. Santiago de Chile.

———. 1965. "Internal Migrations in Latin America." *MMFQ*, 43 (4, part 2): 144–61.

———. 1966. "A Study of Migration to Greater Santiago (Chile)." *Demography*, 3 (2): 352–77.

———. 1969. *Población y migraciones: América latina y el Caribe*. Santiago de Chile.

———. 1970. *Migraciones a las áreas metropolitanas de América latina*. Santiago de Chile.

Ellis Júnior, A. 1934. *Populações paulistas*. São Paulo.

Endrek, E. 1966. *El mestizaje en Córdoba. Siglo XVIII y principios del XIX*. Córdoba.

———. 1967. *El mestizaje en el Tucumán. Siglo XVIII. Demografía comparada*. Córdoba.

Escalante, A. 1964. *El negro en Colombia*. Bogotá.

Espinoza Soriano, W. (ed.). 1964. *Visita hecha a la provincia de Chucuito por Garcí Díez de San Miguel en el año 1567*. Lima.

Fajardo, D. 1969. *El régimen de la encomienda en la provincia de Vélez. Población indígena y economía*. Bogotá.

Fals Borda, O. 1957. "Indian Congregations in the New Kingdom of Granada: Land Tenure Aspects, 1595–1850." *The Americas*, 13 (4): 331–51.

Fischlowitz, E. 1969. "Internal Migration in Brazil." *International Migration Review*, 3 (3): 36–46.

Florescano, E. 1969. *Precios del maíz y crisis agrícolas en Mexico (1708–1810)*. Mexico.

Freyre, G. 1946. *The Masters and the Slaves: A Study in the Development of Brazilian Civilization*. New York.

Friede, J. 1963. *Los Quimbayas bajo la dominación española. Estudio documental (1539–1810).* Bogotá.

*———. 1965. "Algunas consideraciones sobre la evolución demográfica de la provincia de Tunja." *Anuario colombiano de historia social y de la cultura*, 2 (3): 5–19.

———. 1967. "Demographic Changes in the Mining Community of Muzo after the Plague of 1629." *HAHR*, 47 (3): 338–59.

———. 1968. "Las minas de Muzo y la 'peste' acaecida a principios del siglo XVII en el Nuevo Reino de Granada." *Revista de Historia de América*, 65/66: 90–108.

———. 1969. "De la encomienda indiana a la propiedad territorial y su influencia sobre el mestizaje." *Anuario colombiano de historia social y de la cultura*, 4: 35–62.

Friedman, J. 1966. *Regional Development Policy: A Case Study of Venezuela.* Cambridge (Mass.).

Friedman, J., and T. Lackington. 1967. "Hyperurbanization and National Development in Chile: Some Hypotheses." *Urban Affairs Quarterly*, 2 (4): 3–29.

Furtado, C. 1963. *The Economic Growth of Brazil: A Survey from Colonial to Modern Times.* Berkeley.

Gabaldón. A. 1956. "Problemas de población y la campaña contra la malaria." *Revista Shell* (Caracas), 19: 35–47.

*———. 1965. "Leading Causes of Death in Latin America." *MMFQ*, 43 (4, part 2): 242–62.

Galaviz de Capdevielle, M. E. 1967. *Rebeliones indígenas en el Norte del Reino de la Nueva España (siglos XVI y XVII).* Mexico.

Gallardo, M. G. 1961. *Tendencias del crecimiento de la población de Santa Fe, 1769–1960.* Santa Fe.

Gamio, M. 1930. *Mexican Immigration to the United States.* Chicago.

———. 1933. "Comentarios sobre la evolución de los pueblos latino-americanos." *Atti del Congresso Internazionale per gli Studi sulla Popolazione.* Rome, vol. 1, pp. 265–75.

García, M. L. 1970. "Programas de planificación familiar en América latina: 1969." *CRLP*, Mexico, session 2/28.

García Valverde, M. 1950. *Bibliografía estadística de Costa Rica.* San José.

Garzón Maceda, C., and J. W. Dörflinger. 1961. "Esclavos y mulatos en un dominio rural del siglo XVIII en Córdoba. Contribución a la demografía histórica." *Revista de la Universidad Nacional de Córdoba*, 2d series, 2 (3): 625–40.

Gasparini, J. 1969. *Caracas colonial.* Buenos Aires.

*Geiger, P. P. 1963. *Evolução da rêde urbana brasileira.* Rio de Janeiro.

Gendell, M. 1967. "Fertility and Development in Brazil." *Demography*, 4 (1): 143–57.

Gendell, M., and G. Rossel U. 1968. "The Trends and Patterns of the Economic Activity of Women in Latin America during the 1950's." *Estadística*, 26 (100): 561–76.

Gerhard, P. 1968. "Descripciones geográficas (pistas para investigadores)." *Historia mexicana*, 17 (4): 618–27.

Germani, G. 1955. *Estructura social de la Argentina*. Buenos Aires.

————. 1966. *Política y sociedad en una época de transición*. Buenos Aires.

————. 1968. "¿Pertenece América latina al Tercer Mundo?" *Aportes*, 10: 6–32.

————. 1969. *Sociología de la modernización*. Buenos Aires.

*————. 1970. "Mass Immigration and Modernization in Argentina." In I. L. Horowitz (ed.), *Masses in Latin America*. New York, pp. 289–330.

Gibson, Ch. 1955. "The Transformation of the Indian Community in New Spain." *Journal of World History*, 2 (3): 581–607.

*————. 1964. *The Aztecs Under Spanish Rule: A History of the Indians of the Valley of Mexico, 1519–1810*. Stanford.

Gibson, J. R. 1970. *A Demographic Analysis of Urbanization: Evolution of a System of Cities in Honduras, El Salvador and Costa Rica*. Ithaca.

*Glass, D. V., and D. E. G. Eversley (eds.). 1965. *Population in History: Essays in Historical Demography*. London.

Gómez, F. 1970. "Los censos en Colombia antes de 1905." In M. Urrutia and M. Arrubia, *Compendio de estadísticas históricas de Colombia*. Bogotá, pp. 9–30.

Gómez B., M. 1970. "El rápido descenso de la fecundidad en Costa Rica." *Quinto Seminario Nacional de Demografía, San José, Costa Rica*. San José, pp. 271–308.

Góngora, M. 1960. *Origen de los 'inquilinos' de Chile central*. Santiago de Chile.

————. 1962. *Los grupos de conquistadores en Tierra Firme (1509–1530). Fisionomía histórico-social de un tipo de conquista*. Santiago de Chile.

————. 1970. *Encomenderos y estancieros. Estudios acerca de la constitución social aristocrática de Chile después de la Conquista, 1580–1660*. Santiago de Chile.

González, E. R., and R. Mellafe. 1965. "La función de la familia en la historia social hispanoamericana colonial." *AIIH*, 8: 57–71.

González, G. R. 1968. "The Migration of Latin American High-level Manpower." *International Labour Review*, 98 (6): 551–69.

González Navarro, M. 1960. *La colonización en México, 1877–1910*. Mexico.

————. 1968. "La guerra de castas en Yucatán y la venta de mayas a Cuba." *Historia mexicana*, 18 (1): 11–34.

————. 1970. "Mestizaje in Mexico during the National Period." In Mörner, 1970, pp. 145–69.

González Quiñones, F., and J. Debasa R. 1970. "Cuba: evaluación y ajuste del censo de 1953 y las estadísticas de nacimientos y defunciones entre 1943 y 1957. Tabla de mortalidad para el período 1952–1954." *CRLP*, Mexico, Session 1/11.

Gori, G. 1964. *Inmigración y colonización en la Argentina*. Buenos Aires.

*Goulart, M. 1949. *Escravidão africana no Brasil (Das origens à extinção do tráfico)*. São Paulo.

Graña, F. 1908. *El problema de la población en el Perú. Inmigración o autogenia*. Lima.

————. 1916. *La población del Perú a través de la historia*. Lima.

Grebler, L., et al. 1970. *The Mexican-American People, the Nation's Second Largest Minority.* New York.

Guarda, G. 1968. *La ciudad chilena del siglo XVIII.* Buenos Aires.

*Guerra y Sánchez, R., et al. 1958. *A History of the Cuban Nation.* 6 vols. Havana.

Hajnal, J. 1965. "European Marriage Patterns in Perspective." In Glass and Eversley, 1965, pp. 101–43.

*Hardoy, J. E. 1967. *Ciudades precolombinas.* Buenos Aires.

Hardoy, J. E., and C. Aranovich. 1969. "Urbanización en América hispánica entre 1580 y 1630." *Boletín del Centro de Investigaciones Históricas y Estéticas,* 11: 9–89.

————. 1970. "Urban Scales and Functions in Spanish America Toward the Year 1600: First Conclusions." *Latin American Research Review,* 5 (3): 57–110.

Hardoy, J. E., and R. P. Schaedel. 1966. *The Urbanization Process in America from its Origin to the Present.* Buenos Aires.

Hardoy, J. E., and C. Tobar. 1969. *La urbanización en América latina.* Buenos Aires.

Hastings, D. 1969. "Japanese Emigration and Assimilation in Brazil." *International Migration Review,* 3 (8): 32–53.

Hatt, P. K. 1952. *Background of Human Fertility in Puerto Rico: A Sociological Survey.* Princeton.

*Hauser, P. 1962. *L'urbanisation en Amérique latine.* Paris.

Heer, D. M., and E. S. Turner. 1965. "Areal Differences in Latin American Fertility." *Population Studies,* 18 (3): 279–92.

Helmer, M. 1955–56. "La visitación de los yndios chupachos. Inka et encomendero, 1549." *Travaux de l'Institut Français d'Etudes Andines,* 5: 3–50.

*Henry, L. 1967. *Manuel de démographie historique.* Geneva.

Hernández Álvarez, J. 1966. "A Demographic Profile of the Mexican Immigration to the United States, 1910–1950." *Journal of Inter-American Studies,* 8: 470–96.

————. 1967. *Return Migration to Puerto Rico.* Berkeley.

Hernández y Sánchez Barba, M. 1954. "La población hispanoamericana y su distribución racial en el siglo XVIII." *Revista de Estudios Políticos,* 78: 117–18.

Herrick, B. H. 1966. *Urban Migration and Economic Development in Chile.* Cambridge, Mass.

Higuita, J. de D. 1940. "Estudio histórico analítico de la población colombiana en 170 años." *Anales de Economía y Estadística,* 3 (supp. to no. 2): 1–113.

Ho, J. 1971. "Les esclaves dans la zone d'occupation anglaise de Saint-Dominique en 1796." *Population,* 26 (1): 152–57.

Hoetink, H. 1970. "The Dominican Republic in the Nineteenth Century: Some Notes on Stratification, Immigration and Race." In Mörner, 1970, pp. 96–121.

————. 1971. *El pueblo dominicano, 1850–1900. Apuntes para una sociología histórica.* Santiago (Dominican Rep.).

*Hollingsworth, T. H. 1969. *Historical demography*. Ithaca.

Houdaille, J. 1963. "Trois paroisses de Saint-Dominique au XVIIIe siècle. Étude démographique." *Population*, 18 (1): 93–110.

Hübner Gallo, J. 1968. *El mito de la explosión demográfica. La autorregulación natural de las poblaciones*. Buenos Aires.

*Humboldt, A. [1822] 1957. *Political Essay on the Kingdom of New Spain*, Lexington, Ky.

————. 1822–1829. *Personal Narrative of Travels to the Equinoctial Regions of the New Continent During the Years 1799–1804*. 7 vols. London.

IASI, 1941. *Statistical Activities of the American Nations*. Washington, D.C.

————. 1953. *The Story of the 1950 Census of the Americas*. Washington, D.C.

*————. 1959–1960. *La estructura demográfica de las naciones americanas. Análisis estadístico-censal de los resultados obtenidos bajo el programa del Censo de las Américas de 1950 [COTA 1950]* (especially Vol. 1: *Características generales de la población*). Washington, D.C.

I.B.G.E. Conselho Nacional de Estatística. 1951. *Investigações sôbre os recenseamentos da população geral do Império* [J. N. de Souza e Silva, 1870]. Rio de Janeiro.

————. 1961. *Contribuições para o estudo da demografia do Brasil*. Rio de Janeiro.

Instituto de Economía, Universidad de Chile. 1959. *La migración interna de Chile en el período 1940–1942*. Santiago de Chile.

Instituto de Estudios Americanistas. *Censo de la población de la ciudad de Córdoba y su campaña. Año 1813*. 2 vols. Córdoba (forthcoming).

Interamerican Economic and Social Council. 1954. *Causas y efectos del éxodo rural en Venezuela*. Washington. D.C.

*International Labour Office. 1959. *International Migration 1945–1959*. Geneva.

Izard, M. 1970. *Series estadísticas para la historia de Venezuela*. Mérida.

Janer, J. L. 1945. "Population Growth in Puerto Rico and Its Relation to Time Changes in Vital Statistics." *Human Biology*, 17 (4): 267–313.

Jaramillo Gómez, M. 1968. "Medellín: A Case of Strong Resistance to Birth Control." *Demography*, 5 (2): 811–26.

Jaramillo Uribe, J. 1963. "Esclavos y señores en la sociedad colombiana del siglo XVIII." *Anuario colombiano de historia social y de la cultura*, 1 (1): 3–62.

————. 1964. "La población indígena de Colombia en el momento de la Conquista y sus transformaciones posteriores." *Anuario colombiano de historia social y de la cultura*, 1 (2): 239–93.

Jiménez Castro, W. 1956. *Migraciones internas en Costa Rica*. Washington, D.C.

Jiménez de la Espada, M. 1965. *Relaciones geográficas de Indias. Perú*. 3 vols. Madrid.

Jiménez Jiménez, R. 1957. *Exactitud del registro de nacimientos y algunos índices demográficos*. San José.

Jiménez Pastrana, J. 1963. *Los chinos en las luchas por la liberación cubana (1847–1930)*. Havana.

Keith, R. G. 1970. "Origen del sistema de hacienda. El caso de Chancay." In Instituto de Estudios Peruanos, *La hacienda, la comunidad y el campesino en el Perú*. Lima, pp. 13–60.

King, J. F. 1944. "The Latin-American Republics and the Suppression of the Slave Trade." *HAHR*, 24 (3): 387–411.

———. 1953. "A Royalist View of the Colored Castes in the Venezuelan War of Independence." *HAHR*, 33 (4): 526–37.

Kiser, C. V. 1971. "Unresolved Issues in Research of Fertility in Latin America." *MMFQ*, 49 (3, part 1): 379–88.

Klein, H. S. 1969. "The Trade in African Slaves to Rio de Janiero, 1795–1811: Estimates of Mortality and Patterns of Voyages." *Journal of African History*, 10 (4): 533–49.

———. 1969. "The Colored Freedman in Brazilian Slave Society." *Journal of Social History*, 3 (1): 30–52.

Konetzke, R. 1946. "Documentos para la historia y crítica de los registros parroquiales en las Indias." *Revista de Indias*, 7: 581–86.

*———. 1948. "Las fuentes para la historia demográfica de Hispano-América durante la época colonial." *Anuario de estudios americanos*, 5: 267–323.

———. 1953–1962. *Colección de documentos para la historia de la formación social de Hispano-América, 1493–1810*. 3 vols. Madrid.

———. 1970. "Die 'Geographischen Beschriebungen' als Quellen zur hispanoamerikanischen Bevölkerungsgeschichte der Kolonialzeit." *Jahrbuch für Geschichte von Staat, Wirtschaft und Gesellschaft Lateinamerikas*, 7: 1–75.

Kubler, G. 1942. "Population Movements in Mexico 1520–1600." *HAHR*, 22 (4): 606–43.

———. 1946. "The Quechua in the Colonial World." *Handbook of South American Indians*. Washington, D.C. Vol. 2, pp. 334–40.

———. 1952. *The Indian Caste of Peru, 1795–1940. A Population Study Based upon Tax Records and Census Reports*. Washington, D.C.

———. 1964. "Cities and Culture in the Colonial Period in Latin America." *Diogenes*, 47: 53–62.

Lambert, D. 1965. "L'urbanisation accélerée de l'Amérique latine et la formation d'un secteur tertiaire réfuge." *Civilisations*, 15 (2): 158–72; (3): 309–25; and (4): 477–92.

Lannoy, J. L. de, and G. Pérez. 1961. *Estructuras demográficas y sociales de Colombia*. Bogotá.

Lattes, A. E. 1967. *La fecundidad efectiva en la República Argentina*. Santiago de Chile.

———. 1968. *Evaluación y ajuste de algunos resultados de los tres primeros censos nacionales de población*. Buenos Aires.

Lattes, A. E., and R. Poczter. 1968. *Muestra del censo de población de la ciudad de Buenos Aires de 1855*. Buenos Aires.

Leonard, O. E. 1948. "La Paz, Bolivia: Its Population and Growth." *American Sociological Review*, 13 (4): 448–54.

Lerner, V. 1968. "Consideraciones sobre la población de la Nueva España

(1793–1810) según Humboldt y Navarro y Noriega." *Historia mexicana*, 17 (3): 327–48.

Le Roy y Cassá, J. E. 1913. *Estudios sobre la mortalidad de La Habana durante el siglo XIX y los comienzos del actual*. Havana.

Lisanti, L. 1962–1963. "La población de la 'Capitanía de São Paulo' entre la segunda mitad del siglo XVIII y el comienzo del siglo XIX." *AIIH*, 6: 13–26.

Lisanti, L., and M. L. Marcilio. 1969. "Estrutura demográfica social e economica da Vila de Lajes, 1798–1808." *Estudos históricos*, 8: 9–52.

Llano Saavedra, L. 1971–1972. "Rasgos de la población boliviana." *Estudios andinos*, 2 (2): 87–112.

Lobo, E. M. L. 1967. "Imigração e colonização no Chile colonial" (1540–1565). *Revista de história*, 25: 39–60.

Lockart, J. 1968. *Spanish Peru, 1532–1560: A Colonial Society*. Madison.

Lodolini, E. 1958. "Los libros parroquiales y de estado civil en América latina." *Archivium*, 8: 95–113.

Lola Ben, A. 1945. *Estadística*. Managua.

Lombardi, J. V. 1971. *The Decline and Abolition of Negro Slavery in Venezuela, 1820–1854*. Westport, Conn.

Lopes, V. F. 1969. *Problemas que afectan la producción de datos demográficos en América latina*. Santiago de Chile.

López, J. E. 1963. *La expansión demográfica de Venezuela*. Mérida.

López Sarrelangue, D. E. 1963. "Población indígena de la Nueva España en el siglo XVIII." *Historia mexicana*, 12 (4): 516–30.

López Toro, A. 1968. "Migración y cambio social en Antioquia durante el siglo XIX." *D y E*, 2 (3): 351–403.

López de Velasco, J. [1574]. 1894. *Geografía y descripción universal de las Indias*. Madrid.

Love, E. F. 1971. "Marriage Patterns of Persons of African Descent in a Colonial Mexico City Parish." *HAHR*, 51 (1): 79–91.

Loyo, G. 1935. *La política demográfica de México*. Mexico.

Luna Méndez, G. de, 1959. "La natalidad y la mortalidad en el marco de la Revolución mexicana." *Revista mexicana de sociología*, 21 (1): 103–26.

Luna Vegas, R. 1945. "Breve historia de los censos nacionales de población en el hemisferio occidental." *Historia. Revista peruana de cultura*, 10: 229–51. (See also *Estadística*, 9 [1945]: 7–133.)

Macera, P. 1968. *Mapas coloniales de haciendas cuzqueñas*. Lima.

————. n.d. *Población indígena y tenencia de la tierra en el Perú (siglos XVII–XIX)*. Lima (forthcoming).

MacNeish, R. S. 1964. *El origen de la civilización mesoamericana visto desde Tehuacán*. Mexico.

*————. 1970. "Social Implications of Changes in Population and Settlement Pattern of the 12,000 years of Prehistory in the Tehuacán Valley of Mexico." In Deprez, 1970, pp. 215–50.

————. 1971. "Early Man in the Andes." *Scientific American*, 224 (4): 36–46.

Maeder, E. J. A. 1963. "Demografía y potencial humano de Corrientes. El censo provincial de 1814." *Nordeste*, 5: 113–63.

———. 1969. *Evolución demográfica argentina desde 1810 a 1869.* Buenos Aires.

Manrique Castañeda, L. 1963. "Notas sobre la población de Santa María Chigmecatitlán." *Anales* (Instituto Nacional de Antropología e Historia, Mexico), 16: 199–225.

Marcilio, M. L. 1968. *La Ville de São Paulo. Peuplement et population 1750–1850 d'après les registres paroissiaux et les recensements anciens.* Rouen.

Martin, N. F. 1957. *Los vagabundos en la Nueva España, siglo XVI.* Mexico.

Martínez, C. 1968. *Santa Fe de Bogotá.* Buenos Aires.

Martínez, H. 1968. "Las migraciones internas en el Perú." *Aportes*, 10: 136–60.

Martínez Alier, V. 1971. "Virginidad y machismo: el honor de la mujer en Cuba en el siglo XIX." *Cuadernos de Ruedo Ibérico*, 30: 51–79.

Matos Mar, J. 1968. *Urbanización y barriadas en América del Sur.* Lima.

Mattelart, A. and M. 1964. *La problématique du peuplement latino-américain.* Paris.

Mellafe, R. 1964. *La esclavitud en Hispanoamérica.* Buenos Aires.

———. 1965. "Problemas demográficos e historia colonial hispanoamericana." *Nova Americana*, 1: 45–55.

———. 1970. "The Importance of Migration in the Viceroyalty of Peru." In Deprez, 1970, pp. 303–13.

Memorias de los Virreyes que han gobernado el Perú durante el tiempo del coloniaje español. 1859. 6 vols. Lima.

México. Dirección General de Estadística. 1965. "Resumen de la historia estadística de México." *Revista de estadística*, 28: 1245–50.

*Miranda, J. 1963. "La población indígena de México en el siglo XVII." *Historia mexicana*, 12 (2): 182–89.

———. 1966. "La población indígena de Ixmiquilpan y su distrito en la época colonial." *Estudios de historia novohispana*, 1: 121–30.

Miró, C. A. 1963. *Algunos problemas relativos a la evolución de los resultados de los censos de población.* Santiago de Chile.

*———. 1964. "The Population of Latin America." *Demography*, 1 (1): 15–41.

———. 1965. *La población de América latina en el siglo XX.* Santiago de Chile.

———. 1966a. *La población de América Central y Panamá: un ejemplo de multiplicación acelerada.* Santiago de Chile.

*———. 1966b. "The World Population: Two Distinct Blocs." *Latin American Research Review*, 1 (3): 5–16.

———. 1968. *Aspectos demográficos de América latina.* Santiago de Chile.

Miró, C. A., and W. Martens. 1968. "Influences Affecting Fertility in Urban and Rural Latin America." *MMFQ*, 46 (3, part 2): 89–117.

Miró, C. A., and J. L. Somoza. 1964. *Características demográficas de la América latina.* Santiago de Chile.

Moncarz, R. 1970. "Effects of Professional Restriction on Cuban Refugees in Selected Health Professions in the United States, 1959–1969." *International Migration Review*, 8 (½): 22–30.

Montesino Samperio, J. V. 1956. *La población del área metropolitana de Caracas. Factores de crecimiento y tendencia futura.* Caracas.

Montoya Rojas, R. 1966. "Migración interna en el Perú." *Cuadernos de Ruedo Ibérico*, 6: 29–39.

Morales Padrón, F. 1951. "Colonos canarios en Indias." *Anuario de estudios americanos*, 8: 399–441.

Morales-Vergara, J. 1971. "Evaluation of the Magnitude and Structure of International Migratory Movements in Latin America (1958–1967)." *IPC London 1969*, Liège. Pp. 2606–18.

Moreno, J. L. 1965. "La estructura social y demográfica de la ciudad de Buenos Aires en el año 1778." *AIIH*, 8: 151–70.

Mörner, M. 1967. *Race Mixture in the History of Latin America.* Boston.

————— (ed.). 1970. *Race and Class in Latin America.* New York.

Morse, R. M. 1958. *From Community to Metropolis. A Biography of São Paulo, Brazil.* Gainesville, Fla.

—————. 1962. "Cidades latino-americanas: aspectos da função e estrutura." *AL*, 5 (3): 35–64.

—————. 1965. "Recent Research on Latin American Urbanization: A Selective Survey with Commentary." *Latin American Research Review*, 1 (1): 35–74.

—————. 1971a. "Trends and Issues in Latin American Urban Research." *Latin American Research Review*, 6 (1): 3–52; and (2): 19–75.

————— (ed.). 1971b. *The Urban Development of Latin America, 1750–1920.* Stanford.

—————. 1972. "A Prolegomenon to Latin American Urban History." *HAHR*, 52 (3): 359–94.

*Mortara, G. 1940–1942. "Estudos sobre a utilização do censo demográfico para a reconstrução das estatísticas do movimento de população do Brasil." *RBE*, 1 (1): 7–16, (2): 229–42, (3): 443–72, and (4): 674–93; 2 (5): 38–89, (6): 267–76, and (7): 493–538; and 3 (9): 77–90.

—————. 1942. "Contribução ao estudo das influências da imigração sôbre a taxa de natalidade." *RBE*, 3 (12): 575–84.

—————. 1943–1944. "Estudos de demografía interamericana." *Estadística*, 1 (3): 65–75, (4): 89–95; and 2 (5): 72–80.

—————. 1946. "O costo de produção do homen adulto e sua variação em relação à mortalidade." *Estudos brasileiros de demografía*, (1) 2: 1–152.

*—————. 1947. "Pesquisas sôbre populações americanas." *Estudos brasileiros de demografía*, 1 (1) [Monograph no. 3]: 1–227.

—————. 1950. "A fecundidade masculina, na população do Brasil, segundo a idade, a atividade principal e a posição na ocupação." *RBE*, 11 (42): 215–45.

*—————. 1954. "The Brazilian Birth Rate: Its Economic and Social Factors." In F. Lorimer et al., *Culture and Human Fertility.* Paris.

—————. 1957. *A fecundidade da mulher no Brasil. Segundo os resultados do Recenseamento de 1950.* Rio de Janeiro.

*—————. 1961. *Le unioni coniugali libere nell'America Latina.* Rome.

*—————. 1964. *Characteristics of the Demographic Structure of the American Countries.* Washington, D.C.

————. 1965. *Nuovi dati sulle unioni coniugali libere nell'America Latina.* Rome.

Müller, M. S. 1970. "Mortalidad en la ciudad de Buenos Aires desde mediados del siglo XIX." *CRLP,* Mexico, Session 1/20.

Murra, J. 1972. "El 'control vertical' de un máximo de pisos ecológicos en la economía de las sociedades andinas." In Ortiz de Zúñiga, pp. 429–73.

Nadal, J. 1966. *La población española (siglos XVI al XX).* Barcelona.

Narancio, E. M., and F. Capurro Calamet. 1939. *Historia y análisis estadístico de la población del Uruguay.* Montevideo.

Neiva, A. H. 1965. "International Migrations Affecting Latin America." *MMFQ,* 43 (4, part 2): 119–43.

Nogueira, O. 1964. *O desenvolvimento de São Paulo. Imigração estrangeira e nacional e índices demográficos-demo-sanitarios e educacionais.* São Paulo.

Normano, J. F. 1938. "Japanese Emigration to Latin America." *Population,* 2 (4): 77–99.

Normano, J. F., and A. Gerbi. 1943. *The Japanese in South America: An Introductory Survey with Special Reference to Peru.* New York.

Oddone, J. A. 1966a. *La emigración europea al Río de la Plata.* Montevideo.

————. 1966b. *La formación del Uruguay moderno (La inmigración y el desarrollo económico-social).* Buenos Aires.

Omran, A. R. 1971. "The Epidemologic Transition: A Theory of the Epidemiology of Population Change." *MMFQ,* 49 (4, part 1): 509–38.

Orbegoso Rodríguez, E. 1966. *Contribución al estudio de la población peruana.* Lima.

Ortiz de Zúñiga, I. [1562]. 1967–1972. *Visita de la Provincia de León de Huánuco en 1562.* 2 vols. Huánuco.

Oteiza, E. 1969. *La emigración de personal altamente calificado de la Argentina. Un caso de "brain drain" latinoamericano.* Buenos Aires.

————. 1971. "Emigración de profesionales, técnicos y obreros calificados argentinos a los Estados Unidos. Análisis de las fluctuaciones de la emigración bruta, julio de 1950 a junio 1970." *Desarrollo económico,* 39/40: 429–54.

Páez Celis, J. 1962. "Evaluación de las omisiones de los censos de los años 1936, 1941 y 1950 y de las omisiones de las defunciones en los períodos 1936, 1941 y 1950." *Revista de Fomento,* 97: 67–80.

Pan American Union, 1964. *Economic and Social Survey of Latin America, 1961.* Washington, D.C.

*Parsons, J. J. 1968. *Antioqueño Colonization in Western Colombia.* Berkeley.

Parsons, J. R. 1968. "Teotihuacán, Mexico, and Its Impact on Regional Demography." *Science,* 162 (3856): 872–77.

Paz y Miño, L. 1942. *La población del Ecuador.* Quito.

Peláez, C. A. 1967. "The Degree of Success Achieved in the Population Projections for Latin America Made Since 1950. Sources of Error. Data and Studies Needed in Order to Improve the Basis for Calculating Projections." *Proceedings of the World Population Conference, Belgrade 1965.* New York. Vol. 3, pp. 27–33.

Pérez de la Riva, J. 1967. "La population de Cuba et ses problèmes." *Population*, 22 (1): 99–110.

Phelan, J. L. 1956. *The Millenial Kingdom of the Franciscans in the New World: A Study of the Writings of Gerónimo de Mendieta (1525–1604).* Berkeley.

————. 1967. *The Kingdom of Quito in the Seventeenth Century.* Madison.

Population Bulletin. 1958. "Latin America. The 'Fountain of Youth' Overflows." 14 (5): 85–107.

Population Research Center. 1965. *International Population Census Bibliography. Latin America and the Caribbean,* Austin.

Quijano, A. 1967. "La urbanización de la sociedad en América latina." *Revista mexicana de sociología,* 30 (3).

Rama, C. M. 1967. *Los afro-uruguayos.* Montevideo.

Ramos, A. 1944. *Las poblaciones de Brasil,* Mexico.

*Rasini, B. 1965. "Estructura demográfica de Jujuy. Siglo XVIII." *AIIH,* 8: 119–50.

Rasini, B., et al. 1962–1963. "La población de Santa María: el censo de 1771; el padrón militar de 1812; las epidemias de 1882–1889." *AIIH,* 6: 41–118.

Rath, F. J. C. M. 1969. *América central: tendencias pasadas y perspectivas de su población.* San José.

Recchini, Z. L. 1969. *Argentina: la fecundidad en la ciudad de Buenos Aires desde fines del siglo pasado hasta 1936.* Santiago de Chile.

Recchini de Lattes, Z. L. 1967. *República Argentina. Correlación de la serie anual de nacimientos registrados por sexo y jurisdicción, 1911–1947.* Buenos Aires.

————. 1971. *La población de Buenos Aires. Componentes demográficos del crecimiento entre 1855 y 1960.* Buenos Aires.

*Recchini de Lattes, Z. L., and A. E. Lattes. 1969. *Migraciones en la Argentina. Estudio de las migraciones internas e internacionales basado en datos censales, 1869–1960.* Buenos Aires.

*Reinhard, J., et al. 1968. *Histoire générale de la population mondiale.* Paris.

Requena, B. M. 1968. "The Problem of Induced Abortion in Latin America." *Demography,* 5 (2): 785–99.

Reye, U. 1970. "Aspectos sociales de la colonización del Oriente boliviano." *Aportes,* 17: 50–79.

Reyes García, L. 1962. "Movimientos demográficos en la población indígena de Chiapas durante la época colonial." *La Palabra y el hombre. Revista de la Universidad Veracruzana,* 21: 25–48.

Ribeiro, D. 1971. *Fronteras indígenas de la civilización.* Mexico.

Río, M. E. del, 1929. *La inmigración y su desarrollo en el Perú.* Lima.

Rivarola, D. M. 1967. "Aspectos de la migración paraguaya." *Aportes,* 3: 24–71.

Rivarola, D. M., and G. Heisecke (ed.). 1969. *Población, urbanización y recursos humanos en el Paraguay.* Asunción.

Robbins, R. 1958. "Myth and Realities of International Migration into Latin America." *Annals,* 316: 102–10.

Robinson, W. C. 1963. "Urbanization and Fertility: The Non-Western Experience." *MMFQ*, 41 (3): 291–308.

Robinson, W. C., and E. H. Robinson. 1960. "Rural-urban Differentials in Mexico." *American Sociological Review*, 25 (1): 78–81.

Roche, J. 1959. *La colonisation allemande et le Rio Grande do Sul.* Paris.

Rodríguez Barros, J. 1923. "Hacia la despoblación." *Revista Chilena*, 17: 267–95.

Rojas Molina, O. 1964. "El censo de población de la República Oriental del Uruguay." *Estadística*, 83: 272–93.

Romero, H., et al. 1961. *México. Cincuenta años de Revolución.* Mexico.

*Rosenblat, A. 1954. *La población indígena y el mestizaje en América.* Vol. 1: *La población indígena, 1492–1950*; vol. 2: *El mestizaje y las castas coloniales.* Buenos Aires.

———. 1967. *La población de América en 1492.* Mexico.

Rother, H. et al. 1958. *Estudio de población de Bogatá D.E., 1938–1951.* Bogotá.

Rothman, A. M. 1967. *La fecundidad de Buenos Aires según algunas características demográficas y socio-económicas.* Buenos Aires.

———. 1971. "Evolution and Fertility in Argentina and Uruguay." *IPC London 1969.* Liège. Vol. 1, pp. 712–32.

Rowe, J. H. 1946. "Inca Culture at the Time of the Spanish Conquest." *Handbook of South American Indians.* Washington, D. C. Vol. 2, pp. 183–330.

Sacchetti, M. 1965. "Notizie etnographiche sulle popolazioni della provincia di Chucuito (Peru) in una relazione del XVI secolo," *Rivista di Etnografia.* 18: 126–36.

Salinas, S. 1954. "Legislación peruana referente a la estadística." *Estadística*, 12: 270–73.

Salinas Meza, R. 1970. *La población de Valparaíso en la segunda mitad del siglo XVIII. Estudio preliminar del empadronamiento de 1779.* Valparaíso.

Sánchez-Albornoz, N. 1964. "Estudio sobre la demografía histórica del Valle de Santa María." *Universidad*, 62: 93–104.

*———. 1967. "Les registres paroissiaux en Amérique Latine. Quelques considérations sur leur exploitation pour la démographie historique." *Revue Suisse d'Histoire*, 17 (1): 60–71.

———. 1970. "Rural Population and Depopulation in the Province of Buenos Aires, 1869–1960." In Deprez, 1970, pp. 315–34.

Sánchez-Albornoz, N., and J. L. Moreno. 1968. *La población de América latina. Bosquejo histórico.* Buenos Aires.

Sánchez-Albornoz, N., and S. Torrado. 1965. "Perfil y proyecciones de la demógrafía en la Argentina." *AIIH*, 8: 31–56.

Sandner, G. 1961. *Agrarkolonisation in Costa Rica. Siedlung Wirtschaft und Sozialgefüge an der Pionergrenze.* Kiel.

———. 1969. *Die Haupstädte Zentralamerikas Wachtumsprobleme, Gestaltwandel und Sozialgefüge.* Heidelberg.

Sauer, C. O. 1935. *Aboriginal Population of Northwestern Mexico.* Berkeley.

———. 1969. *The Early Spanish Main.* Berkeley.

Saunders, J. V. D. 1958. *Differential Fertility in Brazil.* Gainesville, Fla.

*Sauvy, A. 1962. "Le renversement du courant d'immigration séculaire." *Population,* 17 (1): 51–59.

————. 1963. "La population des pays d'Amérique Latine. Vue générale sur leur état et leur croissance." *Population,* 18 (1): 49–64.

Schaedel, R. P. 1967. *La demografía y los recursos humanos del sur del Perú.* Mexico.

Schwartz, S. B. 1969. "Cities of Empire: Mexico and Bahia in the Sixteenth Century." *Journal of Inter-American Studies,* 11 (4): 616–37.

Segall, M. 1968. "Esclavitud y tráfico de culíes en Chile." *Journal of Inter-American Studies,* 10 (1): 117–33.

Seguí González, L. 1969. *La inmigración y su contribución al desarrollo.* Caracas.

Senior, C. 1947. *Puerto Rican Emigration.* Río Piedras.

Simmons, A. B., and R. Cardona. 1970. "La selectividad de la migración en una perspectiva histórica: el caso de Bogotá (Colombia) 1929–1968." *CRLP,* Mexico, Session 3/11.

Simpson, L. B. 1952. *Exploitation of Land in Central Mexico in the Sixteenth Century.* Berkeley.

————. 1966. *Many Mexicos.* Berkeley.

Sireau, A. 1966. *Teoría de la población. (Ecología urbana y su aplicación a la Argentina).* Buenos Aires.

Smith, C. T. 1967–1968. "Despoblación de los Andes centrales en el siglo XVI." *Revista del Museo Nacional,* 35: 77–91.

Smith, R. C. 1955. "Colonial Towns of Spanish and Portuguese America." *Journal of the Society of Architectural Historians,* 14: 3–12.

Smith, T. L. 1959. "Some Observations Relating to Population Dynamics in Plantation Areas of the New World." In Pan American Union, *Plantation Systems of the New World.* Washington, D.C.

*————. 1961. *Latin American Population Studies.* Gainesville, Fla.

————. 1963. *Brazil: People and Institutions* (3d ed.). Baton Rouge.

————. 1969. "Studies of Colonization and Settlement." *Latin American Research Review,* 4 (1): 93–123.

*————. 1970. *Studies of Latin American Societies.* Garden City, N.Y.

Solari, A. 1967. *El desarrollo social del Uruguay en la postguerra.* Montevideo.

Somoza, J. L. 1965. "Trends of Mortality and Expectation of Life in Latin America." *MMFQ,* 43 (4, part 2): 219–33.

————. 1968. "Fertility and Differentials in Argentina in the nineteenth Century." *MMFQ,* 46 (3, part 2): 53–71.

*————. 1971a. *La mortalidad en la Argentina entre 1869 y 1960.* Buenos Aires.

*————. 1971b. "Mortality in Latin America: Present Level and Projection." *IPC London 1969,* Liège, vol. 2 pp. 889–99.

Somoza, J. L., and A. E. Lattes. 1967. *Muestras de los dos primeros censos nacionales de población, 1869 y 1895.* Buenos Aires.

Stein, S. J. 1970. *Vassouras: A Brazilian Coffee County, 1850–1900.* New York.

Steward, J. H. 1949. "The Native Population of South America." *Handbook of South American Indians*, Washington, D.C. Vol. 5, pp. 655–68.

Stewart, N. R. 1965. "Migration and Settlement in the Peruvian Montaña: The Apurímac Valley." *Geographical Review*, 55 (2): 143–57.

Stewart, W. 1951. *Chinese Bondage in Peru: A History of the Chinese Coolie in Peru, 1849–1874*. Durham, N.C.

Studer, E. F. S. de. 1958. *La trata de negros en el Río de la Plata durante el siglo XVIII*. Buenos Aires.

Stycos, J. M. 1968. *Human Fertility in Latin America: Sociological Perspective*. Ithaca.

*Stycos, J. M., and J. Arias (eds.). 1966. *Population Dilemma in Latin America*. Washington, D.C.

Susto, J. A. 1960. "Censos panameños en el siglo XIX." *Lotería*, 2d época, 5 (53), supp.: 1–52.

Szásdi, A. 1962. "Los registros del siglo XVIII en la parroquia de San Germán." *Historia* (Río Piedras), 1 (1): 51–63.

Tabah, L., and M. E. Cosio. 1970. "Medición de la migración interna a través de la información censal: el caso de México." *D y E*, 4 (1): 43–84.

Taeuber, I. 1944. "The Development of Population Predictions in Europe and the Americas." *Estadística*, 8: 323–46.

Temoche Benites, R. 1947. *Antecedentes históricos del censo de población y ocupación*. Lima.

Thayer Ojeda, L. 1934. *Contribución demográfica para la historia de Valparaíso*. Valparaíso.

*Thiel, B. A. 1951. *Monografía de la población de Costa Rica en el siglo XIX*. San José. (See also *Population*, 1970, (1): 133–34.)

Tormo, L. 1965. "Datos demográficos de la provincia de Chiquitos (Bolivia)." In P. Harsin and E. Hélin (eds.), *Problèmes de mortalité. Méthodes, sources et bibliographie en démographie historique. Actes du Colloque International de Démographie Historique, Liège, 1963*. Paris, pp. 335–47.

Tovar Pinzón, H. 1970. "Estado actual de los estudios de demografía histórica en Colombia." *Anuario Colombiano de Historia Social y de la Cultura*, 5: 65–140.

Ulloa, A. de. 1748. *Relación histórica del viage a la América meridional*. 4 vols. Madrid.

*U.N. 1949–1971. *Demographic Yearbook*. 22 vols.: 1948–1970. New York.

*———. 1953. *The Determinants and Consequences of Population Trends*. New York.

———. 1954. *The Population of Central America (including Mexico) 1950–1980* [Population Studies 16]. New York.

———. 1955a. *The Population of South America 1950–1980* [Population Studies 21]. New York.

———. 1955b. *Handbook of Vital Statistics Methods*. New York.

———. 1958. *Latin American Seminar on Population, Rio de Janeiro, 1955*. New York.

*———. 1966. *World Population Prospects as Assessed in 1963* [Population Studies 41] New York.

*————. 1969. *Growth of the World's Urban and Rural Population, 1920–2000*. New York.

UNESCO. 1955. *The Positive Contribution by Immigrants*. Paris.

Unikel, L. 1968. "El proceso de urbanización en México. Distribución y crecimiento de la población urbana." *D y E*, 2 (2): 139–82.

U.S. Census Bureau. 1944–1945. *Summary of Biostatistics* (different countries). Washington, D.C.

U.S. National Center for Health Statistics. 1964. *Recent Mortality Trends in Chile*. Washington, D.C.

Universidad Nacional de Venezuela. 1967. *Estudio de Caracas*. Caracas.

Urquidi, V. L. 1969. "La ciudad subdesarrollada." *D y E*, 3 (2): 137–55.

Vallois, H. V. 1960. "Vital Statistics in Prehistoric Populations as Determined from Archaeological Data." In R. F. Heizer and S. F. Cook (eds.), *The Application of Quantitative Methods in Archaeology*. Chicago, pp. 188–222.

*Vázquez de Espinosa, A. [1628–1629]. 1942. *Compendium and Description of the Indies*. Washington, D.C.

Vergara, R. 1943. "Los censos de población de Chile." *Proceedings of the American Scientific Congress*, Washington, D.C. Vol. 8 (*Statistics*), pp. 95–108.

Vergara y Velasco, F. J. 1891. *Nueva Geografía de Colombia*, Bogotá.

Verger, P. 1968. *Flux et reflux de la traite des nègres entre le golfe de Benin et Bahía de Todos os Santos du 17e et 19 siècles*. The Hague.

Victor, R. 1944. *Recensement et démographie*. Port-au-Prince.

Vieytez, A. 1969. "La emigración salvadoreña a Honduras," *Estudios Centro-Americanos*, 254/255 (extra issue, *El conflicto Honduras-El Salvador*): 399–406.

Vila, M. A., and J. J. Pericchi. 1968. *Zonificación geoeconómica de Venezuela*. 4 vols. Caracas.

Villaseñor y Sánchez, J. A. 1746–1748. *Theatro mexicano, descripción general de los reynos y provincias de la Nueva España y sus jurisdicciones*. Mexico.

*Vollmer, G. 1967. *Bevölkerungspolitik und Bevölkerungsstruktur im Vizekönigreich Peru zu Ende der Kolonialzeit 1741–1821*. Hamburg.

Wagner, H. O. 1969. "Subsistence Potential and Population Density of the Maya on the Yucatan Peninsula and Causes for the Decline in Population in the Fifteenth (*sic*) Century." *Verhandlugen des 38 Internationalen Amerikanistenkongresses, Stuttgart-München 1968*. Munich. Vol. 1, pp. 179–96.

Warren, D. 1971. "Some Demographic Considerations of the matrícula de Huexotzinco." *The Americas*, 27 (3): 252–70.

Weeks, J. R. 1970. "Urban and Rural Natural Increase in Chile." *MMFQ*, 48 (1): 71–89.

Weller, R. H., et al. 1971. "The Relative Importance of the Components of Urban Growth in Latin America." *Demography*, 8 (2): 225–32.

West, R. C. 1957. *The Pacific Lowlands of Colombia: A Negroid Area of the American Tropics*. Baton Rouge.

————. 1970. "Population Densities and Agricultural Practices in Pre-Columbian Mexico, with Emphasis on Semi-terracing." *Verhandlungen des 38 Internationalen Amerikanistenkongresses, Stuttgart-München 1968.* Munich. Vol. 2, pp. 361–69.

Westphalen, J. 1966. *Bevölkerungsexplosion und Wirtschaftsentwicklung in Lateinamerika.* Hamburg.

*Whetten, N. L., and R. G. Burnight. 1956. "Internal Migration in Mexico." *Estadística,* 16: 65–77.

Wilhelmy, H. 1952. *Südamerika im Spiegel seiner Städte.* Hamburg.

*Willcox, W. F. 1929. *International Migrations.* New York.

Wingo, L. 1967. "Recent Patterns of Urbanization among Latin American Countries." *Urban Affairs Quarterly.* 2 (3): 81–109.

Wrigley, E. A. (ed.). 1966. *An Introduction to English Historical Demography.* London.

*———. 1969. *Population and History.* London.

Young, C. W. 1949. "Some Aspects of Haiti's Population and National Territory Significant in Census Considerations." *Estadística,* 25: 516–19; 26: 69–86; 27: 204–16; and 28: 388–99.

Zañartu, M. 1963. *Necesidad de inmigrantes para el desarrollo económico de América latina.* Geneva.

Zárate, A. O. 1967a. *Principales padrones de migración interna en Guatemala.* Guatemala.

———. 1967b. "Fertility in Urban Areas of Mexico: Implications for the Theory of the Demographic Transition." *Demography,* 4 (1): 363–73.

Zelinsky, W. 1949. "The Historical Geography of the Negro Population of Latin America." *Journal of Negro History,* 34: 153–219.

INDEX

Abascal, census of (1812), 14, 112, 128
Acámbaro, Mexico, 88
Acapulco, Mexico: oriental slaves brought to, 75; growth of port in colonial era, 83; population decline in, 99
Aconcagua, Chile, 135
Actas capitulares, 100
Africa; Africans: origins of Latin American population in, 4, 5, 72–75, 97–98, 125–126; replaced decimated Indian populations, 5, 64, 72; resistance to epidemic diseases, 61, 64; regional origins of slaves, 73, 98, 126; distribution of in late colonial era, 137–142; death rate compared with Latin America, 190. *See also* Slavery
Age distribution: age pyramids, 43, 53, 114–115, 116, 122, 167, 205; effect of war on, 122, 167; effect of migration on, 163, 203; effect of population explosion on, 203–207; predictions, 257, 259, 260
Agricultural revolution, demographic effects of, 4–5, 24–28 *passim*, 29–30
Agriculture: changes in after Conquest, 56–58, 65; effects of introduction of livestock, 57, 123, 124; correlation between food shortages and epidemics, 103; problems causing migration to cities, 227–228, 229; improvements in related to population growth, 238
Alagoas, Brazil, 139
Alberdi, Juan Bautista, 151, 220
Amat, Viceroy, 14
Amazon basin: rural population density in, 229; opening of new lands to settlement, 234, 237
Amezaga, Simón de, 93
Anáhuac, Mexico, pre-Columbian city, 30, 79
Andes: pre-Columbian urbanization in, 30; early settlers in, 71
Angostura, Congress of, 143
Antilles, slaves delivered to, 73
Antioquia, Colombia, 106–108, 123

Apure, Venezuela, 137–138
Araucanian Indians: resistance to Spanish, 71, 84; German immigrants to territory of, 149
Archaeology, as demographic source, 4, 23, 24, 47. *See also* Paleodemography
Archivo General de Indias, 13, 66, 68, 110
Archivo General de la Nación, 94
Arequipa, Peru, 84, 103
Argentina: human sacrifice in, 28; censuses in, 15, 177–178; age distribution in late colonial era, 114–115; growth rate, 114–116, 169, 186; fertility in, 115–116, 172, 176–178, 208, 211, 213; epidemics in, 119; urbanization in, 127, 128, 178–181 *passim*, 230, 233–234, 241, 246–251 *passim*; illegitimacy in, 131; racial groups in, 137; slavery in, 143, 144; immigration to, 149, 152–165 *passim*, 186, 223, 224, 230; immigration policy in, 151–152, 220; life expectancy in, 175, 194, 196; death rates in, 191, 202; opposition to birth control in, 217; migration to U.S.A. from, 226; depopulation of rural areas, 229, 230–234; internal migration, 230–234, 241; migration from neighboring countries to, 239; demographic predictions, 259, 260
Asia: origins of Latin American population in, 4, 23, 37, 150, 151, 161, 221; origins of slaves in, 75, 76; death rate compared to Latin America, 190
Asunción, Paraguay, early Spanish settlement, 80
Atacama Desert, Chile, 229
Atahualpa, civil war with Huáscar, 38, 44, 91
Aymarás Indians, 44
Azores, 69–70
Aztec empire: *guerras floridas*, 28, 50; human sacrifices as birth control, 28, 50; urbanization in, 31, 32, 80; political instability at time of Conquest, 38; records of demo-